The Rise of the
Civilizational State

The Rise of the Civilizational State

Christopher Coker

polity

First published in 2019 by Polity Press
Reprinted: 2019

Polity Press
65 Bridge Street
Cambridge CB2 1UR, UK

Polity Press
101 Station Landing
Suite 300
Medford, MA 02155, USA

ISBN-13: 978-1-5095-3462-3
ISBN-13: 978-1-5095-3463-0 (pb)

A catalogue record for this book is available from the British Library.

Library of Congress Cataloging-in-Publication Data

Names: Coker, Christopher, author.
Title: The rise of the civilizational state / Christopher Coker.
Description: Cambridge, UK ; Medford, MA : Polity Press, 2019. | Includes
  bibliographical references and index.
Identifiers: LCCN 2018012972 (print) | LCCN 2018041094 (ebook) | ISBN
  9781509534647 (Epub) | ISBN 9781509534623 (hardback) | ISBN 9781509534630
  (pbk.)
Subjects: LCSH: State, The--Philosophy. | Nationalism--China. |
  Nationalism--Russia. | Caliphate.
Classification: LCC JC11 (ebook) | LCC JC11 .C57 2019 (print) | DDC
  320.101--dc23
LC record available at https://lccn.loc.gov/2018012972

Typeset in 10.5 on 17pt Utopia Std by
Servis Filmsetting Ltd, Stockport, Cheshire
Printed and bound in the United States by LSC Communications

For further information on Polity, visit our website:
politybooks.com

Contents

Preface

Have you ever given much thought to civilization? It is one of the most important words in the cultural lexicon, but what does the concept actually bring to mind – that's of course if it brings anything to mind at all? It is one of those concepts that you are expected to recognize instantly, along with others with which you are probably more familiar, such as the nation-state. Let's imagine that you are a reader from the West. If so, you might identify with 'Western civilization'. But, when you hear that term, what image does it conjure up, if any? Perhaps the great cathedrals of Europe, such as York Minster and Chartres? Or such intense expressions of beauty as the pictures of Raphael (1483–1520) or Rembrandt (1606–1669)? Or, as you are making the effort to read this book, perhaps you are better acquainted with a unique literary canon that dates back to the epic poems of Homer?

Possibly you may be more interested in ideas. Is Christianity, for you, still a bedrock of Western civilization, as it was for the poet T. S. Eliot (1888–1965) when in 1948 he wrote *Notes on the Definition of Culture*? Or perhaps you are more enthused by secular ideas such as freedom and individualism, which you will find celebrated by Hollywood in films such as *300*, Zack Snyder's over-the-top account of the battle of Thermopylae. If you believe the historian Herodotus (484–425 BCE), claims Victor Davis Hanson (who acted as the historical adviser for the movie), the battle was the centrepiece of a 'clash of civilizations' that set Eastern 'centralism' against a Western belief in individualism (Hanson 2010: 55). Hanson's views are not shared by all, and you may fault Snyder's film for continuing to propagate an ancient myth that has shaped Western thoughts and feelings over the centuries.

Such myths, however, are real enough even if they tend to blur the difference between truth and fantasy in ways that suggest that the boundaries between them may not be as fixed as we would like.

Anyway, you may feel disinclined to regard your own civilization as a Hollywood blockbuster with a fast-moving plot and many leading players, some of them from central casting. You may even be relieved that the Western Civilization 101 courses that used to be part of the standard academic syllabus in the United States were largely abandoned in the 1960s, although on some campuses they are now making a comeback. Perhaps you look at your own civilization through more jaundiced eyes. Back in the 1960s you might have been particularly scornful of those Dead White European Males (DWEM) who are still considered in the popular press to be the 'founders' of your own civilization. The acronym was not, of course, intended to be a mark of approbation. These days it has been superseded by the term WEIRD – Western, Educated, Industrialized, Rich and Democratic – i.e., the people who still tend to form the bulk of the database in the experimental branches of psychology, the cognitive sciences and economics. For a long time researchers in these fields made the mistake of supposing a species-level generality in their findings. But this is now under challenge. As a Westerner, you may indeed be different from everyone else thanks to cultural and social conditioning. If that is indeed the case, then it can no longer be taken that you speak for the rest of humanity; you may count yourself among the weirdest people in the world.

Of course, whether you identify with Western civilization or not, you will be seen by others to come from a distinctive family, and all families, as we know, tend to exclude others. Other people's families cut us out of the conversation, sometimes even when we marry into them. Aldous Huxley (1894–1963), the author of *Brave New World* (1932), put it rather well in an essay he wrote in the 1920s:

'Do you remember Aunt Agatha's ear trumpet? And how Willie made the parrot drunk with sops in wine? And that picnic on Loch Etive, when the boat upset and Uncle Bob was nearly drowned? Do you remember?' And we all do; and we laugh delightedly; and the unfortunate stranger, who happens to have called, feels utterly out of it. Well, that (in its social aspect) is Culture. When we of the great Culture Family meet, we exchange reminiscences about Grandfather Homer, and that awful old Dr. Johnson, and Aunt Sappho, and poor Johnny Keats. 'And do you remember that absolutely priceless thing Uncle Virgil said? You know. *Timeo Danaos* . . . Priceless; I shall never forget it.' No, we shall never forget it; and what's more, we shall take good care that those horrid people who have had the impertinence to call on us, those wretched outsiders who never knew dear mellow old Uncle V., shall never forget it either. (Huxley 1994: 91)

You may not have read 'Uncle Virgil' (70–19 BCE) at school (certainly not as, three generations ago, you might have been expected to in the original language, Latin), but if you visit Ground Zero in New York you will find a wall at the lowest level displaying a phrase from Virgil's great epic poem *The Aeneid*: 'No day shall erase you from the memory of time.' And if you visit the wall that contains the remains of the fallen, you will find another quotation from the original poem about two warriors, Nisus and Euryalus, who gladly embraced death for a greater political cause. It's a noble enough sentiment, isn't it? But, if truth be told, it is also a rather ironic one. Doesn't it, asks one writer, fit the hijackers of September 11 more closely than their victims? (Crawford 2015: 515–16).

The Greeks have been part of the script of the War on Terror since the beginning, and that is important because terrorism is now woven into the fabric of American life: its imagery is omnipresent on the news, in TV series such as *Homeland*, in the political rhetoric of politicians (of all parties), and even in the collective subconscious of the American people. As for the classics, since 2007 Homer's *Iliad* has been translated into English at least seven times. (And why not? Given the state of the world, a poem about rage and the need to defend honour resonates even more on each re-reading.) At West Point, Robert Fagles (1933–2008), the late award-winning translator of Homer, was invited to the college to read out the first lines of his latest translation of the *Iliad* to hundreds of students, some of whom were being sent off to battle (Higgins 2010). When American soldiers went on campaign in Afghanistan in 2010, they found themselves taking part in an operation called 'Operation Achilles'. And when they return from the battlefield, broken in mind if not in body, they are now offered something called Theater of War, a $3.7 million funded programme set up by the Pentagon in 2009 which helps them to deal with their psychic wounds by exposing them to the healing powers of two plays by Sophocles (497/6–406/5 BCE).

Some years later the programme was introduced into Guantánamo Bay, the military prison in Cuba which remains in operation despite the closure order which President Obama signed on his first day in office. The play performed there is *Prometheus Bound*, by the earliest Greek playwright Aeschylus (525/524–456/455 BCE). It is based on the myth of the Titan who defies the gods and gives mankind fire and technology, an act of insubordination for which he is condemned to perpetual punishment. It is interesting that for the most part the guards tend to identify with the victim, Prometheus, not with his judge, Zeus (Doerries 2016). The prisoners, of course, don't get to see the play – they hail from a different culture. And, while all prisoners may dream of freedom, in this case, a Greek tragedy is unlikely to offer much possibility of spiritual escape.

So, although you may not have given much thought to the concept of civilization, there is really no escaping it, is there? Indeed, whenever there is a terrorist attack in Brussels or Paris or London, the newspapers are quick to invoke the Western values that are being attacked. In an article following the Paris attacks of 2015, the journalist Gideon Rachman regretted the fact that cultural reassertion was 'narrowing the space for those who want to push back against the narrative of a "clash of civilizations"', a reference to the famous thesis put forward by the late Harvard professor Samuel Huntington (Rachman 2015). I will return to Huntington in a later chapter, but there is no gainsaying the fact that Rachman had a point. In Malaysia, for example, there has been a significant narrowing of the space for non-Muslims. In Bangladesh, Hindu and other non-Muslim intellectuals and journalists have been murdered by religious fundamentalists. In Indonesia, the Muslim scholar Syafi'i Anwar talks with alarm of the 'creeping Shariaization' of Indonesian society (Sen 2006). And religious minorities around the world now find themselves in trouble. The persecution of Christians in the Middle East is even seen by some as a religious version of ethnic cleansing. Before 1914 they made up 14 per cent of the population; today they have been reduced to 4 per cent as a result of emigration and religious repression, not to mention falling birth rates (usually a sure sign of cultural demoralization).

Even the very concept of civilization is being challenged. 'This is the world's fight . . . This is civilization's fight . . . Either you're with us, or you're with the terrorists.' It is undoubtedly George W. Bush's most famous saying, and it is fashionable these days to make fun both of the man and of the sentiment, but what then of 'cultural vandalism', an instrument of war which is being employed to erase the collective memory of an entire people? Even the most revolutionary regimes in history have chosen to honour the past: the Islamic Republic of Iran has never considered blowing up Persepolis (the damage of course was done by Alexander the Great), and even the Bolshevik revolutionaries decided the past should be preserved in museums rather than reduced to rubble. That is what made ISIS (Islamic State) so different. A few years ago it made a defiantly proud seven-minute video of its organized destruction by bulldozer and dynamite of the buildings of Nimrud, a civilization that dates back to 879 BCE. In Palmyra, the old caravan city at the end of the Silk Road which once brought China's silk to Europe, one of its greatest monuments, the Temple of Bel, was destroyed in August 2015.

Let me importune you one more time. You may not have given civilization a great deal of thought, but others certainly have. In fact you are already living in a world in which civilization is fast becoming the currency of international politics. Take Putin's Russia. As the sociologist Lev Gudkov writes, the great epic of the Soviet period, the Great Patriotic War (1941–5), is now regarded by many Russians as 'a victory not only over Germany but also over the West'. And that reading of history is important because the war is considered by many Russians to be the most important event in their history (which is why, by the way, Stalin, not Peter the Great, regularly tops the list of the ten greatest Russians) (Prus 2015: 3). Academics like me may well find all of this regrettable, a cheapening of the debate, but the language of civilization has allowed politicians such as Putin to prioritize the battles to be fought in the future. My interest in writing this book indeed first took shape in 2013, when for the first time Putin declared Russia to be a 'civilizational state'. Today Russia is busy refabricating its own past to reflect ancient truths and ancestral verities in a bid to inoculate itself against the contagion of liberal ideas and Western norms.

As the book took shape, my aims evolved too. I wanted to include China and, later still, ISIS, with its dream of restoring the Islamic caliphate. China has often been defined as a civilization 'pretending to be a state' (Tsygankov 2016: 146). The present Chinese leadership has chosen to embrace some of the old Confucian verities, repackaging them as part of the rejuvenation of China itself. At the nineteenth party congress in 2017, the regime offered the world a unique example, a Confucian–Leninist model, 'socialism with Chinese characteristics' – an idea that encouraged universities and research institutes across the country to launch 'Xi Jinping Thought Study Centres' by the dozen. The Americans may still hold universal values, but the days when American presidents could lecture the regime on human rights or chastise it for its campaign of ethnocide in Tibet have long since passed. Instead there has been a reaction to what one Chinese writer calls the 'excesses of ideological "globalism" (as opposed to economic globalization) in the past few decades'. The Chinese leadership, he adds, does not believe that the world is moving towards the adoption of a unified set of rules and standards in economics, politics, international relations and even morality. Cultural distinctions will remain; they will not give way to universal values

(Li 2017). Xi Jinping's China has even begun to advance cogent reasons for ignoring 'Western' international law in the South China Sea by reference to a 'geo-cultural birthmark'. Geopolitics, it would seem, is no longer purely geographical or political; it is also socio-cultural or civilizational.

And finally there is Islamic fundamentalism in its most extreme incarnation, ISIS. The movement may have lost most of its territory, but its aspiration to re-establish an Islamic caliphate is unlikely to lose its appeal. What makes the dream so radical is its explicit rejection of the nation-state. People can change nationalities or enjoy more than one, but they cannot do without passports. Countries are as old as history; nation-states are a recent Western invention. And their capacity for self-invention makes them still a chief reference point for a people's identity, whether in Russia or in China. The caliphate, however, offers Muslims a sacrament with God as well as an escape from a Godless secular international order.

Uncertain as we are about what the future may hold, is it so surprising that we are forced back on the landmark institutions and concepts which still define our lives? Neither civilizational identities nor national loyalties can be written off as the delusions of those who cannot make the most of globalization. They exist even if the historical conditions which gave rise to them have changed, and they are likely to be exploited by politicians, even if this means ironing out many of the other complexities of political life.

This book is concerned with the way in which non-Western governments and movements are using the currency of civilization for their own political ends. But it is also about why the Western world is facing its own moment of crisis, as students are taught at increasingly left-wing universities, obsessed with identity politics and no-platforming speakers they dislike, that there are no civilizational values, and as the push back against liberal civilization reveals that there is no widely accepted universal value-system to which everyone subscribes. On the right, on the other hand, there is a despairing denial of the obvious: that the West is not quite as exceptional as it once liked to think. Lurking below the level of consciousness in the rest of the world, the old civilizational values continue to retain their appeal. At the level of consciousness, political regimes are quite cynically tapping into more primal identities. Global citizenship, the great dream of liberal internationalists, is losing traction, as is the dream of liberal civilization itself.

1

Liberal Civilization and its Discontents

Even today, Western intellectuals still like to think that they occupy the commanding heights of intellectual debate; it's their books that are to be found the world over in airport bookshops, though a fight-back of sorts has begun. Indeed, the rumblings of revolution are now becoming audible for the first time. *Can Asians Think?* is the provocative title of a book by Kishore Mahbubani which first appeared in the bookshops in 1998. The book struck a chord at the time, not only because of the argument but because of the author's reputation. He was described by *The Economist* as 'an Asian Toynbee concerned with the rise and fall of civilizations' and by the *Washington Post* as a 'Max Weber of the new Confucian ethic'. Weber and Toynbee (1889–1975) were two of the public intellectuals whose writings were taken as gospel by their followers. Toynbee's book *A Study of History* (1934–61) was a best-seller for twenty years before it finally fell out of fashion.

Mahbubani was only pointing out something that Western thinkers have tended to accept without questioning: the role that ideas played in creating the Western moment in history. It is quite common to speak of the 500-year ascendancy of the Western world and to date it from 1492 and the so-called discovery of the New World. But when one focuses in a little more, the picture is a bit more complicated. Economically, after all, Europe didn't overtake the East until the late eighteenth century. Militarily, its hegemony really dates only from the Industrial Revolution. But, in terms of ideas, the European ascendancy certainly did begin almost 400 years ago. As Mahbubani writes: 'We live in an essentially unbalanced world. The flow of ideas reflecting 500 years of Western domination of the globe remains a one-way street from the West to the East. Most Westerners cannot see that they have arrogated to themselves the moral high ground from which they lecture the world' (1998: 9). The title of his book included two questions folded into one. The first was addressed to his fellow Asians: 'Can we think, and, if so, why have we fallen behind?' The second was addressed to his Western readers: 'Do you *really* think that Asians can think for themselves?'

Putting the answer to one side (I will come back to it in a later chapter), both questions start from the same point of departure: that thinking is not an abstract or abstruse pastime. It is popular of course to imagine academics cloistered away in their ivory towers, but, in the course of the twentieth century, philosophers became public intellectuals and ideas soon seeped from the intellectual salons onto the street. The ideas of the French Revolution eventually found their way into the political and legal systems of almost all European states. And late nineteenth-century imperialism, even if driven partly by industrial cartels and surplus finance capital, also involved the global projection of a civilizing mission. In other words, Europe was able to tap into a large reserve of conceptual capital. In the case of civilizational studies it still can, for most of the books are written by Westerners.

The subject really took off as a popular theme only with the idiosyncratic work by Oswald Spengler (1880–1936), *The Decline of the West* (1918). It brought its author instant fame, rapidly selling 100,000 copies. It has never been out of print since, despite its challenging style, apparent lack of organization and exhausting prolixity. For, if it's not an easy read, the work has panache – who else would have begun his diagnosis of Western decline with a discussion of Euclidean mathematics? Of the many writers who have turned their attention to civilization, Spengler was intellectually by far the most audacious. Not only did he set out to invigorate the style of historical discussion by adopting the widest possible lens, he allowed the civilizations he studied to speak through their own textual and artistic achievements. And although it is fashionable these days to emphasize the tendentious character of Spengler's work, we shouldn't downplay its continuing appeal. It's quite seductive to be drawn into the slipstream of his thought.

Spengler nevertheless was knocked into second place after the Second World War by the British historian Arnold Toynbee. The result of his labours was a much less interesting read – the exhausting twelve-volume *A Study of History*, which brought the author almost instant celebrity status. In 1947 he even achieved every author's ultimate ambition; he appeared on the cover of *Time*. The editors called him the most important intellectual of the twentieth century for challenging Marx's belief that class rather than civilization was the main driving force of history. But very few scholars read his work today – Toynbee was like a brief comet flaring in the academic story, scattering remnants of the tail after him but leaving little impression behind.

Both Spengler and Toynbee were attempting in very different ways to make sense of the complexity of life, to find in the general chaos of history some kind of pattern. 'Homo sapiens is about pattern recognition . . . both a gift and a trap' (the quote comes from William Gibson's novel *Pattern Recognition* (2004)). Or here is Don DeLillo and his most recent novel *Zero K* (2016), in which one of the characters asks: What are long journeys for? 'To see what's back behind you, [to] lengthen the view, find the patterns.' Pattern seeking is merely a way of organizing information, a shorthand heuristic that allows us to make sense of some of the changes that we experience over time. They allow us to generalize, without which it would be impossible to write history.

The problem with both writers was intellectual overreach. Like Marx, they insisted that they had discovered certain invariant historical laws. For Spengler, civilizations have their seasons, beginning with spring and finally entering into winter gloom. For Toynbee, they were determined by the law of 'challenge and response': environmental challenges either spurred people to new heights or quite simply overwhelmed them – the Puritan settlers in North America eventually made the discomforts of New England too familiar to be noticed; the Vikings in Greenland were eventually forced out, leaving behind a treeless wilderness populated by a few Inuit clans. Spengler was eventually discredited by the turn against metaphysical thinking; Toynbee merely fell out of fashion. To the post-colonial era the concept was weighed down by the baggage it carried. By the mid-1960s one of the most famous historians of his time, Fernand Braudel, found himself on the defensive, protesting that while, as a historical category, civilization had always had an uneasy relationship with the granular reality of history, it was 'still useful' in denoting a social and cultural life with its own distinctive rhythms and cycles of growth (Braudel 1994: 30).

It is not possible to give a layered sense of the evolving history of the field in the years that followed. But, then, that is not my intention. The civilization game took off again in the public arena only in 1996 with the publication of Samuel Huntington's *The Clash of Civilizations*, which had begun life three years earlier as an article in the journal *Foreign Affairs*. The book was subsequently translated into forty languages; it helped that it was easy to read – its style was calm and matter-of-fact. To be frank, Huntington's thesis remains popular because the study of civilization is too – when you are selling an idea it makes sense to sell an idea that will sell. It won devotees in the West for another reason. His claim to have discovered the shape of the future offered a refreshing alternative to the micro-histories encouraged by the overproduction of PhDs (one of the scandals of contemporary university scholarship). The public is right to suspect that something has been lost by ignoring questions of large-scale change – the currents, rhythms and recurrences that make history so interesting. If you are writing about these themes you enjoy a built-in advantage: a taste for historical imperatives is something shared by most of us.

Probably what annoyed his critics – and annoys so many of them still – is that the book is a thoroughly uncomfortable read, especially for those of a liberal disposition. It is uncomfortable to read that we all share a need, he insisted, to express our identity and have it recognized and even respected. In the post-Cold War world the most important distinctions among peoples were not ideological, or even political, but cultural. 'Peoples and nations are attempting to answer the most basic question humans can face: Who are we? And they're answering that question in the traditional way human beings have answered it, by reference to the things that mean most to them. People define themselves in terms of ancestry, religion, language, history, values, customs and institutions . . .' (Huntington 1996: 21).

It was even more uncomfortable to be told that civilizations don't always coexist in harmony with each other, or that they often 'clash'. But Huntington's thesis continues to come to mind whenever we read about the persecution of religious groups such as the Yazidis, who were expelled by ISIS from Mosul, Iraq's second city, where they had been a presence for more than sixteen centuries, or the destruction of the last Christian church in Afghanistan by the Taliban in 2010. The trouble is that, once you have read the book, you can't unread it (the idea of a 'clash' comes to mind every time we read of another atrocity by ISIS or another terrorist group).

Huntington's critics were quick, however, to argue that, if civilizations were as invariant as he suggested, they were also incoherent; their unity, such as it was, had often broken down. Aren't most contemporary conflicts intra-civilizational – pitting Catholic against Protestant, Sunni against Shia, Hindu against Muslim and Buddhist in South Asia? They also argued that all civilizations have been marked by cross-fertilization, the adoption of foreign gods and styles and patterns of enquiry. History does indeed show that civilizational encounters can be both constructive and confrontational; more often than not they tend to be the former. But the fact that we must make up our own minds about where the balance should be struck is a fact of political life and not a failure in Huntington's exposition. Remember that he was trying to prepare us for a conversation, not a viva.

We are still reading Huntington twenty years later because he appears to have been swimming with the tide, not against it. 'There are signs that civilization is making something of a comeback', claimed Krishan Kumar in 2014, and some of the reasons he gives are fairly self-explanatory (Kumar 2014: 16–17). One is the rise of militant Islam, which received a shot in the arm with the Iranian Revolution in 1979 which continues to inspire many radical Muslims in the same way that the October Revolution in Russia of 1917 continued to inspire many on the left long after they had lost their illusions about the 'radiant future' that it promised. Then there is the economic rise of China, and latterly India, which has led many commentators – many of them in the West – to conclude that Asian values are far superior to Western ones in generating economic growth. Economists predict that, by 2050, the Chinese economy will be larger than all the Western economies combined, and that India's will be about the same size as that of the United States. Culture here matters too.

And then there was the War on Terror which George W. Bush proclaimed the day after 9/11. It also helped to give Huntington's thesis a renewed lease of life. Critics might claim that the Bush administration saw the threat to Western civilization, as it were, at one remove: through its own overheated imagination. They might well complain that American officials were able to tell a great story without the hindrance of nuance or subtlety. But the story had traction outside the Western world too. In her novel *The Ministry of Utmost Happiness* (2017) Arundhati Roy doesn't mention by name the cast list of the 'War on Terror', but there is no mistaking who they are: 'the planes that flew into the tall buildings in America came as a boon to many in India too. The Poet-Prime Minister of the country and several of his senior ministers were members of an old organization that believed India was essentially a Hindu nation and that just as Pakistan had declared itself an Islamic Republic, India should declare itself a Hindu one.' The 'Poet-Prime Minister' is Atal Bihari Vajpayee, prime minister from 1998 to 2004, and the 'organization' is the Rashtriya Swayamsevak Sangh, the Hindu nationalist missionary movement founded in 1925 that still sustains the BJP, the party that came to power a few years ago.

And finally there was the shock of Donald Trump's victory in 2016. In an article in *Foreign Policy*, Stephen Walt claimed that Trump and his advisers in the new administration were operating from a broad 'clash of civilizations' framework that informed both their aversion to multiculturalism at home and their identification of friends and enemies abroad. 'In this essentially cultural, borderline racialist world view, the (mostly white) Judeo-Christian world is under siege from various "other" forces, especially Muslims.' It was a worldview that explained, in part, the new president's singular sympathy with Putin's Russia. 'For the people who see the world this way, Putin is a natural ally. He declares mother Russia to be the main defender of Christianity and he likes to stress the dangers from Islam . . . And if Islam is the real source of danger, and we are in the middle of a decades-long clash of civilizations, who cares about the balance of power in Asia' (Walt, 2017).

Whether or not this analysis was fair to Trump, it certainly wasn't fair to Huntington or, for that matter, to Vladimir Putin. If we care about fake history, facts should still matter. Huntington never claimed, as Walt insisted in his article, that religion constituted the ideational core of Russian civilization. As for Putin, he is fully cognizant of the fact that, in the near future, the fastest growing ethnic group in Russia will be Muslim. Putin has always been consistent in his insistence that the idea of building a mono-ethnic (Slav) state would not only be contrary to the country's history; it would also represent 'the shortest path to the destruction of . . . the Russian state system' (Tsygankov 2016: 151).

The myth of liberal civilization

In one of Henrik Ibsen's most famous plays, the heroine Hedda Gabler finds herself married to a historian who is writing a book on the domestic industries of Brabant in the High Middle Ages. Her former lover has recently published a popular book on a much bigger theme: the march of civilization. When he calls on Hedda's husband he is quick to inform him that he is already writing a sequel. His first book was on the history of civilization; the second will be about its future. Good heavens, remarks Hedda's husband, we know nothing of the future, to which his academic rival replies, rather archly: 'There is a thing or two to be said about it all the same.' The point is that Hedda's lover is planning to write a book dealing with the biggest theme of all: the route by which Western civilization had become the end state of mankind.

Western writers ever since have shuttled back and forth between two ideas: one, which Spengler and Huntington embraced, that Western civilization is just one of many; the other that it is at the forefront of the historically sanctioned construction of a single normative order. This is why at the end of the Cold War Francis Fukuyama's thesis about the 'end of history' resonated so much in Western minds. 'What we may be witnessing', he wrote, 'is not just the end of the Cold War, or the passing of a particular period of post-war history, but the end of history as such: that is, the endpoint of mankind's ideological evolution and the universalization of Western liberal democracy as the final form of human government' (Fukuyama 1989: 4). There would be no more ideological grounds for major conflict between nations. Even Islamic fundamentalism would have 'no universal significance'. The fact that the process was, as yet, incomplete in much of the world outside Europe and North America – what Fukuyama called those 'most advanced outposts . . . at the vanguard of civilization' – was largely inconsequential: it had no bearing on the underlying logic of history which would continue propelling the world towards a single liberal civilization (ibid.: 5). And Fukuyama, by the way, was not alone in promoting this vision. Other conservative writers embraced it too. Take Charles Krauthammer, who wrote an essay in *The National Interest* the same year proposing what he called 'universal dominion': the creation of a Western super-sovereign state that would establish universal peace even if the price would be 'the conscious depreciation not only of American sovereignty, but the notion of sovereignty itself'.

On the left, too, American politicians sought to structure the public debate in terms of the narrative of globalization. Mindful of what he called a domestic climate of 'apathetic internationalism', Bill Clinton offered the world the Third Way – a chance to externalize an American domestic agenda with the promise that globalization would introduce the rest of the world to American ideas (Romano 2006). In *The Fight is for Democracy* (2003), George Packer argued that 'a vibrant, hard-headed liberalism' could use the American military to promote its values. The subtitle of Peter Beinhart's *The Good Fight* (2006) was 'Why liberals and only liberals can win the War on Terror'.

So there you have it if you are Western: the fact that only you have had an Enlightenment (you can add or subtract the adjective 'European' – it is only a catechistic point) bears witness to the fact that you really did reach the future first. And there are extenuating circumstances for entertaining this delusion, for delusion it most certainly is. You got the Industrial Revolution before anyone else; the West still has a monopoly on 'soft power' – it is still a magnet for other people's thoughts and opinions. And whether or not you may subscribe to any of these opinions, to all or none of the above, you probably find yourself considerably more interesting than anyone else.

But these days it's becoming difficult to regard the West as being at the centre of the *anthropos* in the word 'anthropology', a word derived from Attic Greek. If you are a Western reader you might have to conclude that you are indeed WEIRD. For the 'liberal civilization' – your own – that you once thought universal is now under challenge, and not only from the non-Western world, where it has failed to fire the popular imagination. At home, it has its critics too, those who are not rich, who are often under-educated, who find themselves living in a post-industrial wasteland, and feel that their democratic representatives are largely indifferent to their fate. Their instincts are more tribal – when they think of Western civilization, if they give any thought to it at all, their focus is more parochial. They want to downsize while they still have time; they want to take the 'liberal' out of civilization. And it is their discontents that are being held responsible for some of the challenges liberal Western societies now face at home, from nationalism to populism, from neo-fascist attacks on immigration to neo-Marxist critiques of capitalism. In other words, the liberal civilization that we once took for granted no longer looks robust enough to carry the intellectual freight it once carried.

Liberal civilization and its discontents

In his last years Sigmund Freud (1856–1939) wrote a book on the troubles of his own times. In English the book is called *Civilization and its Discontents*. In German it is known as *Das Unglück in der Kultur*. Unfortunately, there are several problems with the English translation. The first is that Freud didn't use the word 'civilization', he used 'Kultur', and for a German-speaking author the two words are very different. *Kultur* refers to the moral value-system of a society, *Zivilisation* to its technological and technical achievements. It was a distinction, as we shall see later, that played a large role in the German imagination in the run-up to the First World War. For German nationalists, Anglo-American civilization was considered *kulturlos* – i.e., largely valueless precisely because it was so cosmopolitan.

The second problem is that the word *Unglück* is not strictly 'discontent'. 'Uneasiness' would be a better translation. Discontent and uneasiness, of course, are very different. One constitutes a dissatisfaction of the mind, against for example a perceived injustice, the other a feeling that life should be other than it is (Bettelheim 1982: 100–1). Later Freud compounded this problem by advising his English translator to drop her original choice of the word 'malaise' and opt for 'discontent' instead. In his book, Freud argued that civilization repressed our natural inclination for aggressiveness, which he had come to conclude was 'the original, self-substituting, instinctual disposition in Man' ([1936] 1985: 313) So it is not surprising that the work has never been out of print, because we have never been entirely free of the thought that even the most 'civilized' societies can regress very quickly to barbarism. The two states often coexist, calling each other into being.

Freud's argument, in a nutshell, was that the civilizing process had made people very unhappy by persuading them to buy into ideas which their ancestors would have embraced at their peril, such as to love one's neigh-bour as oneself or to turn the other cheek when attacked. Social rules had come to replace natural instincts. Not only that: people were encouraged to feel ashamed of their instincts and to repress them by developing a guilty conscience. In other words, we have paid a high price for civilization: disenchantment. And sometimes disenchantment with disenchantment can lead to violent acts.

If we turn to liberal civilization – the dream of a unified world that followed on from earlier Western thinking – we find that it has generated discontents of its own. Westerners too often tend to forget their privileged position in the world, which stems in part from their remarkable good fortune since the Second World War. For many non-Western societies, the world is a much harder, darker and more unforgiving place than they can ever imagine. And that is exactly what the Canadian journalist Michael Ignatieff discovered in 1993 as he travelled through six politically embattled regions of the world, including the former Yugoslavia, which was then being torn apart by a vicious civil war, and the more remote areas of Kurdistan, which spawned its own ethnic identities and hatreds. What he discovered was a world that was no longer attuned to the civilized values that had once held local nationalities in check. More disturbing still, the values which he had taken for granted were apparently not shared by everyone else (Ignatieff 1994: 189). What distressed him most about the violence in the Balkans was its challenge to what he called 'liberal civilization'. The situation in fact was all too reminiscent of the 1930s, with its pogroms, ethnic cleansing and genocidal acts, and, of course, the burning of books, Freud's among them. Possibly, he concluded, 'liberal civilization runs deeply against the human grain and is achieved and sustained only by the most unremitting struggle against human nature' (cited in Kagan 2014).

Ultimately, Ignatieff's explanation was not that dissimilar from Freud's, even if in this particular case it was 'liberal civilization', and not civilization itself, that was deemed to repress our natural instinct, in this instance to bond with the tribe on ethnic, racial or other lines. What he was questioning is the extent to which the age-old values of civilization (in its liberal incarnation) had penetrated down from a metropolitan elite to the population at large – the extent, in other words, to which they had reshaped, or failed to reshape, the emotional lives of a people. Recently other writers have also come to conclude that the Enlightenment's faith in humanism and rationalism can no longer adequately account for, still less explain away, the violence of the world in which we find ourselves living (Mishra 2016). It just so happens, writes Pankaj Mishra, that the world's discontented have begun 'to mobilize against a civilization based on a false premise, that of gradual progress under liberal-democrat trustees' (Mishra 2017).

It has been argued, by the way, that Freud was not talking about civilization at all so much as the triumph of global capitalism (Bauman 1997: 2). Just at the time that Ignatieff was touring the hot spots of the world, one of my more eminent colleagues, Susan Strange (1923–1998), wrote an article about what she chose to call 'business civilization', a term she coined to describe an informal grouping of transnational corporations, business school graduates and international agencies such as the World Trade Organization (WTO) (Strange 1990: 260–3). For Strange, the concept of civilization needed to be radically redefined. It no longer usefully captured a way of life that had its origins in the Indus Valley, the Yellow River and the Near East five thousand years ago. Instead it constituted something new: a globalized community of bankers and financiers who spent their time cooling their heels in airport business lounges or attending meetings of the World Economic Forum at Davos. These were the people who wanted to optimize globally rather than nationally in order to maximize profits and who were indifferent to national interests. And they were helped by digital technology that seemed to make distance irrelevant, and geography too. These are the people, writes Robert Cox, who are now confronted with an acute existential dilemma: the challenge of 'dual civilization-ship' (Cox 2000: 224).

Politicians usually avoid invoking the 'g-word'. Instead of globalization, they prefer to talk of 'uncontrolled immigration' or 'stagnating wages' or 'the erosion of cultural values'. Looking back, however, it is clear that the 'liberal civilization' that Ignatieff celebrated back in 1993 carried the seeds of its own destruction. Not only did it encourage unbridled greed on the part of bankers and shareholders who expected immediate returns on their investment (there used to be a joke on Wall Street that a long-term investment was a short-term speculation that had gone badly wrong). At the same time, socialist or social democratic parties, having lost many of their basic ideological convictions, were captured by metropolitan elites whose preoccupation with university 'safe spaces' and transgender rights distanced them from their working-class supporters. For those who voted for Donald Trump in the 2016 election, a more immediate apocalypse loomed – Chinese factories which were putting them out of business and Islamic terrorists who were threatening their lives at home. Trump appealed to millions of Americans who weren't so much racist or even right-wing as distressed citizens who were inclined to view an increasingly unrecognizable world through the prism of their own victimization. In Europe and the United States, many workers are experiencing at first hand what it feels like to become a redundant link in a global value-chain. China, not the West, did the best out of globalization by surfing the wave and ignoring the rules – employing trade policies technically prohibited by the WTO, managing its own currency and keeping tight control of international capital flows.

Liberals have come into uneasy contact with another inescapable political reality – they imagined that the rest of the world would find the project equally alluring, but many remain largely unmoved or uninspired by the message. Too often liberal internationalists tended to see themselves as Robespierre's 'armed missionaries' and to treat the project more as an evangelical mission than a political one. They forgot that normative power is largely persuasive – those who espouse it have to persuade, not preach – and that persuasion is the means by which agent action become social structure, ideas become norms, and the subjective becomes, if you're lucky, the intersubjective (Finnemore and Sikkink 1998).

But the crisis of liberal civilization goes much deeper. It involves cultural self-esteem. In the United States, Trump is at war with what he likes to call 'the new barbarity – Davos-inspired crony capitalism' and the dilution of Judeo-Christian values thanks to political correctness, multiculturalism and rampant secularization, all three of which are deemed in a Freudian sense to repress the natural instinct to defend the values of the tribe. Liberal civilization or 'liberal non-democracy' – you get to choose which term you prefer. It would appear that both are having to fight their corner just at the time that the non-Western world, sensing that the West is in eclipse, is re-engaging with its own values and cultural achievements, and this at a time when Western intellectuals have begun to question whether civilization itself is even an ethically acceptable category.

A suspect category?

Let me admit to personal bias. I'm the product of Western civilization. I read the Greek and Latin classics at school (yes, I too spent a lot of time in the company of 'Uncle Virgil', translating one of my set texts, the second book of the *Aeneid*). I confess I am not particularly surprised by the resilience of civilizational identities in the non-Western world, but I am surprised by how weak they are becoming in the West. Rather belatedly, the political class, certainly in Europe, is mounting a rearguard stand to remind its citizens that it was only thanks to a very strong sense of civilizational identity that the liberal powers were able to prevail in the great ideological struggles of the last century.

This is not to deny that civilization is a deeply problematic concept for many Westerners because it carries a lot of cultural baggage. For a start, it brings to mind the former 'civilizing mission' which Europe's Victorian forefathers appropriated for themselves and which finds expression in one of Donald Trump's many tweets following yet another terrorist attack in Europe, in which he demanded that 'the civilized world must change other people's thinking' (Engelke 2017: 65). It confronts the West as it does no one else with its former predisposition to see the 'savage' and the 'barbaric' in binomial terms, introduced into Western thinking by the Greeks, who liked to draw other ontological distinctions between men and women and humans and (other) animals. Binomial thinking, of course, is only a way of organizing knowledge. It's useful in some contexts, but as knowledge increases, not in others. It may not be hardwired into us, but some psychologists argue that it is part of the human condition – it's the way by which we process complex information. Even today it still encourages us to see people as 'types' or to attribute to countries different national characteristics. But, that said, it can also bring one thing into relationship with another and can over time get a person with imagination to think through her own first principles.

Finally, 'civilization' is also a vivid example of what academics call a 'contested concept'. It accredits some kind of valued achievement, though it is not always clear what is being valued. As a concept it always begs the question: What is 'civilized' about civilization? It allows more variations of judgement in this respect than the notion of society, for we can discuss the stability or viability of a society without necessarily asking whether it is especially 'sociable'. And doesn't the word 'civilization' encourage us to trash the achievements of others (their artistic representations and architectural styles)? Doesn't it encourage us to distrust 'otherness' and identify what we consider to be 'barbaric'; and doesn't it also make us insensitive to the plight of our own less fortunate citizens, who may well feel that they are not really part of the civilization that is being celebrated?

Even more regrettable, writes Mohsin Hamid, a Pakistani who spent his childhood in the United States and much of his adult life in London, the term encourages us to deny our common humanity and to allocate power resources and rights on a basis that is intensely discriminatory. 'Civilizations encourage our hypocrisies to flourish. And by so doing they undermine globalization's only plausible promise: that we be free to invent ourselves. Why, exactly, can't a Muslim be European? Why can't an unreligious person be Pakistani? Why can't a man be a woman? Why can't someone who's gay be married?' (Hamid 2015: xvi). To what civilization does a Syrian atheist belong? Or a Muslim soldier in the US Army? Or a lesbian fashion designer in Nigeria? There speaks the voice of Kantian cosmopolitanism, and Hamid's novel *The Reluctant Fundamentalist* (2008) warns us what being forced to choose an identity may lead to and what violent actions it may provoke.

Let us admit that chopping up history into manageable units such as chiefdoms, civilizations and nation-states is a bit like butchery – a job that requires both skill and a measure of brutality. Even so, cultural differences are real enough and cannot be dismissed as an example of what Marxists used to call 'false consciousness'. The fact that a concept may be contested is no reason not to employ it. How many Muslims (or Christians in Russia) are predisposed to atheism? Why are transsexuals welcomed in some cultures (Thailand) but find themselves persecuted in others (India)? Why is gay marriage unpopular with the majority of Russians? The argument that we have many identities – class, race, ethnicity, sexuality – is fair enough, and those identities are clearly deeply felt by many people. But most of us derive our ultimate security from solidarity with the larger tribe, usually still the nation-state. And when a civilization is coterminous with a state, as it is in the case of China and Japan, or with a geographical region, as it is in the case of Russia, or when it runs parallel with a liberal project, as it does in the West, there is also the pull of civilizational affinity.

The historian Joan Kelly (1928–1982) once asked herself whether women ever had a 'Renaissance' (Kelly 1977: 137–61). But the fact that she believed the number of women in powerful positions had actually fallen in early modern Europe did not lead her, as a woman, to reject Europe's Renaissance inheritance, any more than it prompted her, as an American, to deny that it was not a central experience of the civilization with which her own country chose to identify. So, while we all have a responsibility to acknowledge the importance of cross-cutting loyalties in people's lives, we also have a duty to recognize that they may feel a much stronger affinity with those clubs which put them in touch with the largest number of people.

So, when we talk about 'civilization', we must recognize that we are invoking a concept that has not been cooked up solely by academics. It is not detached from the world of everyday experience. If you are Chinese you don't have to be told that your civilization is the oldest on the planet.

But to insist, as does one contemporary Chinese writer, that the Chinese are members of a 'politicised ethnic group' is to identify a potential area of contestation with others (cited in Hughes 2011: 607). People still draw their identity from the group to which they belong – usually still the nation, occasionally reconfigured into a new political entity – the civilizational state. The fact is that the concept of civilization is alive in the imagination because it is deemed, rightly or wrongly, to express all that is best in a people's communal life. And it's not at all certain at this stage in history that it would be wise to dispense with the concept altogether.

2

Civilizational Myths

Before going any further we really do need to ask what a civilization is. And why not, you might well conclude: surely it is a good place to start? Except that it is a little more problematic than you might think.

The history of every major galactic civilization, we are told by Douglas Adams (1952–2001) in *The Restaurant at the End of the Universe*, passes through three distinct phases – survival, enquiry and sophistication (otherwise known as the 'how', 'why' and 'where' phases). For instance:

> The first phase is characterized by the question, '*How* can we eat?'
> The second by the question, '*Why* do we eat?'
> And the third, by the question, '*Where* shall we have lunch?'

The book is the second in a series of five which exploded into the world with the better-known *The Hitchhiker's Guide to the Galaxy* (1979), a best-seller which has been translated into thirty different languages. As a historical shorthand Adams's amusing *aperçu* is not such a bad understanding of the long road that led from hunter-gatherer societies to the very first civilizations. 'In the annals of humanity's biggest accomplishments, cuisine has been underrated', adds Timothy Taylor, a professor of prehistory at Vienna University (Taylor 2010: 184).

The question 'How can we eat?' takes us back to beginning of the human story, 1.5 million years ago, when we discovered fire. As soon as we learnt to cook we went to the top of the food chain. The second step in our cultural evolution opened with the migration of our remote ancestors out of Africa to very different environments which offered a greater range of food. The third step saw the invention of agriculture, though some historians suggest that we would have been much better off staying as hunter-gatherers. One school of historians insists that farming was 'the window of opportunity' which we needed to make history and which we jumped through as soon as we could (Cook 2003: 7). The other insists that we were pushed through it kicking and screaming (Smail 2008: 197). Historians and archaeologists are a contentious lot: they rarely agree with one another on anything. On the evidence available it's certainly true that, until the advent of mechanization in the early twentieth century, farmers lived brutally difficult, hard and exhausting lives. Only 150 years ago it took twenty-five men all day to harvest 1 ton of grain; a combine harvester can do it in 6 minutes. Farming involves much higher workloads and leads to more physical ailments than relying on the wild. The diseases and poverty that agriculture brought with it to Neolithic village life may also explain why it took four thousand years for the first city-states to appear, such as Uruk in 3200 BCE, then the largest city in the world.

The point is that historians used to smuggle all sorts of teleological assumptions into their work; they assumed that history had a direction, if not a purpose, and that civilization was the end state. This way of reading history back from an endpoint allowed them to adopt two contradictory perspectives: history was either continuing progress to a final and permanent civilized state, which the Victorians assumed the Europeans had reached first, or all civilizations, including Western, were fated to decline. In effect, what they were doing was prioritizing civilization not only as an anthropological constant but also as an ultimate historical unit. But both schools of thought were in agreement that human beings were fated to move on. As Immanuel Kant famously remarked, we would eventually escape from our state of 'self-imposed immaturity'; and if we'd spent most of our history in the hunter-gatherer state that was not for lack of ability but for lack of audacity, for not daring to imagine that life might be lived on other terms.

The question 'Why do we eat?' is of course a philosophical one, and philosophy really does require a degree of literacy. The written word is usually taken to be the litmus test of civilized life for that reason. That is not to deny that many oral societies are often more advanced than we think, and many still have much to tell us. What we find in the prehistoric imagination is what we prize most about ourselves: the self-realization of our humanity through symbols, such as art, which is why even today we can still learn something from a painting that was daubed on a cave wall 15,000 years ago. But what is important about literacy is that it allows you to codify laws (and no longer to rely just on social conventions) and to keep archives (enough to establish legal precedents). It facilitates introspection (philosophy) as well as reflection (history) (Goody 1995: 160). And, over time, the unchanging world of oral memory and myth gave way to a more reflective and enquiring mind and in turn to more optimistic thinking. Civilization allowed the thoughts of society to fuse and be reabsorbed by later generations by accessing the first cognitive platform, the clay tablet. In the very first civilization Sumerian scribes made replicas of their minds in mud. If we want to push the analogy further than perhaps we should, we might regard the clay tablet as the world's first silicon chip.

Adams's second and third phases almost fuse because, once you ask why, you have choices and can devise better ways of doing things. In a word, you can be more ambitious. The main difference between merely surviving and going to a restaurant for lunch is that, for us, survival alone has never been enough.

If all this sounds like a theory of evolution, perhaps it is. And although we are always enjoined not to be teleological, not to imagine that the evolution of anything has a purpose, there would seem to be something of a narrative here. If we had surveyed the world on the eve of the Holocene, asks the historian Michael Cook, could we have predicted the emergence of the very first civilizations? Almost certainly not. We are not dealing with a computer game designed by a programmer but with an emergent phenomenon. But knowing what we do, could history have turned out differently? The answer again is probably not. Civilization seems to have been our destiny (Cook 2003: 38–9). There would appear, in other words, to be no bottlenecks in the progression from hunter-gatherer tribes to civilization. And that's not necessarily true of other stages of evolution to complex life (such as the transition to multicellular life forms, which does not always take place). Civilization would appear to be the norm and not an evolutionary anomaly.

To understand why this is the case, let us look at the differences between ourselves and the 9 million other species with which we share the planet, or, in order to narrow the field, the very few with which we share some kind of 'social life'. It might be thought advisable, I suppose, to start with our nearest cousins, chimpanzees, who are very similar to us in their social behaviour. They have brains capable of making intelligent choices and communicating their feelings to other members of the group. They have a rudimentary Machiavellian intelligence: they form alliances and manipulate others; they hatch plots and betray their friends; and, like us, they sulk when their pride is injured. And we have even begun to attribute to them more and more abilities, including the use of tools. Indeed, the fact that chimps can crack a nut with a stone, argue some historians, surely allows them a back entrance into the Stone Age (Barras 2015). But although chimpanzees may have a culture of sorts, not even the most famous primatologists have ever suggested they have a civilization. We need to extend our enquiry further by looking at one of the oldest species to appear on the planet.

The Termite Dean

Twenty years ago the Harvard sociobiologist Edward Wilson engaged in a challenging thought experiment. He conjured up a fictitious Dean of Termites who, in the course of a stirring commencement address, gives a run-down of his species' greatest accomplishments:

Since our ancestors the macrotermitine termites achieved 110kg weight, had larger brains during the rapid evolution through the later Tertiary Period, and learned to write with pheromonal script, termitistic scholarship has elevated and refined ethical philosophy. It is now possible to express the imperatives of moral behaviour with precision. These imperatives are most self-evident and universal. They are the very essence of termicity. They include the love of darkness and of the deep saprophytic dasidiomycetic penetralia of the soil; the centrality of colony life amidst a richness of war and trade with other colonies; the sanctity of the physiological caste system; the evil of personal rights (the colony is ALL!); our deep love for the royal siblings allowed to reproduce; the joy of chemical song; the aesthetic pleasure and deep social satisfaction of eating faeces from nest-mates' anuses after the shedding of our skin, and the ecstasy of cannibalism and surrender of our own bodies for consumption when sick or injured . . .

Some termitistically inclined scientists, particularly the ethnologists and socio-biologists, argue that our social organization is shaped by our genes, and that our ethical precepts simply reflect the peculiarities of termite evolution. They assert that ethical philosophy must take into account the structure of the termite brain and the evolutionary history of the species. Socialization is genetically channelled and some forms of it all but inevitable. (Wilson 1997: 97)

Wilson is not the only writer to have asked how we differ from other social species. Long before Darwin (1809–1882), philosophers were struck by the sociability of insects. Aristotle (384–322 BCE) was the first philosopher to suggest that bees and ants create sociable societies, but he also insisted that there was a major difference when it came to human societies, and that difference was speech. Insects work together because they are genetically programmed to do so. The termite world is genetically networked and intentionally collaborative. Termites follow a series of genetically prescribed rules of interaction and behaviour that have not changed over millions of years. Thanks to language, however, our species insists on arguing out the terms on which we live. Language encourages cooperation. It affords us a way to evaluate reciprocity, to ask whether we are getting the best out of a contract, and to establish how far we can place our trust in the person with whom we are cooperating. Possibly even more important is our ability to talk to ourselves. Daniel Dennett suggests that we might have developed the skill so that we could explain our actions to other people; our minds are 'clearinghouses' in which we can rehearse justifications for our actions and run through the reasons that might persuade other people to follow our advice (Dennett 2017).

But to return to Wilson's termite analogy: Is it possible – stretching a point – to come up with a similar biological take on human civilization? The anthropologist Laura Betzig actually has. Civilizations, she maintains, are merely struggles for genetic representation. Take eusocial emperors in China and the Byzantine Empire who, like eusocial insects, turned their subordinates into sterile castes while remaining overly fertile themselves. Think of the eunuchs who served the later Roman and Chinese emperors. Some of them went on to command armies (Narses (478–573) in the case of Byzantium) and even to command naval expeditions (Zheng He (1371–1433/1435) in the case of China) (Betzig 2015). Eusocial behaviour, by the way, involves a division of labour based not on cooperation among equals but on organized cooperation between groups performing long-term roles. Some groups make sacrifices for the good of the whole. Some of the sterile castes Betzig has in mind are the sons and daughters of aristocrats who became celibate priests, monks or nuns after the eleventh century. Occasionally priests even doubled-up as soldiers: seven Hungarian bishops died on the battlefield of Mohács (1526) fighting the Turks. Later, Western Europe even exported 'drones' across the Atlantic following America's discovery of Columbus; there they were able to breed in freedom, like insect workers whose habitats have opened up. In other words, suggests Betzig, far from emancipating us from biology, our history has a narrative, and it is all about reproduction. Forget the Benin bronzes, or the Parthenon, or the Hindu Vedas, or the

Great Chinese encyclopaedias, or a classical raga of India: all these, while impressive in their own right, are epiphenomena of a larger struggle to leave behind a genetic footprint. I admit that it is an amusing take, but I suspect that, even were we to believe it, we would be reluctant to embrace the thesis, for it would mean reducing our behaviour to nothing more impressive than a series of gene-programmed, profit-maximizing protocols.

The point is that we think of ourselves as agents of our own fate; and it is our imaginative ability to conceive of what *might* be which was responsible for the pyramids of ancient Egypt and the Pantheon in Rome. Unlike the deadening uniformity of a termite kingdom, human civilizations show an extraordinary diversity of expression, which is why both the pyramids and the Pantheon still appear at the top of the tourist checklist of places to visit: we are intrigued by what our ancestors achieved through teamwork, as well as by the breadth of their imagination. Of course, termites can be said to have something that looks like a civilization of sorts. As Wilson reminds us, they have a rudimentary language, a pheromonal script; they have a warrior caste that specializes in warfare; and they have a strong political predisposition to authority. But they are not a society so much as a multicellular organism. True, they may work collectively, but their collective actions are not really so different from those of cells in our own bodies; they are simply more loosely organized.

We are very different. For us too, of course, civilization is a collective enterprise. It rests on a division of cognitive labour: scribes record information; warriors read histories of war or are encouraged to – if they think much about it at all; politicians come up with strategies for realizing their political ambitions. Our ability to work together in teams (whether we call them that or not) is what makes us such a remarkable species. We all rely on collective intelligence: we can access the specialized knowledge of others. In other words, if social insects are sometimes described as eusocial, we should think of ourselves as being *ultra-social* (Pagel 2012: 73).

At the same time – and this is the problem – we are often very unsociable indeed, particularly when the tribe with which we identify seems to be under threat. Termites may well outlive us precisely because they don't have the benefit of civilization. Without it, for example, you can't build a nuclear bomb. If we do destroy ourselves in a nuclear war, termites will almost certainly survive us; but we can rest assured that, even after our disappearance, termite archaeologists are unlikely to be found shifting through the rubble of our long-compacted cities.

So what is a civilization?

'Civilization is . . . a general, hidden, complex fact; very difficult, I allow, to describe, to relate, but which nonetheless for that exists [and] has a right to be described and related' (Guizot [1846] 1997: 31). I have lifted the sentence from *The History of Civilization in Europe* by François Guizot (1787–1874), the first book of its kind anywhere in the world. It was based on a series of lectures which were delivered in 1828. By the time Guizot put pen to paper, he did so in the knowledge that a civilization that has survived several thousand years (like his own) never entirely loses touch with the past; its past continues to live on into the present. His own generation still read Virgil (in Latin) and still saw Greek philosophy as the bedrock of civilized life. It shared the civilization, in other words, with those who had preceded it, but it also took its achievements further. By then the word 'civilization' had come to mean what we understand it to mean today.

We use the term all the time, of course, without giving it much thought. It is a marvellously elastic concept, but it is not that elastic. Guizot established the common minimum. Although it is synonymous with culture in the anthropological sense of a lifestyle, or the beliefs (religious or otherwise) of a particular group of people, we usually apply the term to denote societies that have developed a market of some kind (a system of production and distribution) as well as a developed urban life (with a hierarchical class/caste system at its heart). Add to that a bureaucratic infrastructure based (usually) on literacy which at least allows records to be kept and history to be written. And then there are the material achievements – the unapologetic magnificence of buildings such as the Parthenon, or the extraordinary ambition that lies behind projects such as the Great Wall of China, or such extraordinary imaginative departures as the Bauhaus project in 1920s Germany.

So, when we talk of a civilization, think of it, if you will, as a lifestyle start-up that becomes over time a business conglomerate, though a better metaphor might be a constant 'work in progress'. For, unless a civilization collapses, its evolution never stops. Western civilization is often thought of as distinctly Christian, but the Christian phase of its history is not a particularly long one, and today Europe (but not the United States) is becoming increasingly 'post-Christian'. India is still often thought of as a Hindu civilization, but in medieval China its identity was very different; it used to be known as the 'Buddhist Kingdom'. Civilizations can be counted among the oldest and most resilient social units for a reason; they have survived because they are always adapting to the times while preserving an underlying shape.

Is there a Western civilization?

Isn't it time, however, asks the Harvard philosopher Kwame Appiah, to give up on the very idea that there is something called Western civilization? Has there ever been one? (Appiah 2016). Appiah regards civilizations as being so embedded in historical particularities that they cannot meaningfully be arranged in a single family tree. Instead he prefers to see Western civilization as a palimpsest constituted of so many layers of fact and fiction that it is difficult to tell one from the other. Like many critics, he prefers to identify the fault-lines and fissures that make it difficult, if not impossible, to give any concrete form to the subject being discussed. In other words, there is very little hope of nailing it down.

True, can any civilization be fully explored, mapped or understood? Neither the Greeks nor sixteenth-century Europeans, for example, regarded themselves as 'Western', a term which dates back only to the late eighteenth century. If brought together, however, they would probably still recognize something of themselves in the other beyond their common humanity. Even today Westerners still read Homer. On a quite different plane, computer games such as *Rise of the Argonauts* and *The God of War* franchise offer a portal to the classical world for the young, as do the film adaptations of Rick Riordan's *Percy Jackson and the Olympians*. What is remarkable is that, two thousand years later, Western writers still seek inspiration in Greek mythology to tell their stories of everyday life.

The secret of every surviving civilization's resilience in fact is its ability to evolve. And I use the term quite self-consciously, for it is fashionable these days to employ evolutionary metaphors or frameworks for understanding change. Evolution as a metaphor is ingrained in our thinking. The closest thing we have to a human essence, writes Yuval Noah Harari, is our DNA, and even the DNA molecule is the vehicle of mutation (Harari 2016: 105). So if you want to pin down the civilization of the West, think of it as an organic entity that began with the Roman encounter with Greek culture and evolved from the Greco-Roman to the European (though the Europeans regarded themselves not as Europeans but as members of 'Christendom' until quite late in the day) before eventually mutating into something we call a Euro-Atlantic community. And these different transmutations are easy enough to identify chronologically. Western civilization isn't shapeless.

Let me take just two examples: philosophy and literature. When it comes to philosophy, the Greeks really do seem to have got there first. In all the tens of thousands of surviving cylinders and tablets bearing cuneiform script, there is not a single logogram that expresses a Near Eastern concept (Egyptian or Babylonian) of what might be called the 'pursuit of truth'. Nor can we find even a rudimentary methodical practice or understanding of what might be the best way of capturing it (Dusenbury 2016: 26). So, with justification, I think we can say that philosophy was an invention of the Greeks, at least west of the Indus Valley. Continuity, by the way, doesn't mean an unbroken tradition. What makes a tradition continuous is its constant reappearance at critical times in the life of the civilization concerned. All of Western philosophy, the early twentieth-century philosopher Alfred Whitehead (1861–1947) famously proclaimed, is merely a set of footnotes to Plato (428/427 or 424/423–348/347 BCE). And Plato's name keeps reappearing again and again in the story of Western philosophy. He was the first public intellectual, and the Academy he set up at Athens was the first Western university department where young men could discuss philosophy and were to do so for the next 500 years; it remained at the heart of the Greco-Roman philosophical tradition until it was finally closed down in 529. Long before then neo-Platonism had made a significant contribution to early Christian theology; without it there would be no concept of a Christian God. And Plato's work was still to be found at the core of German philosophical thinking until at least the mid-twentieth century: imagine the work of Martin Heidegger or Hans-Georg Gadamer without it (Sloterdijk 2013: 4).

The Romans borrowed more from the Greeks than their philosophy. They copied their literary forms such as epic and lyric poetry. Indeed, Latin translations of Greek works such as the *Iliad* enabled the Romans to network the Mediterranean world. Dennis Feeney has gone so far as to describe this process as the very first appearance of a 'worldwide web'. He also reminds us that no other people in the ancient world, neither the Egyptians, for example, nor the Phoenicians, translated other people's works. The Romans, in that sense, can be said to have forged Western civilization by deliberately not patenting their own literary conventions and genres but adapting instead the Greek classics to their own uses (Feeney 2016). And what that synthesis produced in turn was the Western canon, a body of work that still remains the bedrock of the humanities which continue to be taught (even in the face of cultural opposition from some) in the schools and universities of North America and Europe.

It is that canon which more than anything else still fixes the idea of Western civilization in most people's minds. It most vividly maps out the contours of its life. And it has a life precisely because it has evolved. As

T. S. Eliot once remarked, it is impossible to gum leaves back on trees; the literature of the past cannot be grafted onto that of the present, but it can be revised and adapted. In the case of early modern Europe and the Renaissance, the great texts of the ancient world – many of which were rediscovered – inspired competition, not emulation. In the sixteenth century, Montaigne (1533–1592) broke with tradition by creating an entirely new literary form – a series of conversational-style essays which took their cue from classical authors such as Cicero (106–43 BCE) – while at the same time transcending them by offering what Cicero couldn't: 'a diversity of judgement' as opposed to a single point of view. His early readers, for example, were doubtless amazed to be told that all religious opinions were merely 'conjectures'.

And the canon is expanding all the time: think of the trademarks or styles specific to modern Western literature such as the Gothic and the historical novel and the *Bildungsroman*, to name but three. With the appearance of the nation-state there arose distinctive national styles and then the first serious literature to take the remotest parts of the world as their theme – think of the South Sea novels of Herman Melville (1819–1891) and the ambition of Ezra Pound (1885–1972) to find a Western equivalent for Chinese ideogrammatic writing (Moretti 2013: 2–14).

Of course, even this story is somewhat reductive. In the end, Western civilization is no different from any other: it offers a series of styles which interact and overlap, and which converge at the poles of the pre-modern/ modern eras, like meridians on a map. So is there a Western civilization? Of course there is, and the same is also true of the few other civilizations to have survived into the twenty-first century. They too are highly diverse, and it is the diversity that is part of their underlying unity. As scientists discovered to their surprise in the 1970s, complexity is not an enemy of order – quite the opposite. The fact that an eco-system is so complex is what makes it so stable.

Let us go back for the last time, however, to Edward Wilson's Termite Dean. Termite societies are highly complex too; termites are an impressive species, to be sure. They have been around for millions of years (far longer than we have). And they have evolved extraordinarily complex systems of cooperation. What they lack is language and what it enables – dreaming. They cannot tell themselves stories about how life might be other than it is. They cannot set off on 'crusades' against other termite realms. They have no civilizing mission or aspiration to make the termite world 'safe for autocracy'. Nor do they share any concept of termite 'rights'; they don't harbour revolutionary ambitions. They have not changed in millions of years because their world is bounded by 'terminicity'. Our world is bounded only by the laws of physics and in the case of our humanity by what we can dream, and our dreams are structured by language which allows us to tell ourselves some stirring stories. We are the supreme storytelling species for that reason.

But storytelling also allows us to spin myths, which tend to lodge themselves strongly in the popular imagination and are often exploited by politicians for their own purposes. Originally a myth was thought to represent a timeless but elusive truth about the human condition, and that is still the case even with specific cultural identities. What can be more striking if you're a Russian nationalist than to be told that your civilization has a 'soul'? No other civilization, after all, advances such a claim. Myths, remember, don't claim to be history; they claim to be *larger* than history, which is why they persist. And, more than historical narratives, myths have much more lasting influence precisely because they don't have much truck with ambiguity or ambivalence; instead they highlight what is most immediate and vivid in a people's collective life. In a word, they help us to *essentialize* life, to reduce it to its basic components.

In an attempt to capture the essence of civilization we have told ourselves the following three myths:

1 Civilizational identities are essentially unchanging.
2 Civilizations are largely self-contained; they have gained little from contact with each other.

3 At the heart of every civilization there is a cultural code – a religion, a worldview, a social imaginary – which is simultaneously ontological and axiological; it defines its essential character and prescribes its expected behaviour.

All three myths tend to fence off existing civilizations from each other just at the very moment when historians are busily writing 'global histories', alongside the globalization of practically everything else. And all three were very much central to the Western imagination too – and to some extent still are; they allowed, as we shall see, Western states to forge a unique political civilization called 'the West'.

Myth 1: Civilizational exceptionalism

In the course of the twentieth century a number of prominent Western intellectuals developed a central narrative of their own civilization and the dangers it now faced. One of the most famous wrote that: 'When we say that our Western civilization comes from the Greeks, we ought to be clear what that means. It means that the Greeks began that greatest of all revolutions, the revolution which started just yesterday as it were, for we are still in its initial stage – the transition from the closed to an open society' (Popper 1946: 33). The quotation comes from one of the seminal texts of the Cold War, *The Open Society and its Enemies*, which was penned by the Austrian philosopher Karl Popper during the Second World War, not in war-torn Europe from which he had fled in 1938 but from the remoteness of Christchurch, New Zealand.

The Greece that Popper's generation recalled was celebrated in many popular histories of the time, such as Edith Hamilton's *The Greek Way* (1930). Reading their work today, one is reminded how distant we are from that era, but they were mining a rich historical seam: a particular version of Greek history. Browse the shelves of any major library or bookshop and you will still find books with titles such as *The Greek Genius, The Greek Triumph, The Greek Enlightenment, The Greek Experiment* and *The Greek Idea*. When I studied classics at school over forty years ago we took all this for granted. Only later did I discover that this was only part of the picture; it was largely the cover story, but what a cover story! As the French writer Paul Valéry pointedly remarked, it was perhaps 'the most beautiful invention of the modern age' (Lilla 2016b: 43).

The prevailing myth that Popper and his generation chose to spin was that of Western exceptionalism – and that view still has traction. For Julia Kristeva, the Greeks – and only the Greeks – came up with 'the idea and practice of subjective freedom' (Kristeva 2000: 116). Not everyone would go that far, besides which it has become quite a fashion to condemn the idea of Greek exceptionalism which Popper and his generation took for granted. The historian Edith Hall thinks it is real enough (Hall 2014: xvii). She feels confident in identifying a certain 'open mentality' that made the Greeks an especially original people. It is only that these days we also remember their perpetual wars, and the slaves, though we also see them in a more critical light: should we celebrate the Greeks for anticipating the 'open society' when we recall their constant wars, their organized slave markets and their endemic misogyny? Or should we, adds Hall, ask a more interesting question: Could a society that did not have slave ownership on such an extensive scale ever have produced such a strong definition of individual freedom? (ibid.: 8).

At the heart of this idea is Herodotus' *History* and one of its sub-themes: the successful defence of the Greek city-states against the Persian invader. It is one thing, however, to celebrate the Greek defeat of the Persians; it is quite another to conclude that is the master narrative of Western history. Such a narrow perspective allows one to conclude – like Anthony Pagden, in his book *Worlds at War*, that the 'long struggle' between East and West won't conclude any time soon – that 'the battle lines drawn during the Persian wars more than twenty-three centuries ago are still in the self-same corner of the world', even if this time they are between Christian Europe and Islam (Pagden 2009: 538). It's one thing to celebrate the Greek achievement, quite another to attribute it to superior reasoning power. It's a different matter again to argue that the Greeks were able to grasp, as no one else succeeded in doing, the essentials of our own humanity, that, as Gertrude Himmelfarb writes, ideas such as justice, reason and the love of humanity are 'predominantly, perhaps even uniquely, Western values' (Himmelfarb 1996: 74–5). If you tell yourself such a story then, instead of seeing history as a series of historical events, most of them contingent, you may really come to believe that it is pre-programmed, that it conforms, if you like, to some previously hidden 'intelligent design'. By definition, writes Amartya Sen, everyone else is condemned to occupy the 'other side' of the historical divide, without access to the values that lie at the heart of rationality, reasoning and social justice. In other words, you might well end up concluding that the Rest is everything that the West isn't (Sen 2006: 285).

Myth 2: Civilizational isolationism

In Gore Vidal's novel *Creation*, a fictitious Persian diplomat called Cyrus Spitama, banished to Athens as an ambassador by his master the Persian King of Kings, remains largely unmoved by the Greek achievement; he is particularly bored by the interminable tragedies he is expected to sit through every other day. For a man who has spoken to the Buddha and debated the finer points of philosophy with Confucius, the Greeks are simply pompous bores. And what of their renowned philosophers? It is true that he makes the acquaintance of Socrates (470/469–399 BCE), but only so that he can hire him to paint the front wall of his house (Vidal 1981). Socrates needs the money. Vidal's novel nicely cuts down to size the most famous philosopher of the ancient world and, in so doing, allows a Western reader to grasp the actual distance of her own past against its deceptive familiarity.

As it happens, we still celebrate the Greeks for their intellectual achievements: the thoughts of Socrates included. But today's historians now know something that the historians of Vidal's day didn't: the extent to which the

Greeks were highly indebted to the civilizations of the East for many of their most ground-breaking ideas. Possibly, writes Walter Burkert (1931–2015), the 'Greek miracle' owed everything to the fact that they were the most *easterly* of Western peoples (Burkert 1992: 129). And that included the privilege of living near to the Persians, the old enemy.

None of this is really surprising. Contacts between civilizations are many and often surprising. The Greeks got their alphabet from the Phoenicians and their astronomy from Babylon. A quarter of the Hellenic vocabulary has a Semitic origin. As for the extent of the collaboration between Greek and Babylonian thinkers, much may well have been lost to history, but we catch a rare glimpse of it when, around 280 BCE, a priest of the god Marduk founded a school of astronomy on the island of Kos, where he wrote a book about his native Babylon in Greek (D'Angour 2011: 55). Some historians even go so far these days as to describe Hellenistic astronomy as 'Greco-Babylonian'.

Even when it comes to philosophy (the Greek trademark) these days, writers such as Orlando Patterson, the author of *Freedom in the Making of Western Culture* (1991), are the first to acknowledge that the originality of Greek thought owed everything to the constant encounter with the 'barbarians' they aspired to despise. Take the case of the pre-Socratics – the philosophers who came before Socrates – and the most famous of them, Heraclitus (535–475 BCE). Like all early Greek thinkers, Heraclitus tried to identify the driving force of the world in which he lived. And just as his countrymen thought metaphorically in terms of the elements such as air or water, he chose fire as a symbol of what he considered most important in life: flux or change. A flame can flare up briefly, illuminating its surroundings, before diminishing and casting us back into the darkness. Knowledge can be said to do the same. We often catch a glimpse of what is real before losing sight of it, and philosophers then try to put us back in touch with reality again. So where did Heraclitus get the idea that fire was the essence of life? Quite possibly from the Persian religion Zoroastrianism. One of its principal tenets was the identification of wisdom with everlasting fire.

The Persians worshipped the god Lord Wisdom. The word *theos* appears nine times in the fragments that have survived from Heraclitus' work. Most translators elect to render the word as 'God', but the smart money these days is on the word 'wisdom' (Heraclitus 2001: xxiii). Hegel, for once, got it right when he wrote that Greek culture was the result of a confrontation with 'the strangeness . . . it contained within itself' (Hegel, *Lectures on the Philosophy of History*).

When we move into the Roman period the contacts are even more transformative. Civilizations can be highly imitative; they are not averse to copying the achievements of their neighbours and rebranding them as their own; they are even open to importing foreign ideas that can be radically transformative. To cite just one example, Jesus, writes Tom Bissell, was both a reflection of and a response to the Jewish encounter with the Greek world following Alexander the Great's campaigns. Greek rule opened up Judaism to a new vocabulary (the word 'synagogue' is Greek rather than Hebrew) and to new concepts which made it possible for Jesus' apostles to imagine him as God, and which also permitted a newly radical Jewish conservatism to reject him along the same lines (Bissell 2016: 90). Much later, Hellenism permeated Roman thinking about Christianity and certainly facilitated its adoption as the official religion of the later empire. The word 'Christ' appears only in the Greek New Testament; it is essentially Hellenistic, and the Trinity (the Father, Son and Holy Ghost) probably comes from the Greek world too – three was a magic number for many Greek sects, including the Pythagoreans, who got the idea from India. And that is important of course because of the role that Christianity has played in defining what Western civilization is.

Myth 3: Civilization and its cultural codes

There is a famous picture by William Blake (1757–1827) of the Old Testament story of Jacob's ladder (1805). It depicts Jacob asleep on the ground, beside his head a spiral staircase. It is an iconic image from the Old Testament for Jews, Christians and Muslims alike, but it also happens to be quite a common image in many near-death experiences the world over. People often record how they saw a bright light at the end of a tunnel as they became detached from their bodies. Often they also report that they experienced a strong feeling of euphoria. On awakening, many will be convinced, especially the religious-minded, that they had been about to embark on the final journey to the afterlife.

These experiences are apparently common to all cultures at all times. And the explanation for that may be biological. A person's heart may have stopped beating, or she may have suffered traumatic brain damage such as an intra-cerebral haemorrhage, or her brain may have put a lock on her body. The experience of meeting the dead may also have something to do with the chemical dopamine and the disruption to the reward pathways in the brain. Even the feeling of euphoria may be accounted for by an endorphin rush; and the light at the end of the tunnel may be the result of a lack of oxygen to the retina of the eye. In other words, we would seem to be dealing with a culturally refracted interpretation of a purely biological experience.

Blake's picture, like the depiction of Jacob's ladder by Johann Baur (1607–1640) or the fifteenth-century take, *The Ascent of the Blessed*, by Hieronymus Bosch (1450–1516), is a striking expression of a Christian culture. In India, near-death experiences more often than not involve Yama – the Hindu god of the dead – and Tibetans seem to see visions of reincarnation. The fact is that, while scientists tell us that actual medical experiences are biological, they also concede that they are often shaped by cultural variation. And near-death experiences do tend to level the playing field by putting us back in touch with the lessons we first learnt when we were young.

Clearly, as far as we know, Blake and Bosch never questioned the truth of the Bible stories or of Christian revelation. They lived a Christian life and expressed their faith in art, and in William Blake's case also in poetry. The world in which they lived was one in which life was mediated through God. If you like, we can say that they were socialized into Christianity. The great artistic renditions of the Nativity, the Crucifixion and the Resurrection can be written off, if you are so inclined, as sacred propaganda or, if you prefer another metaphor, the equivalent of Soviet social realism, but Western art would be the lesser without them.

But the imagination, like language, is always in flux, and the two feed off each other. An economic system such as capitalism can affect the way we think about values, and it had already begun to make its mark two centuries before Blake painted his picture. By then it was even more specifically 'Western' to say that one lived in a world 'defined by market forces' rather than in one 'ordained by God'; but the point is that both were mere 'expressions' of the same social world. Even so, the difference between them was significant. Read Hobbes's *Leviathan* ([1651] 1960) and you will find that an idea such as the value of a person is defined no longer in religious terms but in those of the marketplace – 'the value or worth of a man is as with all other things, his price.' And when Hobbes asks us to be prudent in our actions, he is not talking about virtue allied to practical intelligence; he is talking about thrift – the husbanding of resources, the calculation of balance and loss, 'the virtue that is embodied in life insurance' (MacIntyre 1998: 71).

Now, if you were to conclude from this discussion that Christianity has been at the heart of Western civilization, as T. S. Eliot famously claimed back in 1948, you would not be entirely wrong, but then you might need to ask what Christianity has meant to the faithful in the last 900 years. Try this thought experiment. Imagine yourself standing before the great door of York Minster. It is one of the outstanding cathedrals of Western Europe, a moving testament to the monumental faith of its builders. Sitting as it does hydraulically afloat on a bed of oil which protects its structure from the vibrations of traffic, it is also highly indebted to modern technology. Yet, between the monumental faith and modern technology, what scenes has it witnessed of the devout living out the Christian message? Some of them may surprise you. It saw, for example, one of the earliest pogroms of Jews in Britain, carried out by the very people who built it. Then came a frenzy of witch-burning in the sixteenth century, followed a century later by the solemn trial and execution of a cat for the crime of catching a mouse on the Sabbath and thus breaking the Christian day of rest (Windsor 2002: 86–7). But when the cathedral was struck by lightning in the 1980s and a large part of it was gutted by fire, the Archbishop of York was quick to reassure the faithful that it had not fallen victim to an 'Act of God' (except in the insurance industry sense of the term, for which, alas, the cathedral could not be insured).

This is a vivid picture of a country – my own – in which Christianity has changed over time. It is these constant transformations that have given it its staying power as a religion. Change is the way in which every religion usually renews its message. And Christianity has come a long way from the witchcraft burnings of the early modern era. The archbishop's relaxed attitude to the most recent disaster can be attributed, of course, to the fact that a pre-modern way of life has given way to a post-modern one. Or, to put it bluntly, the technology that shields York Minster from traffic is probably more awe-inspiring in the minds of many Christians these days even than their religious beliefs. What these different stories illustrate is that the faith has remained the same, but that the normative practice of Christianity has changed over time; norms usually change as society constantly interrogates itself and its practices. Such changes are often unarticulated: they tend to creep up on a society largely unannounced, and often untheorized as well. And a change of norms of course is often painful.

And yet the changes which have given Christianity in Britain its narrative propulsion would seem to be almost at an end. The country, insists a former Archbishop of Canterbury, is now post-Christian (BBC News 2014). Indeed, in the world at large, Christianity is ceasing to be a predominantly Western religion. The most important development in recent years has been the rise of Pentecostalism, a Christian confession that offers a far more emotive and ecstatic religious experience than even Catholicism. The spread of Christianity in China is most impressive of all; it is also part of a much wider spiritual revival unfolding across the country. Some think it is the biggest hope for the development of civil society. While Daoist masters are still agonizing over rituals, Christian priests are getting their followers to challenge the official way of looking at things. And that is important because Christianity is now the largest religious constituency in the country (400 million). China is set to become the largest Christian country in the world by the 2030s.

In reality of course it is impossible to find anything like an essence, or a fundamental core, that marks out any civilization. In the words of the historian Paul Veyne, no civilization has historical 'roots'. Its character, in so far as it has one, is largely heterogeneous, contradictory, polymorphous and polychrome (made up of many different colours) (Veyne 2010: 138). A religion such as Christianity or a concept such as democracy is only one of the components of Western civilization, not its matrix. And none of its components is more original than any other. Think of them, Veyne writes, as the product of epigenesis, a phenomenon that occurs when a gene changes thanks to environmental influences. Thus, twins, though sharing a single mother, may have very different personalities and live very different lives (ibid.: 149). Or, if you want a different metaphor, think of those changes as a software developer might, not as a 'bug' but as a central feature of the design.

The continuing importance of myth

Ultimately, I think that one has to accept that civilization lends itself to myth-making; it feeds off another very human tendency – to essentialize life, to strip it down to its core, to reveal the eternal behind the commonplace.

In reality, writes the Chicago historian William McNeill, 'the principal factor promoting historically significant social change is contact with strangers possessing new and unfamiliar skills' (Friedman 2016: 147-8). And civilizations enable change thanks to what most possess: a *lingua franca* or unifying language (the language of the ruling elite) and the ability to network knowledge (think of the 48,000 miles of road built by the Roman state).

Think too of their centres of excellence, such as schools and universities, which tend to attract a community of scholars, many from abroad. All have helped to facilitate profound changes, both material and ideational.

Civilizations don't colonize the future so much as *evolve* into it. Or, if you prefer a more fashionable and now popular term, we might see them as the product of 'emergence'. Instead of referring to the 'nature' of particles, physicists prefer to talk of 'fields and forces' that describe their constant interaction. And biologists tell us that living organisms are no longer composites, put together out of separate hardware and software, but entities that are capable, by working together, of generating patterns spontaneously without any specific instructions. In other words, they emerge through self-organization. Civilizations interact all the time – they trade with each other and even adopt one another's gods. Historians tell us that we are a very special species – *Homo dictyous* (network man): we engage with others in order to barter and trade the things, both material and immaterial, that we value most. That doesn't mean we always bond with each other, but we do tend to seek each other out to strike deals and make money.

But at the same time many people find these encounters and the changes they provoke profoundly disorientating; they often challenge the beliefs and values that civilizations brought into the world and helped to propagate. That is why they can provoke a backlash, a rearguard attempt to protect society from corrupting influences from the outside world. There were times when Japan was open to the outside world and others when it sequestered itself off, banning foreign publications and crucifying Christian missionaries under hard-line shoguns who were anxious to unite the kingdom once and for all. Sometimes Islam was receptive to the other religions of the Book (Jews got a much better deal in fourteenth-century Cairo than they did in fourteenth-century Paris). But they had to flee Baghdad in 1958. And today in the West – democracy notwithstanding – there are siren voices encouraging people to abandon some of the first principles that the Western democracies struggled so hard to sustain over the course of the twentieth century.

The other problem is storytelling. Our stories in turn allow us to construct myths which encourage us to place an emphasis on differences rather than similarities. And that can be problematic if not downright dangerous. As the Athenian stranger remarks in Plato's dialogue *The Sophist*, the forms of sameness and difference are interwoven throughout with all the other forms that comprise reality, and the attempt to separate everything from every other thing would make it impossible to have a conversation with anyone else (*The Sophist*, 259e-260a; Shankman and Durrant 2000: 232). The problem is that sameness is what we often *expect* to find, and we are inclined to feel affronted when we don't find it.

Ultimately, our encounters with other human civilizations always involve an encounter with ourselves. Frequently we may conclude that we *are* superior and more civilized, and perhaps we even congratulate ourselves on being exceptional. Sometimes, however, we may actually see ourselves in an entirely new and not always flattering light. Lévi-Strauss spent much of his academic life telling us that what we find in other cultures is our own in unfamiliar dress. If we are willing to dig deep we will find the same regularities, the same social patterns, the same myths, even the same cognitive maps. In *The Savage Mind*, he claimed that the Australians revealed a taste for erudition and speculation, although it wasn't the sun-bronzed surfers of Bondi Beach that he had in mind but the country's much abused Aboriginal peoples. In other words, occasionally our encounters with others can lead to a major breakthrough; sometimes they can get us to recognize that we are human only to the extent that others can see their own humanity in us.

3

Imagining the West

In a speech delivered in 1937, two years before the outbreak of the Second
World War, Churchill told his audience that as a child he had learnt that
there was a continent called Europe and that he still believed this to be the
case. Geographers, however, now informed him that Europe was not a continent but merely a peninsula of the Asian landmass. He objected that he
found this to be an arid and uninspiring conclusion. The real demarcation
line between Asia and Europe was not a chain of mountains or a national
frontier but 'a system of beliefs and ideas which we call Western civilization' (Burleigh 2010: 76). On that understanding, Churchill later became a
strong advocate of the European Convention on Human Rights as well as
an impassioned supporter of European unity. Throughout his political life
he spoke for a generation that had a very specific understanding of what
Western civilization actually embodied. By the mid-twentieth century, liberal thinkers had come to conclude that our first duty as human beings is
ontological; we have a duty to recognize that human responsibility matters
because the idea of humanity matters, and that our chief responsibility is to
be true to ourselves.

To think ontologically, of course, you have to have an ontology; every
civilization, I would argue, has one, although it often is unaware of the fact.
Read the work of Pitirim Sorokin (1889–1968), a famous American sociologist who is not as well known as he used to be, who thought that every
civilization represents in one form or another a concrete socio-cultural
world. 'Hidden behind the empirically different, seemingly unrelated fragments of the cultural complex lies an identity of meaning which brings

them together into consistent styles, typical forms and significant patterns.' The phrase I want to single out is 'an identity of meaning'. For Sorokin, this encompassed a set of distinctive political ideas or principles that together constituted a 'dominant attitude towards the nature of ultimate reality' (Lee 2012: 97). In other words, every civilization, whether it recognizes the fact or not, has a particular 'worldview'. This is what Michael Oakeshott meant when he claimed that every civilization is 'at bottom a collective dream'.

Oakeshott was famous for his poetic imagination. Sorokin, however, preferred the dry-as-dust language of science and encouraged his readers to think in term of 'systems'. We are more familiar with the systems approach than was Sorokin's generation: we are told, after all, that we live in eco-systems and bio-systems whose stability is under threat (largely through our own actions) and we have known for some time that our planet is part of a larger solar system. Sorokin was merely ahead of his time in applying this idea to a civilization. Every system is made up of interconnected parts whose interconnection produces a certain pattern of behaviour. Behaviour *emerges* like life. Life itself has been described as 'an emergent property' that arises when certain chemical systems interact in certain unpredictable ways. Single-cell organisms had their potential emergence built into them from the beginning; they could, and did, lead to life as we know it today, though there were other possibilities. Play the tape again and something else might happen. What Sorokin was claiming was that at different times in history every civilization has a governing principle, 'a dominant attitude towards the nature of ultimate reality'. Every civilization has a founding myth, and a historical narrative, which combine to give it a sense of purpose.

In the systems world, of course, behaviour emerges; there is no overarching design or even intelligent designer. But for emergence to work there needs to be a 'gateway event' to get it started. The Big Bang was the most significant gateway event of all. And a major historical episode can also spark off a series of events crystallizing around a unifying idea. One such event was America's entry into the Second World War. As the French writer

André Malraux (1901–1976) wrote at the time: 'the modern age . . . shows us with simple clarity and insistence the continuous development of certain principles of life which were defined for the first time at a certain date. That date is a decisive one in a series of dates which make up the modern era' (cited in Mayne 1983: 180–1). What Malraux believed he had witnessed was the birth of history's first 'political civilization' – one that had finally become conscious of itself.

It's a term that might bring you up short if you've not given it much thought, and why should you? The very first reference to it that I've come across was in an interview given to the German newspaper *Bild* by Donald Tusk, the president of the European Council, in the run-up to the British referendum on leaving Europe in 2016. A decision in favour of withdrawal, he warned, might not only provide a boost to radical anti-EU forces, it might also do even more incalculable harm to the Western world. 'As a historian I fear that Brexit could be the beginning of the destruction not only of the EU but also of Western political civilization in its entirety' (Tusk 2016). Let us be the first to admit that it's not a term that trips lightly off the tongue. But it's not a bad term for what the West continues to remain in its own imagination: a civilization that is distinguished by a common political identity.

So, when can the idea of the West be said to have first emerged? Some writers trace it back to the 1840s and the work of a once popular but now much neglected writer, Auguste Comte (1798–1857). Comte is little read these days. If he is remembered at all it is because he coined the term 'sociology' (though he originally planned to call his new discipline 'social physics'). But, if truth be told, he was an indifferent sociologist and never came up with the Holy Grail which he searched for all his life: the invariant laws which he believed governed the social world, just as the laws of physics governed the natural. But the point is that in 1848 he published a book called *The Republic of the West*, which was probably the very first work to conceive of Western Europe as a single political community.

Nearly twenty years later the idea was taken up in England by a writer called Richard Congreve (1818–1899), who picked up Comte's idea but ran with it further in suggesting that the two principal European countries, England and France, had a moral responsibility to export their values to the rest of the world (Varouxakis 2008: 37). It was an idea that gelled with European imperialism and its central legitimating principle: the French called it the *mission civilisatrice* and the English the 'civilizing mission'. It also fitted in comfortably with the English enthusiasm for free trade and everything global: Richard Cobden (1804–1865) had recently coined a new term, 'international'.

Other writers, such as Alastair Bonnett, prefer to trace back the idea of the West no further than the end of the nineteenth century and the then popular predisposition for Social Darwinist thinking, with its stock terms such as 'survival' and 'selection' and its repeated emphasis on the 'struggle for life'. A book that he thinks especially important is *Principles of Western Civilization* (1902), by Benjamin Kidd (1858–1916), which explicitly discussed the West as a racial unit (Bonnett 2004). Beliefs are all important; they influence the way we see ourselves and others. And in the run-up to the First World War there were writers who saw a racial consanguinity between England and France; one even referred to the two countries as 'commensal mates'. For his part, Christopher GoGwilt nominates Kidd's earlier book, *Social Evolution* (1894), in which Western civilization was depicted for the first time as a 'coherent and contemporary entity within world history' (GoGwilt 1995). That too was a comparatively recent concept; it was only in the last decade of the nineteenth century that compound nouns with the word 'world' first began to establish themselves in the popular consciousness – 'world politics', 'world economy', 'world trade' and, most ambitious of all, 'world history' (the first course ever to be taught was at the University of Michigan in the 1890s). It wasn't long before Western writers began to dream of something more ambitious still: a 'world order' shaped by liberal ideas.

Nonetheless, to my mind all these writers tend to miss the point. What the West subsequently became in its own imagination was an exclusive political civilization, and for that to be formulated in the mind of intellectuals there had to be a major 'gateway event': the Franco-Prussian War (1870-1). On one level, the war was not especially remarkable. It was seen at the time as yet another struggle for the balance of power in Europe, between an established power, France, and a rising power, Prussia, which under its astute chancellor, Bismarck (1815-1898), managed to unite Germany. But the unification of Germany represented a sea change in national thinking. 'To be German meant to wonder what it was to be German', Nietzsche once wrote of his countrymen (Raphael 2017: 336); after 1871 they knew that to be German was to be everything that the French and English were not. Indeed, within a few years of France's defeat it soon became clear that the new powerhouse of Europe was not going to follow the French and English example; imperial Germany was an illiberal democracy, not a liberal one, and it was powerful enough to take much of Europe in another direction. Defeat in war forced the French to confront an unsettling reality: not every European power found universally appealing the founding texts of the French Revolution, including the *Declaration of the Rights of Man* (1789).

French revolutionary ideas had very little appeal in England either, but the idea of freedom most certainly did, and human rights soon became part of the English liberal discourse on international relations – beginning with Gladstone's (1809-1898) fulminations against Turkish atrocities in Bulgaria. Today we know the philosophy by another name: 'liberal internationalism' (the Americans tend to favour another formulation, 'liberal interventionism'). In short, if the Germans began to instil some disquiet in European liberal circles after 1871, their stubborn refusal to buy into the liberal package sparked more general apprehension before the century was out. Fearing what the future might hold, two French historians, Henri Martin (1810-1883) and Jules Michelet (1798-1874), led the call for a union of liberal democracies, or what the former called, rather presciently, an 'Atlantic community' (Kohn 1953: 113).

The Mann nobody knew

In Christopher Hampton's play *Tales from Hollywood* (1982), the German novelist Thomas Mann (1875-1955) appears as a pompous bore who puts one of the other characters to sleep by reading out passages from his latest novel. The play is set in Pacific Palisades, a neighbourhood in Los Angeles which hosted a small but distinguished German émigré community during the Second World War and numbered among its members Thomas's brother, Heinrich (1871-1950), and the playwright Berthold Brecht (1898-1956). In real life, Mann was dismissive of his Californian neighbours – the 'gentle barbarians' he liked to call them. He made little attempt to disguise his disdain for their cultural aspirations, and he was especially distrustful of their wish to save the world. He was particularly scathing about what he called 'the unparalleled sacrifice of America: to make other people happy'. It was dangerous, he added, to spurn that love (Craig 1996). In giving voice to such opinions he was betraying some of the deep misgivings he had entertained against liberalism as a young man, and which he had expressed most openly in a book he later tried to suppress, *Reflections of a Non-Political Man* (1918). Although he was unequivocal in his condemnation of Nazism from the very beginning, he was never really a democrat at heart: in later life he seemed to favour an 'enlightened dictatorship', an expression, writes Javier Marias, in which the adjective is far too vague and connotative not to be overruled by the noun (Marias 2006: 68).

Mann himself is not much in vogue these days. In the US his novels remain on the shelves largely unread (thanks to some really awful English translations). Even before his death in 1955 he was considered simply rather boring. However, he appears in these pages not as the Nobel Prize-winning novelist of the 1920s but as a representative spokesman for the social imaginary of imperial Germany. Long before the outbreak of the First World War he could be found complaining: 'I don't want the Parliamentary Party horse-trading that poisons the whole of the national life of politics . . . I don't want politics. I want objectivity, order and decency. If that is Philistine, then

I want to be a Philistine. If that is German, then I want in God's name, to be called a German' (Craig 1996).

This passage captured rather vividly a long-running strain of anti-liberalism in German thinking. Not that this meant that the Germans were not interested in politics, but, like Mann, many of his fellow countrymen claimed that there was more to the life world than the parliamentary politics of France and Britain. And so there was, but they tended to wrap up their political beliefs in a metaphysical language that liberals found deeply disconcerting.

The English, true to their general distrust of overly intellectual thinking, tended to dismiss German thinkers as incorrigible romantics, or even nihilists. The Cambridge philosophers Whitehead, C. D. Broad (1887–1971) and G. E. Moore (1873–1958) considered the mark of a 'civilized' man was a scepticism of any abstractions that could not be proved to be 'real'. As Keynes later wrote, his own generation was imbued with 'Moorism' – the notion that sound ideas needed to be constructed in a language shorn of metaphysical conceits (Woolf 1969: 12). For their part, German writers had reason to complain that the English were far too hasty in dismissing what the great Alexis de Tocqueville (1805–1859) once called 'the habits of the human heart'. The Germans just happened to intertwine their political convictions with an interest in the collective state of the nation, the *Volksgemeinschaft* (or people's community). Yet this in turn led English liberals to find them gravely deficient in prizing what they themselves valued most: the rights of the individual.

It would be quite wrong of course to claim that the Germans were not interested in individualism. The seminal event in modern German history, after all, was Martin Luther's protest against the papacy, which is deemed to have kick-started the Reformation. His most famous remark, when warned that he might lose his life for his beliefs, is: 'I can do no other.' Well, that's the story, though historians now tell us that Luther (1483–1546) probably never said it. Nor, apparently, did he nail ninety-five theses to the door of Wittenberg Cathedral. All of which is entirely beside the point.

Despite its large Catholic population, imperial Germany was in all respects a Protestant state; its dominant intellectual figures, Goethe (1749–1832), Schiller (1759–1805), Kant (1724–1804) and Lessing (1729–1781), were all Protestants. Even the German word for debt – *Schuld* – is the same as that for sin or guilt which figures so prominently in Protestant theology. Imperial Germany may have had a significant Catholic population, but it also had a distinctive Protestant soul. It is perhaps significant that Mann, who was raised a Lutheran, later turned against the church in the Hitler years. 'The prominence of Hitler', he wrote in 1937, 'is not a case of rotten luck but directly in line with Luther and so a truly German phenomenon' (Raphael 2017: 336). This was the Luther of anti-Semitism, the hater not the reformer, but both Luther and Hitler in their very different ways were the supreme revolutionaries of their time.

The real problem was not German Protestantism but the fact that its commitment to Western individualism was very narrowly conceived. In the Western world we are encouraged to celebrate the individual who insists on standing by his convictions. We believe that we are what our actions make us, and we consider that one of the virtues of democracy is that it allows the citizen to confirm his authenticity as a person through his own self-selecting acts. The American novelist E. L. Doctorow (1931–2015) found this starkly elaborated in the last scene of Ernest Hemingway's Spanish Civil War novel, *For Whom the Bell Tolls* (1936). The American hero, Robert Jordan, who travels to Spain to fight for the Republicans, surrenders his own life at the end of the novel so that his Spanish friends can escape and continue the fight. Hemingway lifted the title for the novel from the poem 'No Man is an Island', by John Donne (1572–1631). And his message was simple: in a century which required everyone to make choices, there could be no room for moral isolationism. Jordan's death, as it happens, will hardly serve the cause, but for him this is not the point: it's the final affirmation of his short life. As Doctorow wrote, for him, war is 'the means by which one's cultivated individualism can be raised to the heroic, and therefore never send to ask for whom the bell tolls; it tolls so that I can be me' (Doctorow 2007: 92).

The trouble was that, in liberal eyes, the Germans were moral isolationists. As Mann himself declared, somewhat sententiously, 'Out of the liberty and sovereignty of the Germans Luther made something accomplished by turning them inward and thus keeping them forever out of the sphere of political quarrels' (Dumont 1991: 49). In other words, a German of the pre-1914 generation would not have dreamed of fighting for any cause but his own. The writer Ernst Troelsch later acknowledged this in a book that he published at the height of the First World War – the 'Western idea of liberty', he wrote, was not Germany's. His choice of the pejorative adjective 'Western' was highly illuminating (ibid.: 40).

To this disdain for the 'political' Mann attributed another critical difference between imperial Germany and the Western Europeans, that between French and German literature. Western literature had its own novel of social conscience (think of Voltaire's (1694–1778) *Candide,* or Zola's (1840–1902) novels of working-class life, or Balzac's (1799–1850) *Human Comedy.* Germany, by comparison, had the novel of personal cultivation (*Bildungsroman*) in which there was no place for social or political themes. There is another German term, *Erziehungsroman* – the novel that charts the personal development of a hero who is usually untroubled or untouched by whatever social or political events are engulfing everyone else. Mann put it frankly: 'to ask [a German] to transfer his allegiance to politics . . . to what the peoples of Europe call freedom, would seem to him to amount to a demand that he should do violence to his own nature' (Dumont 1991: 54).

Our memory of the 'other Mann' has diminished as our distance from the twentieth century has deepened. Twenty years later he was among the most trenchant critics of Nazism. Ten years after that he had aligned himself with the West, an irony that was no doubt lost on him. But before the First World War, like many of his fellow countrymen, he was to be found condemning liberalism on many other grounds as well. One was that liberal values were not universal at all; they were merely the product of English and French history. Mann regarded them, as Edmund Burke had originally seen the ideas of the French Revolution, as 'prejudices' (i.e., the long-established beliefs that held a particular society together). Another objection was that they were the prejudices not only of a nation but of a particular social class, the bourgeoisie, and in the German illiberal consciousness there was a large element of bourgeois-phobia.

If we take all this into account it's easy to see why, from the very beginning, the First World War was seen by the Allies as a struggle between two very different social imaginaries. It was, if you like, a clash of values, though we must delve into philosophy a little to understand the true import of that proposition.

In implementing values we introduce some very specific cultural norms into the equation. This is contrary to Kant's belief in absolute values, or Categorical Imperatives, and his claim that, if only we employ correct reasoning, we can argue anyone out of a wrong proposition. In making this claim he appealed to Euclidean mathematics, the geometry of flat surfaces that we learn at school. Kant believed that, in time, we could reason out what was the right thing to do – he called it an increase in moral maturity. In the same way, we once believed – by analogy with the incontrovertible nature of Euclid's geometry – that there was a best system of values in the way of running an economy or managing a society. Unfortunately, mathematicians later robbed us of our illusion by showing us that non-Euclidean geometry is equally valid – triangles constructed from the shortest lines between three points do not have interior angles that add up to 180 degrees. Philosophers have also challenged the rules of logical reasoning that Aristotle took as an absolute. We now know that there is no such thing as an absolute truth in logical mathematics. It is quite possible to have a statement that is true in one logical system and false in another. Apart from which, we also know that life is not logical. As Nils Bohr once rebuked a student, 'Stop being so logical and start thinking.' Ultimately, human beings are what they understand themselves to be. We are comprised entirely of beliefs about ourselves and about the world we inhabit. The difference between the liberal West and Germany before 1949 was the former's belief that values are universal and that moral truth is the same in every culture, in every time and in every place.

Philosophical mills grind exceeding small, and the aim of philosophy is to show that things are trickier than they might seem to be, at first. The point is that, in the absence of universal morality, there are only a series of 'social imaginaries' that are more or less believable at different times. In the end the Germans did buy into the liberal social imaginary, but only after regime change – not in 1918 but in 1945, when the Allies occupied the country and carried out a radical programme of democracy promotion. By then, however, the experience of fascism had discredited the axiology of illiberalism too.

Behaving badly

In 1937 Churchill found himself giving another talk, this time in Leeds, in which he told his audience that he had resolved never to visit the 'Arctic or Antarctic regions in geography or politics'. 'Give me the temperate zone. Give me London, Paris or New York. Let us keep our faith and let us go somewhere and stay where your breath is not frozen on your lips by the secret police.' By then the Nazis had been in power for four years, and already everyone had seen the true face of the Third Reich. What made the Nazi state different again from imperial Germany was the secret police, the mass propaganda, the *Führer* worship. The change, in other words, was axiological. It turned on German behaviour.

If ontology comes from the Greek for a 'thing' (in philosophy it refers to the things we believe to be true through either knowledge or belief; faith requires belief in the unknowable), axiology is yet another word derived from the Greek – from *axia*, meaning worth or value. And it can be extended to cover behaviour: for example, what we think we are permitted to do, and what standards we should set ourselves when interacting with other people. The Nazis are the absolute bogeymen for that reason. That is why the

Second World War is still central to the Western imagination – my parents' generation called it *the war* as if no other conflict was worth remembering. But their parents, in turn, had called the First World War 'the Great War', and of the two conflicts the latter can be thought of as the intellectual Petri dish in which Nazism first germinated. Hitler's state was not some anomaly or aberration – it had its intellectual roots in the illiberal ideas that Thomas Mann himself once espoused.

German Atrocities (1914) was the title of the very first propaganda pamphlet to appear in wartime Britain, which denounced the conduct of the German Army on its march through Belgium. It was popular when I was at university in the early 1970s to dismiss these publications as crude works of propaganda, but historians now tell us that many of the atrocities were indeed committed by the occupying force. And although the Allies too can be held to account for their own crimes, what made Germany different was that it positively boasted of them. Take the U-boat campaign which began in earnest in 1915. Any objection to the killing of civilians tended to be dismissed as *Humanitätsduselei*, or mere 'humanitarian babbling' (Stone 2007: 99). Even more surprisingly, the U-boat campaign was celebrated as a splendid expression of *Deutschtum*, a curious neologism which meant something like the 'ineffable spirit of German-ness'. The subtitle of Will Jaspers's book on the sinking of the passenger liner *Lusitania* says it all: *The Cultural History of a Catastrophe*. Back at home the U-boat crews were seen to embody 'the spirit of heroism'. And it was specifically contrasted in the newspapers with the 'spirit of shop keeping' – the soulless, liberal and mercantile values that were held to be distinctive of British capitalism. It is particularly noteworthy that almost all the surviving U-boat commanders went on to become prominent Nazis in later life (Jaspers 2016).

The glorification of war was another axiological feature which it is worth commenting upon, if only briefly. The *Kriegsideologie* (the ideology of war), a term coined by Thomas Mann, was rooted in German culture. During the war the German people were regularly bombarded with speeches and newspaper articles telling them that war was a regulative element in the life of mankind, and even that it was essential to a nation's biological health. In such writings war functioned more like a religion, a promise of redemption. But this was salvation by faith, not good works, and it is by works that liberal societies preferred to judge not only others but also themselves. Inevitably the language used by German nationalists invited the kind of criticism that you find levelled at the Islamic world today: the claim that an entire culture seemed to be in love with death, sacrifice, blood and belonging (the German term was *Blutsgemeinschaft*). In his book *Merchants and Heroes* (1915), the respected sociologist Werner Sombart (1863–1941) even contrasted the 'heroic' warrior culture of Germany with the depressing commercial spirit of the English. His view of them was grimly sardonic; going to war against England, he complained, was like going to war against a large department store (Losurdo 2001: 12).

Of course, twenty years later Mann was among the first to recognize that under the Nazis Germany was heading towards another war that would be even more destructive, not only of the lives but also of the moral health of an entire society. There is really no need to recount the Nazi war crimes – the callous mistreatment of Soviet prisoners of war (3 million of whom died in captivity); the targeting of civilians in the occupied countries and, of course, the most horrendous crime of all, the Holocaust. The Germans could have chosen to play a different hand and posed as the defenders of Western civilization. Hitler might even have survived had he been more willing to make National Socialism more European (or socialist) and less German (or nationalist) (Lukacs 2010). The invasion of Russia in 1941 was – for propaganda purposes – portrayed by the Nazis as a civilizational struggle against Asiatic Bolshevism, and there were plenty of Europeans who volunteered to serve the German cause: Spaniards, Finns, Italians, Hungarians and Romanians all joined in the fight. Dutch, French and Scandinavian volunteers formed distinct SS divisions. All of them committed atrocities, as did the Hungarian Arrow Cross, the Romanian Iron Guard, the Croatian *Ustashi*, the Slovakian Hlinka Guard and the Ukrainian Insurgent Army (UPA). Far from averting the defeat of Germany, such atrocities merely speeded it up. Once they became widely known, it was quite impossible to legitimize German war aims by reference to any civilizational values, Western or otherwise.

Nazi Germany's defeat was a real game-changer. Even today German politics still bears the imprint of that experience. The state that emerged from the ruins in 1949 considered itself to be part of the West, and on that understanding it was invited to join NATO six years later. The only opportunity left to the Germans after the war, writes the historian Michael Sturmer, was to play the Western card, to become the most European of the European powers, as well as one of the most Atlanticist at the same time (cited in Garton Ash 1994: 21). In an interview which he gave in 1965 to a German newspaper, the philosopher Karl Jaspers reiterated the central theme of his book *The Question of German Guilt* (1947), namely the urgent need 'for every German to transform his approach to the world'. Jaspers insisted that the only way to do this was to become part of the Western community, or what Hannah Arendt, who arranged for the book to be translated into English, described at the time as the 'harmony that can be felt to exist from America to all the European countries' (Watson 1992: 49). The decision to join the West, in other words, can be seen as an expression of a redemptive yearning, the wish to be less exceptional of necessity, not choice. On a more practical note it was also seen as the only guarantee of the country's new commitment to constitutional republicanism.

The graft eventually took. Today, Germany is the most eloquent exponent of the political civilization that defeated the Third Reich. Indeed, in December 2012 *Time* chose Chancellor Angela Merkel of Germany as its 'Person of the Year', adding for further effect that she was also 'Chancellor of the Free World'. A month earlier *The Economist* had named her 'the indispensable European' (Giegerich and Terhalle 2016: 155). But, as she looked at the world from the vantage point of Berlin, she may have been struck by an irony close to home. Inside the European Union, and even in Germany itself, voices are now being raised in favour of the same illiberal values that Thomas Mann had espoused in his youth: the collective against aggressive individualism; the rejection of liberal elitism; the celebration of the 'non-political'; the rejection of the 'poison' of parliamentary factionalism; a return to the community's roots. Indeed, some leading political and intellectual figures in countries such as Poland and Hungary seem determined to take their countries backwards into the past.

Merkel may also have been struck by another irony. Following Donald Trump's surprise victory, she was quick to insist that Europe and the United States were tied by the same values, even though Trump himself later made no mention of them in his acceptance speech. Here was a man who openly wished for a closer relationship with Putin's Russia and who before the election had questioned the strategic relevance of the Atlantic Alliance. A watershed came in a speech in Munich at the end of May 2017, when the German chancellor expressed a fear that had been in people's minds for some time: that the Europeans might no longer be able to rely on their principal ally. 'The times when we could completely depend on others are, to a certain extent, over . . . We Europeans truly have to take our fate into our own hands' ('Trump spells out foreign aims on grand tour' 2017). If America was to be 'first', would Europe be second or third place on the list, or possibly find itself even further down? For Donald Trump, however, the issue is rather different: the West is addressing the wrong enemy – not China, but Russia, hostility to which seems to be constitutive of its own identity.

Russia as the eternal 'Other'

As early as the 1850s the neo-Hegelian theologian Bruno Bauer (1809–1882) had posed a stark question in his book *Russia and the Germanic World* (1853): Russia or the West? Other writers, picking up this theme, spoke to their readers with even greater urgency. Referring to an article that Bauer had gone on to pen thirty years later, the philosopher Friedrich Nietzsche (1844–1900) argued that only a united Europe could successfully prevent itself from being eventually overwhelmed by the Russian colossus. Unlike the countries of Europe, he warned, Russia was a comparatively young nation that had time on its side (Voegelin 1944: 205–8). The eventual showdown would come sooner or later. 'The time for petty politics is over . . . The next century will bring a fight for the dominion of the earth – the *compulsion* to politics on a grand scale' (Nietzsche [1886] 1966: 208). There were only two ways in which the Russian challenge might be seen off: first, if a bourgeois revolution in Russia led to 'the introduction of the parliamentary nonsense, including the obligation for everybody to read his newspaper with his breakfast' (Nietzsche was no democrat); second, if Europe were to unite under a new caste, by which he meant a super-aristocracy, and certainly not the meritocracy that runs the European Union today – a class and an organization which he would have despised.

One has to be careful, of course, whenever quoting Nietzsche, especially out of context. For much of his life he was out of sympathy with the times, and in much of our life we have been out of sympathy with him; he spent his last years in an asylum out of sympathy with himself. But he had a way with words, and the 'dominion of the earth' does call to mind the two world wars and the Cold War that ended only in 1989. The 'compulsion to grand politics' also invokes the great ideological struggles of the short twentieth century which was heralded in by the Russian Revolution in 1917 and which concluded with the collapse of the Soviet Union in 1991.

Was the Soviet Union, the new enemy after Nazi Germany's defeat, more Soviet or Russian? The question is not academic, given the principal theme of this study. Can the Cold War even be seen as an early 'clash of civilizations'? The Russian Revolution, to borrow a phrase from Gershom Scholem, the historian of Jewish Messianism, was one of history's 'plastic hours' when anything became possible. In the 1930s there were attempts to introduce Soviet genetics, Soviet ethnography and Soviet linguistics into everyday life, all with the stated aim of uprooting what was left of the Western influence in Russian life. Those who still subscribed to their initial revolutionary idealism hoped to forge *Homo sovieticus*, a Soviet person, a possibility in which many really did believe. Students in the 1950s working on the virgin lands of Kazakhstan and Siberia often pooled their wages so that they could practise the complementary virtues of self-reliance and mutual support that had been held up to them as civilizational ideals since childhood (Dobson 2017: 32).

However, it didn't take very long for Russia to revert to type. If its ambitions were scripted by Marx, the possibilities open to the new regime were delimited by Russian history. In addition, the Great Patriotic War (1941–5) ensured the eventual triumph of Russian history over any attempt to create a specifically 'Soviet' civilization. Take the substitution of the Soviet Russian national anthem for the *Internationale* and the adoption for the highest military medals of the Red Army of names such as Kutuzov (1745–1813) and Suvorov (1729/1730–1800), the heroes of the 1812 war against Napoleon (1769–1821). Such gestures, together with Stalin's support of the Orthodox Russian Church, can be regarded as authentic examples of what became after 1940 an increasingly nationalist ideology (Lukacs 2005: 134).

The philosopher Nikolai Berdyaev (1874–1948) probably hit the nail on the head when he claimed that, far from communism swallowing up Russia, Russia had swallowed up communism. In other words, Russia was strong enough culturally to assimilate communism, while communism was never strong enough to master Russia. Indeed, to explain away seventy years or more of communism without reference to Russian history or culture is really impossible.

Unfortunately, today's Russia has not yet escaped its past, and it is possible that it never will. As Yuri Trifonov writes in his novel *Another Life*, 'Nothing . . . breaks off without leaving a trace of some kind. There is no such thing as a total break with the past.' There are those who argue that it was the Soviet system which so reshaped the national character that the Russian people have positively acquiesced in the authoritarian rule of Vladimir Putin; there are others who point out that the Russians have always delegated their power to a single person – a tsar, or Stalin, or Vladimir Putin. Whatever the truth, Russia continues to remain for the West the eternal 'Other', and that reality is unlikely to change any time soon. Maybe, writes

Masha Gessen (2017), when a totalitarian society reconstitutes itself rather than being shaped by a totalitarian regime, the ideology congeals last. History for her is the future – now subject to manipulation by those in power who are anxious to reshape the country not as a socialist republic but as a civilizational state.

It's a grim conclusion to reach but one that suggests that Russia and the West will continue to see each other as an existential challenge for years to come. By contrast, the Germans since 1945 have never been allowed to forget, or in fairness allowed themselves to forget, what was specifically 'German' about National Socialism. The trouble is that Russia is once again back in the frame as the most immediate threat to the Western world. The Western Balkans are subject to Russian influence; the Baltic States live with the fear of a Russian occupation; Ukraine has effectively been sundered in two. This time the threat comes not from a competing ideology, communism, but from a civilizational state that claims its own rights and privileges. It even claims a cultural *droit de seigneur* with respect to its immediate neighbours, the countries with which it coexists often uneasily in what it regards as its own 'civilizational space', or what is often called 'the Near Abroad'.

For many Russians, too, the West remains the eternal enemy. Its political class, or, to be more accurate, what Mark Galeotti calls its 'security elites', still see themselves as holding the front line of a long struggle to defend not only Russia's place in the world but the country's distinctive culture and identity (Lipman 2015). If you look at it from Putin's perspective, what you find is a 'civilizational schism' in Europe (the words are his), not between Europe and Russia but between the 'political West' and the Russian people, between Russia as a civilizational state and the 'political community' that emerged after 1941 and divorced the Russian people from the historical West with which it had lived mostly in peace in the nineteenth century (Shevtsova 2010).

But it is precisely at this moment that the future of the West as a political community has been thrown into doubt. Is the US beginning to lose faith in the project? Could the European Union instead transform itself into a separate 'civilizational community'? Is the new slogan of the future going to be 'Europe for the Europeans'? And all these questions are being asked just at the moment that the Trump administration's promise to make America 'great again' may involve turning its back on the whole Western project.

Trump's America

Among the papers which Woodrow Wilson (1856-1924) took to the Versailles conference in 1919 was a much underlined memorandum from an American academic, Frederick Jackson Turner (1861-1932), a scholar whom Wilson greatly admired. If he is thought of at all these days, Turner is remembered as the historian who described how the frontier had moulded American nationality. He is an excellent example of how one man can help forge a national myth. For in 1893, at the age of thirty-three, he presented a paper at a special meeting of the American Historical Association at the Chicago World Fair. His contention was that the 'factors of space and social evolution' had fed into each other. Geographical space was lived experience and therefore socially produced. Consequently, the American West was a form of socialization:

The frontier is the line of most rapid and effective Americanization. The wilderness masters the colonist. It finds him a European in dress, industries, tools, modes of travel, and thought . . . at the frontier the environment is at first too strong for the man. He must accept the conditions which it furnishes or perish . . . Little by little he transforms the wilderness, but the outcome is not the old Europe, not simply the development of Germanic germs . . . The fact is, that here is a new product that is American . . . Thus the advance of the frontier has meant a steady movement away from the influence of Europe, a steady growth of independence on American lines. (Turner [1894] 1963)

Turner was not an elegant writer but he was good at spinning a tale. And in the paper commissioned by Wilson he span a new one. He now contended that, having closed in 1890, the frontier had turned back on itself. Americans could venture back to Europe and mould its different nationalities and ethnicities into a coherent political unit, the West (Gardner 1982: 23). And there were many American historians who were quick to join in the understanding that Europe and the US were moved by the same rhythms, stirred by the same impulses, and inescapably involved in the same crises. Here was another myth that was equally compelling, at least for those early liberal internationalists who chose to buy into it.

Wilson himself later tried to translate this vision into a League of Nations, which we should remember was intended from the beginning to be a league of 'like-minded nations' (essentially Western democracies). And, although the US never joined the League, Wilson's vision continued to have enormous appeal throughout the Cold War.

All that now seems to be history, or perhaps it would be more correct to say that Americans are beginning to tell themselves a different story. What was the purpose of the United States?, asked the author John Updike back in 1993 in his commencement address at Amherst. As he told the students, they were graduating in bewildering times; history appeared to be more like a collection of short stories than a novel (Updike 2011: 478). It had become shapeless. But Donald Trump thinks there is a story. It's time for America to be true to itself and not take part in the narrative of someone else, namely Europe. The West as a distinctive political civilization has little claim on his emotional loyalty. At times Trump makes little secret of the fact that he believes that the West as a political civilization no longer has the will or self-belief to defend Western values with the conviction it once displayed. Like all good storylines, the West had its beginnings in the 1870s; perhaps its end is now in sight. Alliances and alignments, after all, have their take-offs and landings too, and, to extend the metaphor further than is probably wise, the Western community may be running out of fuel.

European communitarianism

If the West does fracture, what hope is there that the European Union might strike out on its own as a civilizational community? The problem when it comes to values is that many Eastern Europeans are beginning to ask whether Europe is a Judeo-Christian construction or a product of Latin Christendom. Or, for that matter, is it more Jewish than Christian?, asks a character in one of the stories from the collection of the Czech writer Bohumil Hrabal (1914–1997) entitled *Mr Kafka and Other Tales*.

> 'Things are getting much better, Doctor', said Barta, the loader.
> 'Christian Europe is consolidating.'
> 'What Europe?' asked the Doctor of Philosophy derisively. 'And what do you mean Christian? It's more Jewish than ever before . . .'
> 'It's Christian,' said the merchant.
> 'That's crap,' said the Doctor of Philosophy, raising his hand. 'At one end of the spectrum you've got one brilliant Jew, Christ, and at the other end you've got another genius, Marx. Two specialists in macro-cosmics, in the big picture. All the rest is Mother Goose territory.'
> (Hrabal 2015: 89)

And what of Islam? Even in Germany, one of the most liberal countries in Europe, there are deep misgivings about Muslims and immigrants of all religious hues and none. The satirical novel *Look Who's Back*, which appeared in 2015, is based on the conceit that Hitler returns to present-day Germany and becomes a media celebrity. Its author, Timur Vermes, turned to satire to warn his countrymen that one day they might be lured again by the anti-Western sentiment that was the trademark not only of the Third Reich but also of imperial Germany. As it is, Muslim immigration is eating away at German liberalism all the time. A Leipzig University study in 2016 found that 40 per cent of the respondents wanted to ban all further immigration, and one in five longed for a single strong party that embodied the 'national community as a whole' (*Sunday Times*, 23 October 2016). It is just one poll, of course, but beneath the surface broader tectonic shifts can be detected. The electoral success in 2017 of the extreme right-wing Alternative for Germany (AfD) is evidence of this.

Why is this particularly telling? Because the most important evidence of Germany's Westernization following its defeat in 1945 was its rejection of the idea that a successful nation has to be ethnically homogeneous. No longer was it acceptable to draw a distinction between a *Staatsbürger* (citizen) and a *Stammgenosse* (member of a tribe). The experience of the Holocaust even made this a national duty. But now the Germans have the choice of voting for the AfD and its anti-immigrant stance. Invoking a language that has not been heard in political life since the 1940s, the party likes to refer to German culture as *einheimische Kultur* – a native culture – and goes so far as to describe the German nation itself as a 'cultural unit'. Such language may call to mind the old debate in imperial Germany about the superiority of German *Kultur* over Western *Zivilisation. Kultur* is a way of life; it pre-dates civilization. It is considered to be a sensibility, a unique expression of a particular national spirit. For the AfD, Germany is not a cosmopolitan community so much as an ontological entity. Even if every Muslim were to be a good secularist and willing to abide by the tribal conventions, he could never be truly German – only a visitor under sufferance (Sauerbrey 2016).

Are all these examples yet another case of what the historian Fritz Stern called 'cultural despair' – a condition not unique to Germany but which he considered definitively German and which Thomas Mann would have recognized immediately for what it was? That is the main impression one gets from reading works such as Thilo Sarrazin's *Deutschland schafft sich ab* (Germany's abolishing itself) (2010) and Henryk Broder's *Hurra, wir kapitulieren!* (Hurray, we surrender!) (2004). Both authors are peddling an ideology that we have seen before, but on a much less extensive scale: a 'racism without races' and an 'anti-Semitism without Jews' (Gunther Anders's phrase for the treatment of Turkish guest workers in post-war Germany). Whatever the future electoral success of the AfD – whether it has peaked, for example, and is not a grim foreshadowing of what is to come – its presence in the Bundestag is likely to coarsen the political discourse.

Even so, we should get the rise of the AfD into perspective. Its electoral success in 2017 was still modest historically. Much more worrying is what is happening across the German border: a Hungarian government that trumpets that it is an illiberal democracy, deeply opposed to globalization; a Polish government that has embraced a form of Catholic nationalism; and a Romania that has yet fully to honour the commitment it made when it joined the EU to enforce the rule of law at home. According to the Democratic Index published by *The Economist* in 2016, all three countries were recognized as flawed democracies (The Economist Intelligence Unit 2017). At the Bratislava summit in 2016, Hungary's prime minister called for a 'cultural counter-revolution' against the cosmopolitanism of European institutions. He went further in proclaiming his desire to make Hungary an 'illiberal' state, and even to close its borders to 'global capitalism' (*The Times*, 8 September 2016, p. 9).

To be fair to the Eastern Europeans who think this way, they believed they were joining a Judeo-Christian club. The fact that it had long since ceased to be one escaped their attention – not surprisingly, perhaps. After all, they had no experience of multiculturalism; people left communist countries, if they could; they didn't emigrate to them. And unlike Britain and France they had no experience of mass migration from former colonies. In addition, unlike West Germany, they never experienced an influx of Turkish 'guest workers' who were lured into the country by the German economic miracle of the 1960s.

And here is another critical historical difference. Western Europe may be largely 'post-Christian', but religion remains a powerful force in some Eastern European countries, notably Poland. It is unimaginable that a Polish government would accept the findings of a government-sponsored study such as *Living with Difference* (CORAB 2015), which concluded that Britain was no longer Christian and that anyone who objected to the conclusion should try to 'get over it'. In Poland, the Catholic Church played an

important role in the resistance to communism and in defending the right
of the people to be members of a Christian club. In its own eyes the Polish
government is defending what it deems to be best in the European tradition.
'It's us who are the bulwark of real Europe', the Polish president declared on
a visit to Hungary in March 2016. 'In today's Europe there is, without doubt,
a crisis of values on which European civilization has been built, and I am
thinking about a civilization with Latin roots supported by Christianity . . .
All those ideals have been lost in today's Europe. They are being forgotten
and trampled by other ideologies that debase the essence of humanity and
the human being' (Balcer et al. 2016: 7).

To be sure, writes one Polish social psychologist, what we are witnessing
is a fierce debate between two different tribes, or two different 'cultures'.
Both adhere to different and opposing value-systems. One is conservative,
Catholic and nationalistic, the other cosmopolitan and West European
(Balcer et al. 2016: 3). One is convinced that security lies in strengthening
the nation-state, the other believes that it lies in strengthening international
bodies such as the EU. As James Davison-Hunter once said of the culture
wars in the United States, what is ultimately at issue is far more than disa-
greements about values or opinions. 'What is ultimately at issue are deeply
rooted and fundamentally different understandings of "being" and "purpose"' (Davison-Hunter 1991: 131). And those differences are now coming
to a head.

In January 2016, the European Commission took the unprecedented step
of opening an investigation into the laws passed by the Polish government
which had been condemned by human rights organizations, in particular
the laws that were intended to give the government much greater control
over the state media and the constitutional court the power to block legislation passed by parliament, even if it was deemed to be in breach of the
country's constitution. This followed real concerns entertained in Brussels
about some of the actions of Viktor Orbán's government in Hungary. And
that is precisely what has happened: there is no longer an independent
judiciary; the ruling party controls a media committee with powers over

the press, broadcasting and libel laws that are unrecognizable in Western Europe. On the periphery of Europe, where democratic institutions traditionally have been weak, there has been a slide backwards into the simplicities of the past.

And governments are quite unapologetic about what is happening. The Polish government's insistence that Polish membership of the EU is a 'right', not a 'special privilege', was an implicit rebuke to the Western Europeans for what it considers to be one of the great cultural crimes of the twentieth century: the indifference with which they treated the fate of Central Europe (*Financial Times*, 16 January 2016). Many Hungarians also have not forgiven what happened in 1956. What does it mean to be European anyway? That, as a contemporary Hamlet might have added at the time, was indeed the question. It was posed rather poignantly in November of that year when the director of the Hungarian News Agency dispatched a telex to the world alerting it to a Russian invasion. The dispatch ended on a ringing note: 'We are going to die for Hungary and for Europe.' The plight of the unfortunate director was revealing, wrote Milan Kundera thirty years later. For a Hungarian or a Czech in the mid-1950s, Europe was more than a geographical expression; it was 'a spiritual notion synonymous with the word "West"' (Kundera 1984: 37). The West's failure to come to Hungary's aid in 1956 revealed that it had become instead merely an economic project.

In fact it signalled much more. Back in 1946 the Hungarian writer István Bibó wrote that it had become clear that the Western Europeans considered their Eastern cousins to be defined by an 'innate barbarism' – they tended to regard them as a people who were as much a danger to Western Europe as historically they had always been to themselves.

This was why the admission of countries such as Hungary to the European Union, followed later of course by Romania and others, meant so much to the intellectuals of Eastern Europe. As the Czech president, Václav Havel (1936-2011), reminded Western politicians at the time, if his countrymen wanted to join Europe it was not only because of fears for their own security: 'We are concerned about the destiny of the values and principles that communism denies . . . the traditional values of Western civilization' (Havel 1994: 4). But what are those values, and do they still obtain? Or, more to the point, do you honour those values today by introducing different norms such as multiculturalism and secularism? Europe, after all, is less Christian than it used to be. In the Czech Republic itself, a small majority of its citizens even declare themselves to be atheists. It is the Muslims who are a new force in European political life; 12 million of them have migrated to Europe in the last twenty years. How much more comforting, if you're the Hungarian prime minister Viktor Orbán, were the days when Europe was split between those who subscribed to the Judeo-Christian ethos and those who chose Marx and historical materialism as their guide, the two Jews of Hrabal's tale – one of the reasons perhaps why, when Putin visited Budapest in February 2017, Orbán, rather pointedly, welcomed him back 'home'.

A Byzantine option?

Let's wax optimistic for once! Let's imagine that populism burns itself out; that the campaign against 'liberal civilization' peaks; that the EU recovers its vision and stands by its cosmopolitan values in the face of a communitarian challenge from the right. Let's imagine that even Trump's America proves to be a passing phenomenon. Reality, wrote the science fiction author Philip K. Dick (1928–1982) (who, thanks to his drug addiction and incipient schizophrenia, was not always in touch with it), is that which, 'when you stop believing it, doesn't go away' (Dick [1978] 1995). The most important feature of most civilizational narratives is that they are historical even if those who promote them often have an imperfect grasp of their own history. It just so happens that the historical narratives which give Western civilization its shape tend to be more robust than most.

If the Western world does manage to hold together, even in a much looser form, I suspect that it will continue to harp back to its Ur-text, the Greco-Roman world. In 2016, nineteen of the twenty-seven professors in the US whose work focused on any aspect of humanity before 600 CE worked chiefly on Rome and Greece. And a survey of the websites of other leading American universities revealed that twice as many faculty members devoted their research time to both civilizations as they did to the rest of the ancient world combined (Morris and Scheidel 2016: 116). Not that this is really surprising. The great historical caesura of Western civilization was the fall of Rome (in China it was the period of the Warring Kingdoms, the bloodiest and most traumatic era in its history: one calculation estimates that there were 256 wars between 656 and 221 BCE. And defeat often meant total state annihilation (Toner 2015: 109). It took the Western world a thousand years to recover from the fall of the Western Empire, much longer than it took China to recover from its own 'dark ages'. No other civilization that has survived into the twenty-first century has ever suffered such a catastrophic fall from grace, at least in its own imagination. And when the recovery eventually came, in the late fifteenth century, it also took a typically Western form: a dialogue with the past. For Aldo Schiavone, Western civilization is a constant counterpoint between the ancient and modern worlds, the taking further, if you like, of classical thought. 'The symmetry of abandonment and revival (virtually a contrapuntal movement beyond deprivation and recovery)', he writes, 'has proved to be, we might say, a *style* of the Western world' (Schiavone 2000: 204).

But hold that thought for a moment. One of the great European intellectuals, Ernst Bloch (1885–1977), used to talk of the 'still undischarged future in the past' (Eagleton 2016: 32). I venture that the West could reconnect with a quite different past, with the Eastern Roman Empire (the Byzantine), which amazingly survived the great crisis of the mid-fifth century and continued in one form or another for another thousand years. That is why Greece invested in its cultural identity by joining China and ten other countries in launching the Ancient Civilizations Forum in 2017. The forum's declaration recognizes civilization as 'soft and smart power' and hails the defence of one's cultural heritage as a defence against terrorism and political extremism and 'other forms of related intolerance'. For the Greeks, the

Byzantine world is as important as what used to be called the 'C5th Greek Enlightenment' in establishing its Western credentials: if it were possible, the Greek government in its debt relief negotiations with the EU might like to put a value on its contribution to Western civilization, adjusted for inflation, of course!

So, what was the secret of Byzantium's success? It began life as a regional superpower before witnessing a dramatic decline in status and ending up as a city-state. At all times, though, it was a cultural magnet whose influence ran from Russia to the Caucasus and even beyond. And even when it was not militarily strong it was an object lesson in long-term survival. Because it was never as powerful as the Western Empire at its height, it had to be more resourceful; it couldn't afford to rely on force alone. It rarely invaded other countries. It relied on diplomacy and deception and religious conversion to manipulate its enemies, sometimes into fighting each other. It made a particular point of studying its enemies and mastering their languages, the better to enmesh them in its own designs (Luttwak 2010).

But what really made it different was its reliance on what we now call 'soft power'. This mustn't be confused with our present understanding of the term. Byzantium didn't have permanent missions at multilateral organizations; it had no UNESCO World Heritage sites, or chart-topping music albums, or football followings, or world-class universities. Back in the Middle Ages this is not how soft power was measured. What it did have was a capital city that topped the list of any outside Baghdad, as well as a world-class product, Christianity, with a distinctive brand – its distinctive church architecture and its religious art, most notably its icons. Unlike the countries that boast of soft power today, it wasn't a member of a globalized world, of course. The Byzantine brand did not carry across to the Indus or sub-Saharan Africa, but it was exported successfully to the Middle East, and to Russia, and even to Western Europe. In addition, its ceremonial, its antiquarianism and its church decoration allowed it to pull off what Jonathan Harris calls one of the great deceptions of history – to present itself as 'Roman' to the very end (Harris 2015: 4–5). In other words, while contemplating the limits of its own achievement, it was able to retain its identity and, thanks to a remarkably resilient and appealing brand, to keep its ideas afloat for almost ten centuries.

On today's soft power index, all but one of the top ten places are accounted for by Western countries (the exception is Japan). And that is unlikely to change in the immediate future despite the rise of China and India. At the very least, soft power may permit the West to compensate for its diminished political status; at best, it may even help it secure for itself the values in which it still professes to believe. Contrary to appearances, the West may not be shrinking, but merely changing shape. 'We may find to our surprise', writes Peter Brown, an emeritus professor of history at Princeton, 'that Byzantium – that wily old survivor, may have more to say to us, in our own dangerous times, than those tired platitudes on the fall of Rome . . . that are so often uttered these days by anxious xenophobes and by would-be imitators of Edward Gibbon' (Brown 2016).

4

Cultural Darwinism

In recent years historians have taken us beyond the usual clichéd descriptions of civilization. To be sure, cities, roads and libraries are all important, but they constitute a checklist, an intellectual tool kit for historians. More recently, civilizational studies have begun to encompass more intimate questions of the emotions and the imagination; historians have begun to study civilization as lived experience. The phenomenologists of early twentieth-century Europe called it a *Lebenswelt*, or life world; it is the world we construct in the presence of others.

The best-known writer who set out to capture this was Oswald Spengler. No other writer tried to explain so thoroughly the relationship between civilization and styles of enquiry. In *The Decline of the West* ([1918] 1980) he offered his readers what might be called a cultural morphology. Famously, for example, he claimed to have found connections between the differential calculus of Leibniz (1646–1716) and the dynastic principles of politics in the world of Louis XIV (1638–1715); between the classical Greek city-state and Euclidean geometry; between the space perspective of Western oil painting and the conquest of space thanks to the railroads, telephone and long-range weapons built by Western scientists. He even claimed to have found a link between Western contrapuntal music and credit economics (Graham 1997: 153–4). A bridge too far?

In the West, academics have little time for Spengler's metaphysical musings or his famous signature skills, one of which was to segue almost seamlessly from the general to the particular. Thus he insisted on tracing what he identified as 'the central idea' of Western civilization – individualism

– to contemporary mathematics and the history of art. It is not an idea that has found much favour with historians, not only on the grounds for example that much in Greek mathematics came originally from outside the Greek world. It is also faulted on the grounds that a characteristic of Western civilization such as individualism is only part of the story. What of the totalitarian temptation that Karl Popper traced all the way back to Plato?

Spengler's intention, I think, was admirable enough: he wished to show how civilization is not only shaped by our own imagination, reflecting back to us the colour of our own desires, but can actually shape our desires in ways in which, at the time, and even later, we are often unaware. The trouble was that many of his observations, though often fascinating, were far too sweeping; his brush was so broad that, in the end, very little that he painted is truly illuminating. Re-reading his book tends to generate fewer and smaller rewards.

Nevertheless, the morphology of culture has come back into popular discourse through the back door in countries that take Spengler more seriously than do people in the West – Russia for one. Many Russian conservatives buy into what I call Cultural Darwinism, a philosophy which taps into an idealized existential version of civilization in the often openly declared hope of giving a country a competitive edge in the zero-sum struggle for life. Immediately you may think of Social Darwinism, which remained popular until it was finally discredited by the Second World War. It retained a following largely because of its pseudo-scientific claims. It suggested that there were inescapable biological laws which it was unwise to ignore. Race was considered to be a biological reality as well as the driving force behind history. And part of its appeal was that it could be invoked to justify the most ruthless market capitalism as well as the most ambitious projects of social engineering. Its most famous formulation, 'the survival of the fittest', was coined, after all, by a renowned liberal writer, Herbert Spencer (1820–1903) (one-time editor of *The Economist*).

Cultural Darwinism, too, allows politicians of different persuasions to claim that civilizations find themselves locked into a struggle with eternal enemies (usually the West). And, like Social Darwinism before it, it offers people a collective identity that is both inclusive and exclusive at the same time. It helps solidify the in-group while helping it to identify an out-group, which is to be defended against, not ignored in the discourse between the two.

Every discourse, wrote the Nobel Prize-winning poet Octavio Paz (1914–1998), can be reduced to a simple phrase: 'I am'. Where imagination comes in is the point where this admits to numerous variations, such as 'I am a member of the "Chosen People"', or of the 'Master Race'. Ironically, such claims can be made only in conversation with others. As Aristotle tells us, the verb 'to be' is really empty unless it realizes itself for an attribute such as 'I am stronger than you', or 'I am an American, First.' We are what we think we are, again thanks to the distinctive group or tribe with which we identify (Paz 1990: 157).

If you want to conjure up a world in which different cultures cannot engage with one another in discourse, watch an episode in the *Star Trek* franchise, in the course of which Jean-Luc Picard debates his fate with an alien species called the Borg Collective, a collection of former species who have been turned into a cybernetic organism with a hive mind – not quite a termite 'civilization', but certainly not a human one either. For, unlike human beings, they have no desires, other than an insatiable appetite to expand and absorb every culture that they come across. Following his capture Picard does his best to live up to his own Western cultural code:

Picard: I will resist you to my last ounce of strength.

Borg: Strength is irrelevant. Resistance is futile – your culture will adapt to serve ours.

Picard: Impossible! My culture is based on freedom and self-determination.

Borg: Freedom is irrelevant. Self-determination is irrelevant. You must comply.

Picard: We'd rather die.

Borg: Death is irrelevant.

What is this, if not a dialogue of the deaf? As the sci-fi writer Adam Roberts observes, what is most striking about the conversation – if that's what it can be called – is that Picard is quite unable to enter into the mind of the Borg any more than the Borg can imagine what it would be like to share his philosophy. The point is that they have no imagination (Roberts 2000: 166–7). The Borg don't claim that they are stronger than the Federation; they claim that strength is beside the point. And they have no truck with Picard's very American belief in a species' right to self-determination. Note that they don't dismiss it as a myth; they dismiss all storytelling as irrelevant. Even death is irrelevant. And yet of course it's death that defines us, the knowledge that we are here only for a short while and that we will be judged, and sometimes we will judge ourselves at the end of our lives by what we have achieved or failed to achieve while we were alive. Strength is important for that reason – it is what you do with it that counts, though it can take many different forms: one society may be stronger in its moral conviction, another in its ability to go to war, yet another in its spiritual stamina. And each variation may be celebrated at different times in its history.

It is because we *are* the conversation that we conduct with others that Cultural Darwinism has such appeal, however bizarre its claims. Let me discuss three claims that have gained some traction in China and Russia. The first is that a civilization has a unique cultural DNA, thanks to gene-culture co-evolution. The second is that some languages are different – so very different as to make it next to impossible to engage in a cross-cultural conversation. And the third is the claim that we are shaped by the interaction between genes and geography. And all these myths share one thing in common: their use of metaphysical sledgehammers to prise out hitherto unsuspected linguistic, genetic and genetic-geographical realities that are deemed to lock the world's respective civilizations into a confrontational future.

All three discourses feed off the earlier myths I discussed, but what makes them so depressing is that they are also unapologetically *transgressive*. They throw into question the cultural diversity which is a hallmark of our species – the fact that, although we all wrestle with the fear of losing touch with the familiar, we all have to deal at some stage in life with the problematic encounter with difference.

Gene–culture co-evolution

One of the publishing sensations in China in the early twenty-first century was a novel called *Wolf Totem* (2004). Its subject is life in the remote steppes of Inner Mongolia, the most northerly of China's provinces, a life that is shared both by wolves and Man. In an unremittingly hard existence, both compete for scarce resources. But both have also found a way to live in harmony, though this is now threatened by the demands of modern life. *Wolf Totem* is a totemic book. It has sold more copies than any work except Mao's *Little Red Book* and been translated into several Western languages. It has even been turned into a movie.

Its author Jiang Rong (a pseudonym) was a victim of the Cultural Revolution (1966–76), a period of particular political turmoil in China's history. Jiang Rong was exiled to Inner Mongolia, where he eventually learnt to prize a way of life even older than Chinese civilization itself. For the nomadic peoples among whom he lived, Mao (1893–1976) was not god; the Sky was. And in place of Mao's famous *Little Red Book* with its revolutionary catechism, there was the wolf, in the role of both totem and teacher. You will find many monologues in the novel; let me single out one of them:

Out here the grass and the grasslands are the life, the big life. All else is little life that depends on the big life for survival. Even wolves and humans are little life . . . So, the grass isn't to be pitied? Grass is the big life, yet it's the most fragile, the most miserable . . . Anyone can step on it, eat it . . . When they graze the land, isn't that killing? . . . When you kill off the big life of the grassland, all the little lives are doomed. (Jiang 2008: 66)

Such homilies tend to pall after a while. What is surprising, however, is that, given its depiction of the damage that has been inflicted on the environment in China's relentless push for economic growth, the novel passed the state censors. When the narrator goes back to the grasslands thirty years later, what does he find but a 'yellow dragon sandstorm' blowing from the steppes towards the country's cities. The reason why the novel probably got past the censors is that it embraces several different levels of reality at the same time. On one level, of course, it is an attack on the disharmony of political life in a world when a leader such as Mao can plunge an entire country into mayhem on nothing more than a senile whim. On another, it presents itself as a useful military tract, if you believe the author's claim that the tactics of the wolf pack were the secret that allowed the Mongols in the thirteenth century to conquer half the world, including China itself. The book, as it happened, was a popular Chinese New Year present for the generals in the People's Liberation Army (Coonan 2008). Indeed, the military may be the most attuned to its message.

There is a quite different explanation, however, for the book's popularity in the West. It is deemed to be ecologically sound. It is a favourite of many environmental campaigners, who tend to take away a simple message: the goal of life should be the urgent need for coexistence with nature. But what they won't find in any of the translations is the epilogue with its quasi-Cultural Darwinist message. They won't find the bizarre claim that a country's history is determined by its peculiar genetic inheritance, the fact that over the centuries various nomadic tribes crossed the frontier into China. During the Song dynasty they included Tanguts, Khitans and Jurchens, to name but a few. Over time, they gradually intermarried with the local population. Today's China is home to fifty-six different nationalities or ethnicities. Its great genius as a civilization has been to persuade nearly all of them that they are Han Chinese.

But that is not actually the real message that Jiang Rong wants to get across. Instead he reminds his Chinese readers that their civilization is a product of two different sets of genes: its 'wolfish' traits are inherited from the northern nomadic races and its commercial 'sheepish' traits from the original Han people. And the distinctive rhythm of Chinese history – the rise and fall of its many dynasties – can be attributed to the fact that, in every period in which the country has cut a figure in the world, its warlike genes have come to the fore. The author advocates returning to a 'purer' form of Confucianism, to the period when the values of 'steely fortitude and valour' were dominant. Indeed, the message of his book is to be found in an aphorism from *The Book of Changes*: a people should always strive for 'self-strengthening' (Hughes 2011: 611).

I suspect that *Wolf Totem* is popular in China with some because of these ethno-racial connotations. To be told that the differences between oneself and others are not entirely cultural but also biological allows you to entertain a belief in your own racial superiority. It offers a curious psychic retreat into a fantasy world. It permits a return to the geo-racial politics of the 1930s which set Japan and China at odds with each other. It pitches political life ambiguously between history and metaphysics (Callahan 2012: 39). Tatar genes, by the way, also make an appearance in another socially constructed myth which tells the Russians that they are not a European or even a Slavic people so much as a Eurasian one. Even Hungary's right-wing Jobbik Party links the Hungarians to the Turkic–Tartar peoples of Central Asia. For politicians looking for the main chance, a country's genetic inheritance is a blank screen onto which they can project whatever primordial fantasies they think their supporters will find most appealing.

Now, if all of this sounds very bogus, gene–culture co-evolution is real enough. Take lactase deficiency. In those societies where cow's milk has been drunk for more than 300 generations, 90 per cent of people have the enzyme, lactase, which allows the absorption of milk sugar, lactose. In groups that don't enjoy a history of dairy farming, 80 per cent carry a different version of the enzyme and have difficulty drinking milk. Or take the Tibetans, who are able to thrive at high altitude because over time they have developed elevated levels of nitric oxide which causes their blood vessels to dilate, allowing more blood to flow through them and at a faster rate than the rest of us (Solomon 2017: 60). Culture really does influence biology. The most telling example perhaps is the caste system in India. As Andrew Rutherford tells us, if you opt for elective surgery in Hyderabad, the first question you will be asked is whether you are from the Vaishya (merchant) caste. This isn't a case of social prejudice; it is simply rooted in the evolution of the Indian genome. If you are a Vaishya you will be particularly prone to pseudocholinesterase deficiency, which means that you may remain unconscious under general anaesthetic for much longer than anyone else. This may be the result either of inbreeding or of diet (the Vaishya are famous for eating especially fatty foods). Since arranged marriages have been the norm in Indian social life, the custom of marrying-in is probably the correct explanation (Rutherford 2016).

But consider another argument which takes us back to China. Some years ago, two Western writers put forward another claim that I imagine the author of *Wolf Totem* would find less congenial than his own. There is indeed, they insist, a genetic determinant in the Chinese character that owes everything to a particular allele. What is an allele? Adam Rutherford defines it as a variant of a gene akin to an alternative spelling, such as the difference between 'affect' and 'effect'. The first means 'to change', the second 'a result'. In other words, changing a single letter of a word can make all the difference to its meaning (Rutherford 2016: 382). In the case of China, our two authors claim, there is an interesting genetic deficit that we tend to associate in industrial societies with a particular syndrome, attention deficit hyperactivity disorder (ADHD). This, in turn, is often traced to the 7R (47-repeat) allele of the DRD4 (dopamine receptor D4) gene. If you are to believe child psychologists, Western children would seem to be particularly plagued by the disorder. Many are heavily medicated. What is interesting is that, while the alleles derived from the 7R are as common in China as they are elsewhere, the 7R allele itself is comparatively rare.

So, were individuals with these alleles selected against by a culture that put an emphasis on social conformity? Was cultural bias strong enough at a very early stage in China's history to select for submission to authority? 'The

Japanese say, "the nail that sticks out is hammered down", but in China it may have been pulled out and thrown away' (Cochran and Harpending 2009: 112). It is one of several examples that are deemed to show how civilization has accelerated human evolution. In this case it would suggest that the Chinese really have only 'sheepish' not 'wolfish' traits. But then everything depends on the story you want to tell, and the story of *Wolf Totem* almost certainly won't be the last tale that Chinese nationalists will spin.

Language

There is a short story by the Argentinean writer Jorge Luis Borges (1899–1986), 'The Analytical Language of John Wilkins'. It is the story of a Dr Franz Kuhn who attributes to a Chinese encyclopaedia, 'The Celestial Empire of Benevolent Knowledge', certain striking ambiguities, redundancies and deficiencies:

> In its remote pages it is written that the animals are divided into: (a) belonging to the Emperor; (b) embalmed; (c) tame; (d) sucking pigs; (e) sirens; (f) fabulous; (g) stray dogs; (h) included in the present classification; (i) frenzied; (j) innumerable; (k) drawn with a fine camel hair brush; (l) et cetera; (m) having just broken the water pitcher; (n) that from a long way off looked like flies. (Borges [1937–52] 1973: 52)

The passage was made famous by the French philosopher Michel Foucault, who wrote that, thanks to Borges' story, we can apprehend 'the exotic charm of another's system of thought' – that of a culture that apprehends the world by using very different classifications from those employed by Westerners.

Culture, as Charles Taylor tells us in *The Language Animal*, is behind the expression of every thought. A word has a meaning only within a cultural context. It is not possible to understand a word or a sentence in isolation; or, to put it more directly, we often have to know the cultural background to make sense of the linguistic foreground. Language structures our way of seeing the world and thus profoundly alters our experience of it, often in life-changing ways (Taylor 2016). In other words, there are indeed very different ways of apprehending reality. In a real Chinese classical text you won't find the Aristotelian distinctions between *genera/species* that are so common in the West (Hall 2000: 206). And in the past Chinese writers did indeed like to subdivide species by applying aesthetic rather than logical criteria. They used to distinguish 'noble' animals such as the lion from ones considered to be 'ignoble', such as the fox, and to identify what were considered to be more aesthetically pleasing trees, such as the pine, from the very unpleasing thistle. Indeed, adds David Hall, there is something positively Borgesian about classical Chinese texts; one could almost come to the conclusion that the Chinese did not seem to know what a single definition actually was (Hall and Ames 1999).

But the Chinese don't hail from a different planet. What we have here are two very different cultural styles – between the Greek demand for a mode of understanding based on deductive reasoning (which was carried over time into European thinking) and a very Chinese preoccupation with associate understanding (Lloyd 2012: 104). In both China and Japan the social ideal is harmony: *wa* in Japanese, *he* in Chinese (with no discordant notes allowed as in an atonal musical composition). We find this in the Chinese novel, which is all about relationships, or *guanxi* – the different connections in a social network. It even has its own lexicon, such as *jangqing* (sentiment), *renging* (human feeling), *mianzi* (face) and *bao* (reciprocity), all of which capture a world which is neither individual- nor society-based so much as relation-based (Moretti 2013: 237). Thus there is not a single Chinese classical novel that has the name of the principal character in the title; there is no equivalent, for example, of a *Don Quixote*, a *David Copperfield* or a *Madame Bovary*. And while there certainly are leading characters they are always part of a vast network. There are 975 characters in one of China's most famous novels, *The Dream of the Red Chamber* (compare this with the work of Charles Dickens (1812–1870), who probably created more characters than any other Western author – 2,000 in all, but they appear in fourteen different novels and thirty short stories).

That is not to say that the Chinese are not interested in individuals, but the country's history clearly has impelled it in another direction. Group harmony has always been more important than the cultivation of the self that was encouraged in Europe by the Greeks, and the reason may have a lot to do with geography. The Chinese landscape encouraged massive water irrigation projects and farming programmes for the cultivation of rice, which, in turn, put a premium on teamwork and a belief reflected in philosophies such as Confucianism about the interconnectedness of all things. The fact that even today discordant notes are not encouraged by the state doesn't mean that the state considers all 'notes' to be the same. But it is one thing for people to hold different opinions, quite another to voice them. If that sounds oppressive, we must remember that China's emperors usually expressed little interest in what people were thinking. They didn't burn people at the stake for their religious beliefs; there was no equivalent of the Catholic Inquisition (the notable exception in East Asia was the persecution of Christians in early seventeenth-century Japan. Christianity was deemed to be un-Japanese, just as communism in the early 1950s was deemed to be un-American). Instead of orthodoxy, it's better to talk of orthopraxy; what mattered was the right behaviour, not the right beliefs. The great break with tradition came with Mao and communism, a European rather than an Asian philosophy, which claimed the lives of 9 million Chinese in the Cultural Revolution alone.

Now the point is that, whatever linguistic differences there may be, the major works of every culture are open to translation. And yet in today's China there is a movement called cultural nativism (*ben tuzhuyi*) which contends that the Chinese language is unique and that Chinese characters are an expression of the 'national soul'; they penetrate its people's thoughts and its collective unconscious (or dreams). In other words, they can be considered part of the Chinese people's cultural DNA. Consistent with this belief, cultural nativists are demanding a return to 'native studies', as well as an end to the practice of reformatting classical Chinese texts using modern (i.e., in this case Western) categories. And they are particularly scornful of Western sinologists, however gifted, for lacking what they call 'cultural consanguinity' (Jullien 1995: 166). What is being claimed is that a non-Chinese speaker, even one who has mastered the language, can never really understand China or its people. In other words, the Chinese language is essentially unintelligible to non-Chinese.

All of this is nonsense, of course. However foreign a text may appear on first encounter it can always be translated into another language: that is why we have a world literature. Ideas can be communicated across time and culture. Ultimately, cultural nativism is a telling example of an objection to an age-old civilized belief that every educated person on the planet should make an effort to learn a language other than his own. That is why, to quote the Nobel Prize-winner Gao Xingjian, language is 'the ultimate crystallisation of human civilisation'. 'The written word is also magical for it allows communication between separate individuals, even if they are from different races and times. It is also in this way that the shared present time in the writing and reading of literature is connected to its eternal spiritual value' (Gao 2007: 85–6).

And what is the practice of international relations, asked Michael Oakeshott, if it is not what he famously called 'the conversation of mankind? It's worth quoting him at length:

In conversation, 'facts' appear only to be resolved once more into the possibilities from which they were made; 'certainties' are shown to be combustible, not by being brought in contact with other 'certainties' or with doubts, but by being kindled by the presence of ideas of another order; approximations are revealed between notions normally remote from one another. Thoughts of different species take wing and play round one another, responding to each other's movements and provoking one another to fresh exertions. Nobody asks where they have come from or on what authority they are present; nobody cares what will become of them when they have played their part. There is no . . . doorkeeper to examine credentials. (Oakeshott 2007).

Unfortunately, the nativists want to reshape a culture with which they claim to have privileged intimacy. The doorkeepers are out there, intent on hobbling the conversation at the cost of narrowing the range of thought.

Geographical determinism

The writer Iain Banks (1954–2013) is famous for identifying what he liked to call the 'Outside Context Problem': what happens when an advanced civilization encounters another and when the former is so advanced that it's totally outside the latter's frame of reference. The concept first appears in *Excession*, the fifth novel to feature 'the Culture', a fictional interstellar society. As Banks wrote, an OCP is the kind of problem 'most civilizations would encounter just once, and which they tended to encounter rather in the same way as a sentence encounters a full stop.'

> The usual example given to illustrate an Outside Context Problem was imagining you were a tribe on a largish, fertile island; you'd tamed the land, invented the wheel or writing or whatever, the neighbours were cooperative or enslaved but at any rate peaceful and you were busy raising temples to yourself with all the excess productive capacity you had, you were in a position of near-absolute power and control which your hallowed ancestors could hardly have dreamed of and the whole situation was just running along nicely like a canoe on wet grass . . . when suddenly this bristling lump of iron appears sailless and trailing steam in the bay and these guys carrying long, funny-looking sticks come ashore and announce you've just been discovered, you're all subjects of the Emperor now, he's keen on presents called tax and these bright-eyed holy men would like a word with your priests. (Banks 1996)

Banks later admitted that when he wasn't busy writing he had spent much of the time playing the computer game *Civilization* and that it had actually inspired the concept of the OCP, which is one of its central conceits. The game itself is a mark of our age. Deemed by the magazine *Computer Gaming World* as the 'computer game of all time', it has now been included in Stanford University library as a cultural artefact in its own right (*New York Times*, 12 March 2007).

The whole object of the game, by the way, is to build an empire, starting all the way back in 4000 BCE and reaching into the near future. With a little luck you might even make it to 2100 and manage to reach Alpha Centauri. The only problem is that the early version of the game Banks played was incorrigibly Eurocentric. If you were successful you could fast-track to the classical world or the Renaissance – two historical eras that might have little resonance for a non-Western player. The world of video games is actually well placed to introduce players to the history of civilization, but history cannot be reduced to one central story that used to be called 'the triumph of the West'. And there is another problem. Every computer game presupposes a program and a programmer who will have a view of how she thinks the world works. In *Civilization*, the program presupposes an idea that is definitively 'Western' – that being 'discovered' is the price you pay for progress, whether you survive the experience or not.

But then again the Outside Context Problem has applied, as far as we know, to only one *civilizational* contact in history, as opposed to many often fatal contacts between different tribes and the outside world, which have usually ended badly in drunkenness, petty criminality, economic dependency and a life of beggary. Contact between civilizations usually is very different. Often traumatic, it is rarely catastrophic; the one exception is the disastrous encounter between the Spanish and the native civilizations living in what the Europeans chose to call the New World (even if the lands that Columbus (1451–1506) purportedly 'discovered' probably hadn't escaped the notice of the people who had lived there for 12,000 years).

The problem was that, in the absence of contact with the outside world, there was little selective pressure to drive evolution, which is why the Aztecs were still stuck in the Bronze Age when the Spanish arrived. More striking still was the case of the Inca, a civilization that, despite its many accomplishments, was without the wheel, without an alphabet and without the arch or the dome – the hallmarks of all other Bronze Age civilizations. But it is also important to remind ourselves that what took place was historically unique. 'Two cultural experiments running in isolation for 15,000 years or more, at last came face to face' (Wright 2004: 112). It had never happened before and it won't happen again, and there is a reason for that: global communication.

The famous Silk Road, in the words of Peter Frankopan (2015), was 'the key artery', the international highway which for thousands of years brought China and the West into contact with each other. Alexander's armies marched east along it, bringing with it their own civilization – Hellenism. The historian Felipe Fernández-Armesto argues that the intellectual achievements of Plato and Aristotle, the Hundred Schools of Thought in China and the Nyaya School in India owed everything to the long-range cultural exchanges opened up by one geographical region in particular. Eurasia really is the world's greatest highway (Fernández-Armesto 2011: 130–58). The Silk Road in turn brought the Mongols to the gates of Europe in the thirteenth century and the Black Death a little later. The latter in retrospect was possibly the most significant export of all. For, in reducing Europe's population by two-thirds, it encouraged mass migration to the cities and led to the creation of a modern labour market which kick-started Europe into the next phase of its economic development. In other words, if you were not part of the Eurasian world, you really were marginalized in one way or another. Cut off from both Asia and Europe, Latin America and sub-Saharan Africa were both dealt a poor hand by history.

Unfortunately, Eurasia today has taken on a quite different connotation in contemporary Russian thinking. For some nationalist writers, geography translates very conveniently into geopolitics. Russia, they insist, is both northern and eastern at the same time: it is the fulcrum of the Aryan race and it has an inner oriental nature. Geography makes it unique: racially Western, but Asian by culture, and possibly even inclination (Laruelle 2006: 15)?

We are back to metaphysics and in this case Oswald Spengler, who was at his best when he left his wilder theories behind him in favour of memorable insights, which, though not always demonstrably true, are nonetheless thought-provoking. One such idea was that, whenever two civilizations interact with each other, one is bound to be more powerful, the other more creative. In this situation, the more creative will be forced to conform outwardly to the more powerful civilization's cultural configuration, although the latter's ideas will never really take root. Spengler called the phenomenon 'pseudo-morphosis' and thought it applied particularly to Russia – a satellite society that in the reign of Peter the Great was drawn into the field of European civilization of which it never really became part.

Some Russian writers would agree with him; they prefer to see their country as a civilizational state as opposed to a nation-state and argue that the country when a young and undeveloped culture was set back by the attempts of Peter the Great (1672–1725) to modernize it along European lines. In Spengler's rendering of the story, the burning of Moscow in 1812 by its own citizens can be seen as a de-programming exercise, a rejection of Peter's programme, even a primitive expression of a wish to return to its roots (Neumann 2016: 1387). The modernizing Bolsheviks took a very different view: the novelist Maxim Gorky (1868–1936) famously saw the Russian peasant as a 'non-Russian nomad' and argued that the country's 'Asiatic Mongol biological heritage' had significantly 'retarded' its historical development (Losurdo 2015: 202). Yet it is precisely that historical inheritance that now divides Russian historians, with liberals insisting that their country should continue to see Peter the Great in the traditional light, as the great modernizer, and conservatives insisting that Russia can be true to itself only if it re-engages with its Asiatic Mongol heritage.

The latter will tell you that on the great Eurasian steppes a variant of Tatar genes, or so we are told, got recoded. The process was described by one of the first Eurasianists, Lev Gumilev (the estranged son of the poet Anna Akhmatova), as 'passionarity'. It is not a word that most Russians would recognize even though it occasionally appears in some of Putin's speeches. It is the process by which organisms absorb biochemical energy from nature, in this case from the soil of Eurasia. Another writer, Peter Savitsky, later developed the concept of topogenesis, or 'place development', to explain the deep link between geography and culture. Cultural Darwinism doesn't recommend itself only to novelists or poets; in Russia it's become a concert familiar to many political scientists. Group mentalities and invariant forms of biosocial organization, write Peter Katzenstein and Nicole Weygandt, unanchored in history, ethology or even mainstream textbooks on civilization, have become legitimate topics in teaching and research, and they are now well known to the country's leading politicians. And that is one of the reasons, they add, why Russians are coming to self-identify in increasingly civilizational terms (Katzenstein and Weygandt 2017: 431).

Not that the idea is to be dismissed entirely out of hand. Like the caste question in Hyderabad and genetic/cultural imprinting in general, some countries may well be governed by an ethological imprint. As the Harvard professor David Haig suggests, writing of genomic imprinting, just as the way in which the imprint on a mother's ovary or a father's testes marks DNA as maternal or paternal and accordingly influences its pattern of expression – what the gene does in the next generation – so historical inputs from the environment might be transmitted over several generations and influence the genetic expression of a country. Would it be possible if your great-grandmother experienced a famine or lived in time of war that one or both might have an imprint on the genome (Haig 2016: 19)? Some Russian scientists certainly think so: they contend that children of citizens who lived through the siege of Leningrad are linked by a single manner of behaviour – a high sense of civic duty. From the blood samples of 206 survivors they have found variants that help to slow down the metabolism and allow the cells to be more efficient in using energy.

The lucky group of super-patriots includes Putin, of course, but also some members of his regime, such as the director of the Foreign Intelligence Service and Putin's former chief of staff (*The Times*, 24 January 2018). It is a convenient finding, though challenged by many geneticists, including the children of the siege survivors.

But when you come to think of it, the idea that civilization is an organic entity is similar to Spengler's belief that it is an organism that experiences life cycles from birth to death. Like Spengler, there are Russian nationalists who feel that their own civilization is measured by the seasons and pace of growth – and the more pessimistic, feeling that winter is already setting in, are given to dreaming of one heroic last act. If you visit Moscow you may see cars with bumper stickers proclaiming 'To Berlin!' and 'We can do it again!' (Both are rather crude allusions to the Second World War). In the West most people are metaphysically tone deaf, but Russia is different; it always has been. And the concept of 'passionarity' shows an interest in exteriorizing the nation's psychic state in a physical setting. Although distinctly strange to a Western audience, it offers Russians an emotional engagement with the environment – it allows them to reconnect with a history much older than the era of the great modernizer Peter the Great.

And the message? It is a rather bleak one. Much of the recent writing on why Russia is a civilizational state turns, as we shall see, on the antagonistic relationship between two opposing forces – Western cosmopolitanism and Russian nativism – which may one day end in war. Unfortunately, all this is a telling testament to how the imagination can shape identities in bizarre ways, and how intellectuals in bed with a political class can hoodwink both themselves and others.

Myth-making

In Ismail Kadare's novel *The Palace of Dreams* (2001), an empire (which is loosely based on the Ottoman) has a department which monitors its subjects' dreams for signs and portents of disaffection. Once collected, they are sifted through, classified and ultimately interpreted to identify the 'master dream' that they share. Every country, Kadare implies, has dreams that are distinctive; every civilization has a collective unconscious. If only it were possible to put a country and its people on the couch. (One can't, of course, but then perhaps it will be possible one day – Cambridge Analytica, the data analysis firm credited with helping Trump win the election, harvested masses of consumer and personal information from Facebook to build a 'psychographic profile' of the US electorate. If you know the personality of a people and what they are dreaming, you can adjust your message to resonate more effectively. Anton Vaino, Putin's chief of staff, is even more ambitious: he is working on a 'nooscope', a device to measure humanity's collective consciousness (*The Times*, 24 February 2018). So, perhaps, Kadare's novel is not that much off-field. Except for the fact that, while electorates may dream, civilizations don't. Unlike states, they are not unitary actors, but that doesn't stop governments from seeding dreams in the mind of their own citizens.

Regrettably, today's political regimes in China and Russia prefer to exploit history quite cynically for their own purposes, usually to bolster their own legitimacy. And they tend to hype up the elements of conflict in the encounters between societies in order to rally support for the status quo. Cultural Darwinism is useful for that reason, even if at the moment the competitive advantage it promises falls short of the 'winner takes all' message of the Social Darwinism that preceded it. The message, nevertheless, is stark enough. Once again, writes one Chinese nationalist:

> we need to let the citizens know the truth, that we are totally alone in the world, that Westerners are jackals from the same lair; dispel illusions about any Western country: not to dream that there is any good person among them who will be better disposed toward China, that in a situation of isolation and adversity, the Chinese must ceaselessly strive for self-strengthening. (Cited in Hughes 2011: 604)

Such 'self-striving' may be the basis for future international conflict, especially should the West still wish to export its own values, true to character as history's very first 'political civilization'. For the West, too, tells its own stories and subscribes to its own myths, and the US in particular has been particularly aggressive in asserting them. But then again the West may be out of the business of shaping history for everyone else, or even itself; history may be shaped by different countries with very different values in the name not of 'liberal civilization' but of a new and perhaps more appealing slogan – 'unity in diversity' – as we shall see in the last chapter. But first we must discuss how Cultural Darwinism has abetted the rise of the civilizational state.

5

The Civilizational State

During the Nuremberg Trials (1946) Hermann Goering (1893–1946) spent some of his time reading a book by an American-Chinese philosopher, Lin Yutang (1895–1976). The book, *The Importance of Living* (1937), had topped the *New York Times* best-seller list for over fifty weeks (Williams 2010). I have no idea what Goering made of the author's discussion of national character types. Taking R for a sense of reality (or realism), D for dreams (idealism), H for humour and S for sensitivity, Lin came up with the following evaluation:

R3D3H2S2 – American.
R3D4H1S2 – German.
R2D4H1S1 – Russian.

Goering would not have been surprised to read that the Germans dreamed as much as the Russians, though both had little humour and that the Americans dreamed less than either (evidence perhaps of their main philosophical tradition, pragmatism). But what then of Manifest Destiny and the role of Providence in American history? Both were invoked when the editor of *Time* and *Life*, Henry Luce (1898–1967), announced the coming of the American Century in 1944. Only a few years later, addressing what he identified as 'the crisis in Western civilization', he insisted that dreams and other 'psychic forces' were the decisive factors in the making of history. 'The real drama unfolds within the minds of Man. It is determined by his response to the challenges of life' (McNeill 1989: 213–16).

If you were to conclude that Lin Yutang's exercise has little academic merit, you would certainly be right. Nations don't have characters that lend themselves to analysis. But, to be fair, he was the first to concede that his classifications were both reductive and formulaic, though his system was popular enough at the time to attribute national characteristics to different people (Lin [1937] 1949: 6–9). The main point, to quote Mario Cuomo, is that we dream in poetry but governments govern in prose. And poetic visions of the future have a metaphysical pull of their own. And yet here is a downside: they also tend to lock countries into thinking that history confronts us with a series of existential challenges, when in fact the reality is often much more mundane.

But hold that thought for a moment. We seem to be back to dreaming again. *The China Dream*, *The China Wave*, *The Fourth Protocol Theory* and *The Eurasian Mission* are all books which speak for themselves, loudly and insistently, though with no single authorial voice. And all exploit the three civilizational myths I identified in the second chapter. Sometimes, wrote Wittgenstein, you have to pull a concept out of a language, send it to be cleaned, and then send it back into circulation. Civilization may be a perfect example. It gives rise to many different definitions; for some it denotes an organic structure, for others a discourse, and even a value-system, or all or none of the above. If you define it much more narrowly, however, as politicians often do, as a political community (the West) or as a belief system that is coterminous with a state (China/Russia), then you can move on to different ground. Some states are dreaming of transforming themselves into civilizational states that will rival the nation-states that over time they have become.

Imperial Japan: the first civilizational state

The very first was imperial Japan in the 1930s. Even today the Japanese like to think of themselves as citizens of a unique country with a heavily indented coastline, extensive mountain ranges, and particular customs and conventions that are as distinctive as sushi and the haiku. In truth theirs is also a great assimilating culture. From the seventh century they introduced Chinese ideas, techniques and institutions, including writing and Buddhism, and transformed themselves into something authentically Japanese. The same is true of the techniques and ideas that were introduced from the West some years after Commodore Perry arrived in 1853 with a fleet of four American warships to force Japan to open itself to free trade. With the Meiji Restoration (1868), the old order was overthrown, and a new regime took power that was intent on modernizing society to save its cultural heritage, not transform it. And Japan has remained distinctive ever since thanks partly to the fact that it came to modernization late, a fact which allowed its indigenous tradition time enough to adapt.

Modernization remained highly controversial, of course. There was always the fear that the country had surrendered a little too much of its soul in return for doubtful material gains. 'Japanization' soon became a pejorative term to describe a culture that had lost its self-respect in the process of modernizing itself. Ironically even the term was Western. It was coined by the Spanish philosopher Miguel de Unamuno (1864–1936) to describe his own country's often violent attempt to come to terms with modernity (Castro and Lafuente 2007).

How the Japanese dealt with this challenge is instructive. First, they went into denial by turning on their parental father, China. If you are a Freudian you might see it as a reassertion of a childhood struggle against parental domination. In an essay, 'Farewell to Asia' (1885), Fukuzawa Yukichi (1835–1901) insisted that Japan was geopolitically but no longer culturally part of Asia and as a result had finally overtaken the Celestial Empire in its cultural life (Osterhammel 2014: 84). By the 1920s the Chinese had sunk even lower in Japan's estimation. They were now considered *chankoro*, a Japanese term for the Chinese that was the equivalent of the Western term 'chink' (Tanaka 1993: 277). But at the same time the Japanese found themselves challenged on two fronts: they had to locate themselves in Asia without being Asian and in the West without becoming thoroughly Westernized. The trick was to transform the country into a civilizational state.

The process involved the rewriting of school textbooks. Take the *Kokutai no Hongi*. Published by the wonderfully named Bureau of Thought Control, a division of the Ministry of Education, it sold over 2 million copies in 1937 and was used as a text in most Japanese schools. Japanese schoolchildren were reminded that they lived in a state in which the emperor represented the 'essence' of the nation. Even to talk of a nation, they were told, was meaningless, since a nation in the Western understanding was considered to be an embodiment of the 'will of the people'; in imperial Japan, the people were deemed to have no will of their own. Quite the contrary, they found themselves locked into an apodictic belief that there was nothing of greater importance than unconditional love for an emperor who was considered to be divine and an unconditional willingness to sacrifice oneself for the imperial family (Hall 1949). The old *bushido* ethos of the samurai class survived the Meiji Restoration in a dangerously transfigured form. Being prepared to die for one's country replaced the idea of dying for one's lord.

The transformation into a civilizational state also involved the transformation of Buddhism in the 1920s into something that was distinctively un-Buddhist, but very Japanese. Warrior Zen, as Brian Victoria calls it, became a national religion which translated the Buddhist idea of the surrender of the self into an unconditional commitment to sacrifice for the emperor. Death became a variant of life, not a negation of it. Many young Kamikaze pilots later in the war steeled themselves before going into battle through Zen meditation. Zen became a religion of willpower, and thus central to the Japanese war effort after 1943 and the end of its run of victories when the only thing left was the will to fight on (Victoria 1997).

As a civilizational state, imperial Japan was driven by unconscious psychic needs. The *Kokutai no Hongi* taught that death for the emperor was not self-sacrifice but 'a casting aside of our little selves . . . and the enhancing of the genuine life of the people' (Blomberg 1994: 191–2). But there was little that was genuinely modern in the vision. Japanese militarism in the 1930s may have been modern in the use of words such as 'innovation' and 'self-creation'; it shared with other political religions such as Marxism the language of hope, transcendence and immanence, but it was very unmodern in sacralizing the nation and in promising the Japanese people that they could defy the rational material circumstances of life by the exercise of will alone. Ultimately late imperial Japan was a country composed of multiple identities that tapped into magic and science, feudalism and modernity, rationality and irrationality: all coexisted somewhat uncomfortably in a complex reality, if indeed it can be called 'real'. Even as a ghost, wrote the commander at Iwo Jima to his wife before taking his life, he wished to return in the vanguard of the next war. If he did, adds P. J. O'Rourke mischievously, he is more likely to be found haunting a Toyota factory than a future battlefield (O'Rourke 2004: 96).

Looking back at the Japan of these years, we find a society that faced a crisis of self-belief. One of the country's greatest twentieth-century writers, Natsume Soseki (1867–1916), had warned his countrymen that the speed and intensity of modernization along Western lines could lead to a collective nervous breakdown. In 1941, adds Ian Buruma, the breakdown appears to have been complete. By then the feeling of humiliation had turned lethal (Buruma 2014: 151–2). In 1943 a great conference was convened in Kyoto to discuss how Japanese civilization might be saved. One attendee accused modernity of being 'a European thing'. Others blamed science and the scientific method for hollowing out the nation's soul. A film critic blamed Hollywood for contaminating Japan with degenerate American ideas. Another writer put the main blame on capitalism (Buruma and Margalit 2004: 2). The irony of the exercise, to be sure, did not escape every participant. Though some expressed the hope that a Japanese victory might help the country to 'overcome modernity' and to move to a higher stage of development, they were unable to agree on what form that might take without further modernization. One seemed to presuppose the other, while at the same time contradicting it (Tanaka 1993: 277).

What was this if not a veritable 'clash of civilizations'? Even after the war the national mind-set changed slowly. Many Japanese nationalists tended to dismiss their fellow citizens whom they considered to be too Westernized as *shinjinrui* – 'new editions of a human being recast according to Western specifications' (Conrad 1998: 80). But eventually the graft did take, as did democracy. Seventy years on, Prime Minister Shinzo Abe would like to 'rescue' the country from its Americanization – to get rid of its constitutional obligations to refrain from armed conflict and revive the 'moral education' of the nation by redoubling national pride and downplaying war crimes such as the Rape of Nanjing. He would like to replace the reference in the constitution to 'universal rights' with one to Japan's 'unique culture'. He has even gone on record as wanting to restore the pre-war *Kokutai* and with it the idea of the country's 'national essence'. But, for the moment at least, the country is still wedded to a normative agenda that will keep it closely allied to the liberal West. As long as it needs the United States as an ally it will be predisposed to stick to the script the Americans wrote for it during the occupation. To unpack the post-war order would require a two-thirds majority in the Diet as well as victory in a popular referendum. And the second is by no means a certainty. Japan, after all, is still a democratic country in which people are allowed to express their own opinions. It is not Japan but China – the country with which Japan was once at war – that is staking out claims to be a civilizational state, with all the political prerogatives that are deemed to come with it.

The China way

When Xi Jinping looks at the United States and Europe, he sees a significant decline in Western power. Chinese officials these days like to think of the West as being in terminal decline. China, by contrast, they know is continuing to rise. The US may still double its national income every thirty years, but China has been doubling it every ten. The stated goal is to attain a per capita GDP of $30,000 by 2049, when the regime will celebrate a hundred years in power. By then, if the goal is achieved, China will be producing 1.5 times more than the proportion of global GDP produced at present by the United States.

If you are an American president you may see it very differently. The US is not going to be displaced from the number one position yet. Historically, it is still the short-priced favourite. Trump holds all the aces – the world's most powerful military, its reserve currency, and an enviable geopolitical position – the US finds itself in the safest neighbourhood of all, even without the promised wall separating it from Mexico. In thirty years' time it will have the youngest population of all the developed economies, and it is already almost self-sufficient in energy. It happens to have the most competitive industries in the high-tech sector and attracts the world's most gifted immigrants. Not a bad hand, all things considered, from the point of view of the man sitting in the Oval Office.

Nevertheless, China's rise is the main topic of debate, and the secret of its success is very germane to the theme of this book – it's cultural. One of the problems with contemporary debates is the fact that so many commentators have such foreshortened historical perspectives. Remember Japan when it was the world's number 2 economic power? Japan, too, didn't spring into life in the 1960s. By the end of the eighteenth century it had overtaken China and India in per capita wealth. Modernization a hundred years later served to turbo-charge its economic growth. It was one of the top five economies of the world in 1941, with world-beating industries in new sectors such as automobiles and aircraft production. China at the end of the eighteenth century also accounted for 37 per cent of the world's economic output (Pye 2000: 246–7). In other words, writes Lucian Pye, culture clearly counts in both cases. It wasn't people who changed in that period, nor was it their views, only the historical context in which the two countries found themselves operating. We do not need to adopt a teleological approach to history. Indeed, we should divest it of any claims to have any particular 'shape'. But we can invest it with renewed significance by recognizing that culture actually matters. In the case of China, we are dealing with a civilization that is not only the longest surviving but also the most culturally self-sufficient on the planet. What is surprising is not the claim that it is a civilizational state but the fact that it has taken so long to make that claim.

You will find the claim in a stream of books that have come online in recent years. The best known in the West is probably *The China Wave* (2012), the best-seller by Zhang Weiwei. Following its publication, the author toured the West with his message: there is a distinctive Chinese path of economic, social and cultural development that is very different from the West's because it is not for export. And there is another critical difference. As a political civilization, the West is dangerous. The Chinese way, by contrast, is inherently peaceful, non-expansionist and non-imperialist. Unlike the West, China has no wish to instruct the rest of the world about how it should behave.

If all this were indeed the case, China would be truly exceptional; it would be very similar, in fact, to the United States. In reality, civilizational states also seem to need to establish forward positions and engage in PR. There are hundreds of Confucius institutes embedded in universities around the world (my own country, at the last count, had about twenty). There is a UK edition of the *China Daily*. And then there is the news agency Xin Hua, as well as China Central Television's multilingual programming. In 2015 the government launched a series of televised ads in Times Square featuring the smiling faces of Jackie Chan, Yao Ming and John Woo, which played on six giant screens, 300 times a day (Tan 2012). What the average New Yorker made of this is unclear, assuming it had any impact at all, but it may well be an intimation of what is to come. Far from being endemically incapable of reaching out to other people, China, too, would now seem to have a civilizing mission of sorts: to show the world how to behave (preferably to keep its thoughts about China to itself) and to push ahead with a more harmonious world order (one in which China itself will be beyond criticism).

Indeed, the speed with which China is staking out its claims to the future is increasing all the time. At the nineteenth Party Congress in 2017, Xi

Jinping told the world that the country's peculiar blend of Leninism and Confucianism offered an alternative model to that presented by the West. As soon as he proposed his 'thoughts on socialism with Chinese characteristics for a new era' – the opening phrase of his report – universities and research institutes across the country launched 'Xi Jinping Thought Study Centres' to unpack every word of his seminal speech. What he is offering the Chinese people is a break with two centuries in which they have been subordinate to outside influences. But here is the rub. Back at home China's citizens are required to buy into a version of history that underpins that agenda, threatening to imprison them in the past.

History as a life sentence

A few years ago a British journalist recounted a story about a friend who wanted to marry a Chinese-American woman whose parents many years earlier had emigrated from mainland China. When he was introduced to her father he detected a distinct chill in the air which seemed to grow as the evening wore on. Finally, the old man asked him a question: 'Before marrying my daughter, will you be good enough to apologize?' 'For what?', he asked. The answer took him by surprise: 'For the Opium Wars' (Webb 2013). I doubt whether many Chinese fathers would go out of their way to demand historical satisfaction from their children's Western friends. Don't forget that the man was an immigrant, and ex-pats tend to cling onto history as part of their identity. They tend to pack their historical consciousness in the same suitcases that they bring with them when they travel abroad.

The First Opium War (1839–42) was triggered by Britain's insistence that the Chinese allow the unrestricted sale of opium. And it can be considered, writes Johann Arnason, to be one of the most momentous encounters in history 'for which the term "clash of civilizations" seems far too benign' (Arnason 2006: 48). What made it so traumatic was the violence with which China was dragged into an international order that challenged many of its most strongly held beliefs. What it confronted, in effect, was a threat to its ontological security. And that is why the 'century of humiliation' is to be found at the core of the Patriotic History courses that are compulsory for Chinese children and that have shaped a whole generation's view of the humiliations visited upon their ancestors by the Western barbarians. But then who is doing the remembering, and what exactly is being remembered?

The official story of the Opium War isn't exactly fake history, but it offers a very incomplete version of it. Take the opium trade itself. If the British pushed it in the name of free trade the claim wasn't entirely specious. In 1847 *The Economist* condemned China's ban on opium as misguided, as the journal does the war on drugs today. Until 1916 it continued to list opium in its weekly list of commodity prices. Only in the 1920s did the British themselves need a doctor's prescription to buy opium; before that they could buy it over the counter ('The Opium Wars still shape China's view of the West', *The Economist*, 19 December 2017, p. 34)

Then there is the war itself. Back in 1840 the British, who knew very little about China or its history, were astonished one day to see a fleet of five treadmill vessels bearing down on them, powered not by steam, but by sailors. In his memoirs, one British commander wrote: 'What showed the ingenuity of the Chinese character was the construction of several large-wheeled vessels, which were afterwards brought forward against us with great confidence . . . The idea must have been suggested to them by the reports they received concerning the wonderful power of our steamers or wheeled vehicles' (cited in James and Thorpe 1994: xviii). British commanders were enormously proud of their armoured gunboats, which allowed them to sail against the wind 200 miles up the Yangtze, all the way to Nanking. What this particular British commander did not know was that the Chinese paddle boats were not crude attempts to copy British designs but copies of designs of paddle-wheelers that over a thousand years earlier had been powered by sailors, each of which had been capable of transporting 800 men. If you are, say, a young Chinese schoolgirl, you probably won't have been told about the human-operated paddle boats – until recently the Chinese themselves remained largely ignorant of their own extraordinary technological achievements. It was a British historian, Joseph Needham (1900–1995), who was the first person to catalogue them beginning in the 1930s. It became his lifetime's mission. Needham was amazed to discover that the Chinese had invented much more than gunpowder and printing with movable type, which the Europeans had seized upon in the course of their own rise to power. They had also invented clockwork escapement mechanisms, magnetic compasses and waterwheels. The catalogue which Needham drew up runs to seven pages and includes everything from the collapsible umbrella to the toothbrush. Long before the Industrial Revolution, the Chinese were using hinged pistons in their forges and mechanical reciprocators for sifting grain, and Chinese steam engines were puffing away long before those of James Watt (Steiner 2008: 13–14). What is really surprising is that it should have been the Europeans and not the Chinese who had the Industrial Revolution first.

What our young Chinese schoolgirl won't learn from her Patriotic History courses is that it would have been quite easy to have defeated the British in 1840 had the government set its mind to it. The court in Peking ignored the advice given to it by local officials to arm the peasants, to intermingle professional soldiers among them in civilian dress, and to lure the foreigners inland where they would not have had the numbers to have made much of an impression. These were exactly to become Mao's tactics a century later. The emperor rejected the advice, not because of fear of arming the peasants but because of the related fear that it would be difficult to disarm them after the war. He may well have been right. Twenty years later the peasants rose up in what was a Christian fundamentalist revolt in the course of which 20 million people lost their lives. It was the most devastating civil war in modern history.

And here is one other point: resentment of its past treatment by the Europeans is based on a selective reading of its own history. The government insists that it was wrong of the Europeans to impose 'unequal treaties', though the term itself was not used by the Chinese until 1923. It tends also to forget its own high-handed treatment of its neighbours in the past. The European demand for trading rights in Chinese ports and jurisdiction over their own citizens actually conformed to Chinese practices during the Tang dynasty a thousand years before British warships entered Chinese waters (Gelber 2016). A Great Power, after all, is one which can interfere in the affairs of a lesser power in a way in which the latter cannot interfere in its own. In forgetting this 'inconvenient truth', the Chinese government does itself no favours. In using the past in such a cavalier fashion, it only sells it short.

For its own ends, however, the Patriotic History courses are here to stay. So too are historic sites such as the Yuanmingyuan, or Garden of Perfect Brightness, which was torched by the British and French at the end of the Second Opium War. It was renamed by the party in 1997 a 'national base for patriotic education'. The list of such sites has since grown to 428, and for schoolchildren pilgrimages to the sites are all but obligatory. The way that the party interprets the Opium Wars is a vivid example, in fact, of how a historical event can elude a country's grasp of history while at the same time lodging itself firmly in its historical memory.

It also provides an alibi for not confronting the tragedies of the recent past. Regrettably, writes Milan Kundera in *The Book of Laughter and Forgetting* ([1979] 1992), we are separated from the past by two forces that go instantly to work and cooperate: the force of forgetting (which erases) and the force of memory (which transforms). We all have a responsibility to produce a version of history that is, at the very least, life-affirming. If you read Zhang's *The China Wave*, you will find that the force of forgetting is as powerful as the force of memory, for there is no mention of recent history, especially the crimes of Mao. Western political scientists still tend to claim that 20 million people died in the Great Leap Forward. In fact, an internal CCP report admitted that the true figure was probably twice that number, which, if true, would make it the greatest man-made disaster in human history (Walden 2011). In trying to eliminate the worst consequences of China's 'four olds' – culture, ideas, customs and habits – Mao later launched the Cultural Revolution, which achieved what one writer calls 'auto-cultural' genocide on an immeasurable scale (Johnson 2017). The Communist Party may well have lifted millions out of poverty, but it killed millions more in bizarre social experiments, and the collateral damage should not be forgotten whenever Chinese officials claim that India has lagged behind in its own path to modernization.

When I was studying history at Cambridge in the early 1970s, personalities tended to be airbrushed out of the picture almost entirely, to be replaced by social movements and economic trends. But it is people of course who make history, which is why political leadership is so critical. Daniel Kahneman makes this point when discussing the ideological giants of the twentieth century: Hitler, Stalin and Mao. Each came to a movement which would never have tolerated a female leader, but each man's genetic origins can be traced to an unfertilized egg that had a 50 per cent chance of being fertilized by different sperm cells and thus ending in a female baby. Or, to put it another way, there was only a 12.5 per cent chance that all three leaders would be born male and an 87.5 per cent chance that at least one would be born female (Kahneman 2012: 248–9). Imagine the history of twentieth-century China if Mao had come into the world as a girl, like his adopted sister Zejian. Imagine a communist China spared the horrors of the Great Leap Forward and the Cultural Revolution.

If it could confront the past with greater honesty, the party might not have to make so much of 'the century of humiliation'. Unfortunately, the 'victimization' narrative encourages what Wang Zheng calls 'the arrogance of self-pity', which plays unhelpfully into an acute status anxiety about its relations with the outside world (Wang 2012). Those who do not remember the past are condemned to repeat it – such is the Chinese Communist Party's line. Yet those who cannot let go of the past are always at risk of finding themselves imprisoned by it. As Susan Sontag once warned her fellow Americans: 'devotion to the past is one of the most disastrous forms of unrequited love' (Sontag 1977).

Does all this matter? It does, I think, if you acknowledge the fact that two decades of patriotic education have seeded China's youth, at least superficially, with a virulent strain of state-mandated nationalism. And look at Chinese national security thinking and the extent to which the 'never again' attitude extends to operational domains that were not in existence in the nineteenth century. Take the internet, which Xi Jinping claims is an 'achievement of civilization', one that his own government can use as a social and political engineering tool as part of the rejuvenation of China. The rather disturbing language that he used in a speech in 2016, with its references to 'promoting mainstream values', reflects the need to defend sovereignty, this time not against gunships but against Western attempts to undermine 'the social atmosphere' and the country's 'cultural security' – code words that suggest that, in present Chinese security thinking, cyber-deterrence has a strong cultural slant (Xinhuanet 2016). There is a defensiveness to such thinking that bodes ill for the future. It is especially disconcerting to an outside observer to see a people's deepest resentments take shape through the medium of history. For one day, of course, such thinking could eventually take on a life of its own.

The new Confucianism

China's President Xi Jinping likes to think of the Communist Party as part of the 'unbroken line of Chinese civilization' (*The Economist*, 24 December 2016, p. 46). A case in point is its rediscovery of the country's most famous philosophy, Confucianism. And the party is now keen to exploit the untapped potential of one of its most ancient traditions. Communism and Confucianism may well be strange bedfellows, but, concerned about the rampant inequality which has resulted from years of rapid economic growth, the party has found it useful to rediscover the core message of Confucianism – social harmony (Bell 2000). But there's a problem – it is all very well to turn to Confucianism to promote social harmony, but it is pretty meaningless to do so without locating it in a specific historical context. What do Confucian values mean in a society in which family life has changed out of all recognition and in which the individual and the state coexist on very different terms from even fifty years ago?

The turn to Confucianism began in 2005, when President Hu Jintao applauded the Confucian concept of social harmony and instructed party cadres to build a 'harmonious society'. As recently as 2011, a statue of Confucius was removed from Tiananmen Square following a hundred days of heated online debates between party members. Only three years later, however, Xi became the first communist leader to attend celebrations marking Confucius' death. Party officials are now expected to attend lectures on China's greatest philosopher, while his writings are being revived in the nation's schools in an attempt to reconnect children with such Confucian concepts as *zhong* (loyalty), *shu* (consideration) and *yi* (righteousness). The Chinese leadership also taps into Confucianism to emphasize its peace-loving credentials and its wish to build a more 'harmonious world'. The claim here is that Chinese philosophy had always disparaged the 'absolute subjectivity of the self' and the top-down stratification of the present rules-based international order in favour of an accommodation between different cultures, or what Jiang Zemin used to call 'harmonious inclusion-ism' (Zhang 2016). It is the novelty of linking a philosophical position with a political aim such as 'peaceful development', claims Zhang Weiwei (2012), that reinforces the country's claim to be a civilizational state.

Whatever the consequences, Confucianism is for the moment the agreed pathway to the truth – and it is a perfect fit for an authoritarian society. After all, in the words of one nineteenth-century Confucian scholar, it stresses 'proper relations between ruler and minister, father and son, superior and subordinate, the high and low, all in their proper place, just as hats and shoes are not interchangeable' (cited in Fenby 2014: 12). The upshot of all this, of course, is that the regime in the eyes of some of its critics is coming to look more and more like the Confucian-inspired mandarinate which the communist revolution overthrew. At present it is proving to be an ideal cover for what the political philosopher Christopher Ford calls 'merito-garcic thinking' – the belief of a self-selecting elite that only it can be trusted with power because only it has sufficient wisdom to guide the state (Ford 2012).

Perhaps it is facile to point out that the party's understanding of Confucianism might not be recognized as authentic by Confucius himself. Does it actually matter? Ideas after all constantly evolve; if they didn't they could not be recycled. They have to be equal to the times. Take the attempt in the late nineteenth century to make Confucianism into the equivalent of Shinto in Japan – a national religion, which it had never been before. Or the use made of Confucius in the 1920s by writers such as Feng Youlan (1895–1990) and Mou Zongsan (1909–1995), who both put an emphasis on individual self-fulfilment, which is today condemned by many self-confessed Confucians as an assault on family values. That is the point: if Confucianism has been a recurring theme of the country's history, it has continued to evolve over time. What is called neo-Confucianism even drew on Buddhist thinking from India. And there have also been several periods when Confucianism has been held in little regard by those who employed the 'funny story' (*hsiaohua*) and the 'side-sweep' (*ku-chi*) to attack what they regarded as its dismissal of individual aspirations for freedom (Zeldin 2015: 183). Anti-Confucian thinkers who were critical of its traditions of autocracy and hierarchy were many, including Zhuangzi (d. 287 BCE), the fourth-century BCE thinker whose example inspired the so-called humanist literary movement of the 1920s. Between the first and fourth centuries CE, the young even denounced Confucian collective social norms as 'unnatural', or essentially un-Chinese (ibid.: 244).

And here's another problem. Of all the values that Confucianism traditionally extolls, the most important is justice. So, what are you to do if you are not permitted to criticize the injustices of party rule? If it really wants the reform of the manners and morals of the people, shouldn't the government try to govern by example rather than force (quite the reverse of what has happened since Xi's return to repression)? And, for all its insistence on cracking down on corruption, there is still a huge moral vacuum in China: there is no real rule of law. If the injustices of the system allow for no legal resort to obtain redress, writes Xu Zhiyuan, then there is no alternative to asserting the last shred of dignity left to the citizen: the opportunity to criticize one's rulers. But where should your criticisms be given expression: in blogs exposing the venality of the petty bureaucrats, or in calls for serious democratic reform (for which the Nobel Peace Prize-winner Liu Xiaobo was sentenced in 2010 to eleven years in prison)? (Xu 2016).

But, then again, could Confucianism ironically and eventually ease the country's transition to democracy? (Qing 2013). Confucians used to talk of 'the Way of the Humane Authority', and many political Confucians today advance a specific Chinese model of political power which derives its legitimacy from three sources: that of Heaven (a transcendent sense of natural morality); that of Earth (the wisdom of the ancestors); and that of the Human (the popular will). In an ideal world, Human Authority would be exercised by a tri-cameral legislature – a House of Exemplary Persons, a House of the Nation and a House of the People. A Western reader might be surprised to learn that the leader of the House of Exemplary Persons should be a great scholar, one examined on his knowledge of the Confucian classics. He would probably be even more surprised to learn that the leader of the House of the Nation should be a direct descendant of Confucius himself (Qing and Bell 2012). Fortunately, there is a large field on which to draw. Almost 2 million people claim descent from the great sage; 1.3 million have been added to the list since the Confucian Register was revised in 1998 to allow the inclusion of women (Spencer 2008).

Of course, there is no reason why the Western democratic model should apply outside the Western world. More importantly, there is no reason why China should evolve a democratic form of government, Confucian or otherwise. But that is not the point. In the end, what strikes one as most especially ironical (and which invites scepticism, whether justified or not) is the fact that the party's return to Confucianism is so self-serving. Irony has many meanings, to be sure, and what one culture finds ironic may not be so in the case of another. But a Western reader may agree with Richard Rorty (1931–2007): it is possible to find everything ironical if you finally abandon the idea that the beliefs you consider central in the here and now are beyond the reach of time and chance (Rorty 1989: xv). As Rorty adds sardonically, ironists – liberal or otherwise – are not popular with politicians for that reason. And the Communist Party claims to be defending two truths that it considers to be eternal and therefore beyond criticism: the truth of communism (which transcends time and place) and the innate superiority of Chinese civilization (which spans the last four thousand years of human history).

In an excoriating piece in 2015, Slavoj Žižek highlighted some other ironies: the irony of a Communist Party that claims to be the only true guarantor of capitalism; the irony of a regime which, because it is officially committed to atheism, claims that only it can be relied upon to guarantee different religious faiths continued freedom of expression; and the irony of a government that presides over aggressive individualism in the marketplace while also insisting it is committed to social harmony at home. Of course, what is being defended, he insists, is not the 'Chinese way', but Communist Party rule. But, if all this is ironical, some ironies can be truer than others. And the party would argue that it is the only organization capable of preventing the rise of the nihilistic capitalism that engulfed the Western world in 2007–8. After all, it faulted the West at the time for not regulating the banks strictly enough and for allowing companies to sell products like derivatives that nobody really understands, including those who sell them. All of which might well be true, but for the fact that the government has allowed the debt mountain to account for 260 per cent of national income.

And what of the argument that the party members who are discouraged from embracing any religion are above the narrow sectarianism that divides society? This might be true, too, but for the continuing harassment of Muslims in Xinjiang and the tearing down of crosses from the roofs of Christian churches in Zhejiang province. Not to mention the suppression of the indigenous culture of Tibet. Religious repression reaches quite a level of surrealism when, under Order No. 5 (which has been in force since

2007), the government in Beijing can even forbid a Tibetan lama from rein-carnating without prior approval! You really couldn't make it up. ↙

What the Chinese people are being presented with is a specious claim, namely that the security of a 'timeless' civilization and its 'timeless' values, such as harmony, equality and human dignity, are consistent with the party's continued commitment to communism (Žižek 2015). For what is abundantly clear is that the leadership is not yet ready to renounce communism altogether, or even by name. Whatever the 'mistakes' of Mao (as they are called euphemistically), the leaders grew up as children in Mao's China; they lived through the growth years of the post-Mao period and are now reaping the rewards. Why should they want to turn on their own intellectual forebears? Moreover, why should they do so when the country, as they themselves argue, is threatened by an old enemy: the West.

Certain countries, warned the party secretary of the Academy of Social Sciences in June 2014:

advertise their own values as 'universal values' and claim that their interpretations of freedom, democracy and human rights are the standard by which all others must be measured. They spare no expense when it comes to hawking their goods and peddling their wares to every corner of the planet, and stir up 'colour revolutions' both before and behind the curtain . . . They scheme to use Western value systems to change China, with the goal of letting the Chinese people renounce the Chinese Communist Party's leadership and 'socialism with Chinese characteristics' and allow China to once again become a colony of some developed capitalist country. (Žižek 2015)

This is now a regular theme of Chinese propaganda. You can find a host of videos on the social media platform Weibo posted by state organizations such as the Communist Youth League which usually go viral as soon as they appear. A song called 'Colour Revolution' was posted in 2016 by a hip-hop group blaming US democracy-promotion for all the ills of the world. A prominent Shanghai businessman wrote an op-ed piece in the *Washington Post* warning of the dangers of 'Maidanocracy' (a reference to the central square in Kiev which served as the epicentre of the protests that brought down the former pro-Russian president) (Huang 2014). Remember that what really upset the leadership in 1989 when 6 million people took to the streets was the disturbing picture of a scaled-down Statue of Liberty in Tiananmen Square which the students erected to inspire them in their democratic demands.

The party is still fearful of the appeal of Western ideas, which is why it has fallen back on civilizational values. And indeed there is much to be mined from tradition, and much that China can contribute to the world. The country is just beginning to develop its own theories about its place in the world, based on what one Chinese commentator calls the country's 'geo-cultural birthmark' (Yaqing 2011: 38). But there is also a tendency to follow the worst of Western practices and assert its own brand of exceptionalism. There is a tendency among some Chinese scholars, adopting a Confucian perspective, to claim that their country is not only unique, special or exceptional but actually superior in its moral standing. Because its political culture is deemed to represent the 'Way of Humane Authority', its role in the world centuries past is also deemed to have been more enlightened than that of any other Great Power (Qing 2013: 18). In the speeches of China's former leaders, including Jiang Zemin and Hu Jintao, runs a common theme: Confucianism is seen as part of a pacifist tradition that underlies the country's peaceful development. And it's the continuity of that tradition despite sometimes violent changes in political dynasty that is deemed to represent the Chinese 'differential'. Harmony at home has been accompanied by harmony abroad – no colonies, no civilizing mission, no neo-imperial fantasies. Only the development of what Deng Xiaoping once called a unique 'spiritual civilization' grounded in the Confucian tradition that has always had to fight its corner in history against 'foreign barbaric forces' (Callahan 2012: 24).

The Chinese state, declares China's premier, has inherited from ancient times a fine tradition of honesty, harmony and good faith – values that

China consistently abides by in the conduct of relations with other countries (Curtis 2016: 545). It's a wonderful tale to tell others, and especially yourself – really to believe that you are the only Great Power to have broken the mould, to have behaved as no other Great Power has before – but you have to believe what you overhear yourselves telling others as well as yourself. Americans also used to think (many still do, but with an increasing lack of conviction) that they had somehow bucked the European trend – that they were more righteous and peace-loving than any European Great Power. 'There's an eagle in me and a mockingbird', cried Carl Sandberg. The eagle was America's providential mission, its Manifest Destiny, its belief that it was 'God's own country'. The mockingbird was what Reinhold Niebuhr famously called the 'irony of American history' – if Americans had been as morally virtuous as they claimed, they would never have risen to such a pre-eminent position; for that matter, there would never have been an American Century.

Putin's Russia

In an update of the novel *The Great Gatsby*, Vesna Goldsworthy casts her anti-hero as a Russian arms-dealing billionaire living not in New York, but in early twenty-first-century London. Gorsky/Gatsby remarks, 'Vronsky was my kind of hero – one part Pan-Slavism, two parts death-wish' (Goldsworthy 2015). Scott Fitzgerald's subject was not only Gatsby but America in the tawdry Jazz Age, a power that was clearly going places. Gorsky's Russia is a very different country, a predatory sub-prime Great Power that, despite its decline, is still intent on once again making a mark on the world stage. If Goldsworthy had written twenty years earlier she might have portrayed a very different country. This was a time when Western academics believed that the Russian people would soon set themselves free. Even Samuel Huntington, who was not noted for his optimism, thought that Russia was a 'swing' society and that it might eventually swing back towards the West.

Even at the time, however, other voices were warning of the road that Russia would probably take. On a journey through the country in 1994, the Polish journalist Ryszard Kapuściński (1932–2007) predicted that, as Russian society became more polarized, the rich would get richer and the poor much poorer, and the contrast between the two would become even more pronounced (Kapuściński 1993: 321). Kapuściński coined a new term, 'enclave development', to describe an underdeveloped country with a rich oligarchic core. The challenge for Russia is that it remains a relatively under-developed country which will probably never be able to tap into its vast social and human capital as long as the present regime remains in power. True, by its own standards it has performed quite well over the past twenty years (in the decade 1998 to 2008 the economy grew much more rapidly than America's did in the period 1938 to 1948). But even at the peak of the energy boom (2008) its GDP per capita was still lower than that of the US back in 1950. Incredible though it may sound, the Russian economy is less developed than that of the United States was half a century ago.

Not that there is any possibility of its returning to communism. Visit Moscow and you may well see slogans like 'Back in the USSR' and 'Welcome to the Soviet Union 2.0' bandied about quite often. But the country is not isolated from the world as it was in the Soviet era. It is no longer de-linked from the world economy. Russian businessmen now travel the world, and the rich have second homes in foreign countries. The super-rich even send their children to British public schools and the best American universities. Unlike the Soviet Union, Russia looks like a modern state in terms of its institutions.

Nonetheless, at times it does appear that the past life of the Soviet Union is being shaken back into fragmented being. Potential rivals to Putin are poisoned or locked up. Journalists are regularly murdered (some over-seas); lawyers are constantly intimidated. Not quite a return to Stalinism, to be sure. When the dissident oligarch Mikhail Khodorkovsky was sent to a labour camp in the Russian Far East (the old Gulag camp Yak-14-10 in the Soviet era), he was not sent to work in a uranium mine, an experience he almost certainly would not have survived. Spared that particular horror, he spent his days sewing mittens. But, in its bid to forge a civilizational state, the regime (like that in Beijing) is imprisoning the Russian people in what Putin likes to call 'the unbrokenness of Russian history' (Macintyre 2016: 35).

The unbrokenness of Russian history

In as far as its history is indeed unbroken, that is its greatest challenge. Russia has always been less a functioning state than a collection of vested interests. Putin likes to see himself as one of the country's strong tsars, but Russia has never had a strong state – strong enough, that is, to devolve authority and power to representative institutions and independent courts in which the Russian people could place their trust. The tsarist system offered protection to its subjects at a price. Higher up, people made deals with the tsar and his officials; lower down, they had to make their own accommodation with power-brokers such as patriarchs, boyars and local politicians (Hosking 2001). According to Vladimir Gel'man (2015), it is precisely such micro-strategies of coping that have helped to perpetuate Russia's authoritarian politics for centuries. In this respect, not much has changed except for the fact that businessmen and oligarchs have now been added to the list of power-brokers.

To get a better idea of how the system works, rent a DVD of the film *Leviathan* (2014), a bleak epic about the abuse of power in contemporary Russia by many different actors. One of the power-brokers in the film is a corrupt bishop, another a corrupt businessman. The cynical collusion between church and state is a feature of the new Russia. It is so blatant that at times it's absurd. Thus the FSB, the successor to the KGB for domestic affairs, has its own church dedicated to St Sofia. And the current patriarch has told the Russian people without a trace of irony that they should consider Putin to be 'a miracle of God'. With striking complicity, the Church now opposes any attempt to remove the embalmed body of Lenin (1870–1924) from public display on the grounds that it would stoke foreign-inspired 'de-Russification' (*The Times*, 20 March 2017). As for Russia's businessmen, one remarked in the 1990s: 'the truth is, everything you see around you, all our success, is not thanks to our wonderful economic laws. It's thanks to the fact that we do not obey them' (Handelman 1997). Nothing much has changed there, either.

Unfortunately, there is also another feature of its unbroken history which plays into the idea of Russia as a civilizational state, a term that Putin himself first embraced at a Valdai Club meeting in 2013. When in the following year the West imposed sanctions to punish Russia for illegally occupying Crimea, the then deputy prime minister, Dimitry Rogozin, told the Western press that the Russian people have always been willing to suffer for a good cause (Ioffe 2016). The regime knows that, however bad things are at home, the Russian people still long for an identity and a role in the world in which they can take pride. And that yearning is driven by a sense of wanting a place in the world. The Russians, in short, still want to be noticed.

According to the historian Vladimir Pashtukhov, Putin has reawakened Russian Messianism – a phenomenon that largely disappeared after 1991. 'Russians do not fulfil a mission, all the more so when it's unfulfillable; they live it and are its function.' What is surprising, Pashtukhov adds, is not that Messianism is back, but that it should have disappeared for almost a quarter of a century, for it is an essential part of what he calls 'the Russian cultural code' (Goble 2014). Do countries have unchanging codes? I argued in chapter 2 that they don't, but regimes like to claim otherwise, and anyway, if not a cultural code, Messianism might be seen as a recurring historical theme which can be traced back to the writings of philosophers such as Pyotr Chaadayev (1794–1856) in the 1820s:

> We are one of those nations which do not appear to be an integral part
> of the human race but exist only in order to teach some great lesson
> to the world. Surely the lesson we are destined to teach will not be

wasted; but who knows when we shall rejoin the rest of mankind and how much misery we must suffer before accomplishing our destiny. (Cited in Brzezinski 1983: 541)

I find it particularly telling that President Carter's national security advisor, Zbigniew Brzezinski (1928–2017), should have chosen to conclude his memoirs with this quotation. For the US too has frequently entertained a Messianic vision of its own destiny. Back in 1968 the English historian J. H. Plumb (1911–2001) wrote a book, *The Death of the Past*, in which he reminded his readers that every great society has its historical myths. The nation-state indeed could not really be understood without them. Plumb called it 'the Past' and distinguished it from history – the Past offered a politically driven interpretation of events which had given meaning and purpose to the American people themselves at critical points in its history (Plumb 1972: 149–56). When Plumb wrote his book, however, the US was suffering from its moment of crisis – the Vietnam War, which was being fought in the name of the Past. One day he hoped the Past would lose its appeal and that metaphors such as 'Manifest Destiny' would eventually become 'a threadbare refuge for the ageing rulers of a society . . . from which all strong emotion is rapidly draining away.' 'The Past has served the few', he added. 'Perhaps history may serve the many' (Plumb 1969: 121).

This may be one reason why the US seems to be turning away from its historical mission. But then, unlike the Russians, the Americans have always entertained a more optimistic outlook on life. It was the Jewish philosopher Baruch Spinoza who once remarked that we must love God without ever expecting Him to love us in return. The Americans, adds Harold Bloom, have an excessive need to be loved by God; the Russians haven't (their history has not been a happy one) (Bloom 2000: 249). If the Russian people have a unique historical role to play in the world, suffering seems to be part of the package. And who, if anyone in particular, is to be held responsible for the suffering? The West, of course. Indeed, the Russian state is constantly urging the Russian people to treat opposition to all things Western as constitutive of their own identity.

It is also worth adding, however, that the state is facing an uphill struggle. Most Russians have a love–hate relation with the West, embracing Western culture and consuming it even as they resent the West and the US in particular. Russians in general, especially members of the elite, feel culturally European. In the spring of 2014 the bald statement that 'Russia is not Europe' was included in the draft of a document called *The Foundations of the Russian Cultural Policy* that was cobbled together by the Russian Ministry of Culture. One month later the line was struck out. A clear majority still think of themselves, if not as Western, then definitely as European, and that's a challenge for those politicians who would prefer the citizens to identify themselves as Eurasian instead.

The Eurasian delusion

What do you do when you find yourself in a hole? Obviously, stop digging. It is a famous saying, which is sometimes attributed to the American humourist Will Rogers (1879–1935), but of course, if you are seeking a way out, you can also dig deeper. Take the Izborsk Club, whose members like to see themselves as a policy-shaping patriotic club of intellectuals. Remarkably, they look forward to the day when Russia will cease to be a nation-state. For when the Russian people become a nation, warns one of them, Russia will cease to exist as a civilization (Yanov 2013).

The logic behind this belief – and there is a logic – is that Russia has never been a nation or, for that matter, even an empire in the traditional understanding of the term: it has always been a civilizational state. And the attempt to forge a nation-state has been a disaster, beginning in the early eighteenth century with Peter the Great's programme of reforms. Peter is not popular with the Izborsk Club members, nor is he popular with the Eurasianists, whose most prominent member, Alexander Dugin, although not a member of Putin's personal circle, is credited with selling him the idea that Russia is not so much a country as 'a project for the preservation of the identity of the peoples of Eurasia in the twenty-first century'.

It is time to meet Alexander Dugin. Once a guitar-strumming bohemian, he used to lecture on geopolitics at the Russian General Staff Academy (his lectures later formed the kernel of a book, *The Foundations of Geopolitics: The Geopolitical Future of Russia*, in which he argued that the Cold War had not been what most of us think it – an ideological clash between communism and liberal democracy – but a civilizational contest between Eurasia and the Euro-Atlantic world). In a recent interview he railed against Western cosmopolitanism and its threat to all previous Russian identities: 'civilizational', 'historical', 'national', 'political', 'ethnic', 'religious' and 'cultural'. The real word for 'cosmopolitanism', he insisted, was 'Americanism', 'Atlanticism', 'post-modernism', 'globalization', 'liberalism', 'industrialism'. The civilizational state demands a redrawing of the 'anthropological map' of the world, which requires in turn that Russia tap into a variety of disparate ideas: 'Traditionalism, geopolitics, Sociology of imagination, Ethnosociology, Conservative Revolution, National Bolshevism, Eurasianism, the Fourth Political Theory, National-structuralism, Russian Schmittianism, the concept of the three paradigms, the eschatological gnosis, New Metaphysics and Radical Theory of the Subject, Conspiracy theories, Russian *haydeggerianstvo*, a post-modern alternative, and so on . . .' (Dugin 2014). I will not go on, even if Dugin would. By the way, the Fourth Political Theory is considered to be an alternative to liberalism, Marxism and fascism; it represents a fight-back against globalization and its prevailing ideology, globalism.

These endless lists bring to mind a chapter heading in a novel by John Barth: 'The Poet Wonders Whether the Course of Human History is a Progress, a Drama, a Retrogression, a Cycle, an Undulation, a Vortex, a Right- or Left-Handed Spiral, a Mere Continuum, or What Have You. Certain Evidence is Brought Forward, but of an Ambiguous and Inconclusive Nature' (Barth 1960: 37). As Barth tells us, 'the sum of history is no more than the stuff of metaphors.' And the world for Dugin is one in which metaphors are not so much deployed as battered into submission. But Barth's novel comes to mind for another reason; it is a striking example of what the author himself called the 'literature of exhaustion', by which he meant that, once all the stories are told, or are no longer tellable, all a writer has left is the empty but still functioning fictional machine.

Dugin's pronouncements also bring to mind a little-remembered book by Leonard Woolf (1880–1969) (Virginia's long-suffering husband). Appalled by the turn of events in Europe in the 1930s, he wrote an engaging work called *Quack, Quack!*, in which he set out to analyse the deep roots of European authoritarianism. Civilizations are destroyed, he insisted, by intellectual 'quacks', with their talk of destiny, and the 'logic of the time' and the rhythm of 'cosmic beats'. And although cultural codes are always being repackaged for a new audience, the main themes of political quackery remain timeless: the 'Man of Destiny', the 'Elixir of Life', the Philosopher's Stone, and Dr Ben Ezra's Magic Panacea for the Cure of Rheumatism and Cancer (Woolf 1935: 140). Dugin too can be criticized for telling the same story over and over, obsessively teasing out different resonances from the same tale in overheated and often embarrassing prose.

What is the punchline? The underlying message is stark and unrelenting. There is no international community. What Western liberals call the 'community' is only a metaphor for a collage of different civilizations remaining true to very different cultural 'codes' of behaviour. And it will be the civilizational elite who will give the state its specific personality. If nations were once thought to have a national character, civilizational states are deemed to have distinctive personalities of their own. As we have seen, there are those who would like China to become a 'sea wolf' combining the nomadic energy of Genghis Khan with the buccaneering flair of sixteenth-century Japanese pirates. Dugin is offering something different again, something that taps into an ancient tradition of Russian mysticism. But, like the *Wolf Totem* vision, it is geographically rooted. Russia is deemed to be neither European nor Asian, but Eurasian.

Am I attaching too much importance to one man? Dugin is something of an oddball even in his own country. He is merely the most famous of the current crop of Eurasianists largely because of his over-the-top rebarbative language, which lends itself inevitably to parody. But for many Russians what counts is not only the tale, but the telling. And Dugin has many followers. One is Alexandra Bovdunova, who doesn't want a changing of the guard so much as the destruction of the West 'in its present form as a civilization'. She finds it such a threat to Russia that she wants to undermine it by exploiting a network of 'totalitarian sects, secessionist movements, movements of neo-Nazis and racists, anarchists and anti-globalization activists, radical ecologists, Eurosceptics, isolationists, illegal migrants and so on' (Harding 2015). And so on. Indeed, as the lists grow ever longer, they tend to induce an intellectual listlessness in her non-Russian readership. But let us acknowledge that many such groups in Western Europe are being funded by Russia and their message is being actively promoted by Russian media. The Russians regularly mount cyber-attacks to knock broadcasters off the air (in April 2015 they shut down transmissions of TV5Monde), and they are particularly astute at propagating fake news. Putin's propaganda, in fact, is far more effective in undermining the West than that of the old Soviet state which he served so loyally as a member of the KGB. The Americans discovered this for themselves in the 2016 election.

Can we get beyond all this verbiage to the Kantian *Ding an sich* – 'the thing as it is' – the world as it is in itself, not just for us as we encounter it through the mediating lens of political interpretation or popular (mis)perception? I certainly think we can because, if there is a strong magnetic force that holds Dugin and other extreme nationalists together, it is a clear identity crisis that can be traced back to Peter the Great's reforms. Russia, they insist, is not European, and certainly not Western. That, too, is also a reflection of what Putin calls the 'unbrokenness of Russian history'.

For the Izborsk Club, the true Russia traces its roots back to the centuries of Tatar occupation. And liberal historians such as Alexander Yanov find all this deeply disturbing in so far as it whitewashes one of the grimmest moments of Russian history. Didn't the great poet Pushkin (1799–1837) write that, whereas the Arabs had at least brought algebra and Aristotle to Europe, the Tatars had brought nothing with them to Russia (MacMillan 2013: 180)? True up to a point: but they also brought with them a tax system that was incredibly efficient. Hence the Tatar origins of many related Russian words such as *dengi* (money) and *kazna* (treasury). And the Tatar khanates survived as long as they did – nearly 300 years – only because they were able to count on extensive Russian collaboration, a fact which many Russians nationalists prefer to pass over. Even so, it is probably grossly unfair to depict this episode in Russian history as an early version of *Game of Thrones*, without of course the dragons and White Walkers. Under Tatar rule, after all, the Christian churches and monasteries remained in business, largely untouched. And that is what really matters. Russia remained distinctly European where it counted most, in its own imagination.

Yanov attacks the Eurasian version on many fronts, but his primary argument is that Russia was European long before Peter the Great introduced his reforms. Back in the early sixteenth century it was more like Sweden at the time, which is why it attracted so many migrants from Lithuania and Poland in the reign of Ivan IV. The difference between the two countries was geographical: Russia had an eastern frontier, Sweden didn't. And, when the Swedes began to expand, they went south into Germany during the Thirty Years' War. Russia, by contrast, went east to Siberia, at which point it began to diverge from the European model. And that is where you might well conclude we should leave the debate, except that it would be wrong to do so. For the idea of the civilizational state has also now entered national security thinking.

The spirit of the nation

It is not often that you find in a country's national security concept a reference to 'the spirit of the nation'. But you will find it in *Russia's National*

Security Strategy to 2020 (Russian Federation 2009). You will also find a reference to the need to adopt 'a dignified attitude to [the] historical memory' of the nation. The problem is: whose memory, and who is doing the remembering? And what precisely is being secured? As you might expect, you will read about the 'freedom and independence of the Russian state', but it may come as a surprise to find that the term also encompasses what is called 'the cultural unity' of the Russian people. More surprising still, the paper includes a reference to the defence of the nation's 'ideals and spirituality'. As Daniel Payne adds, what we are dealing with is something that is quite new in the discourse of international politics, but one very germane to the idea of a civilizational state: the idea that every society also needs to secure its *'spiritual security'* (cited in Marsh 2013: 29). All this in Western eyes may be yet another example of overblown nineteenth-century romanticism, a sad reminder in fact of how even apparently sane people can fall prey to their obsessions. But it is also a fine example of rhetoric, as defined by the Irish poet Yeats: 'the will struggling to do the work of the imagination'. And many Russian nationalists have replaced the imagination with will because they have ceased to be able to perceive the world in pragmatic or practical terms, the terms on which the rest of us prefer to live our lives.

For what is this spiritual core that needs to be secured from foreign corruption? One man who gave the matter much thought towards the end of his life was the Russian novelist Alexander Solzhenitsyn (1918–2008). It is surprising that in his declining years the former Soviet dissident should have become such a fan of Putin, though it is less surprising, perhaps, that the respect was apparently reciprocated. In 2007 Putin visited the ailing novelist at his home to award him a state prize for his humanitarian work. But the novelist himself had another agenda. For Solzhenitsyn was the great cheerleader of Greater Russia, even if he was critical of former Soviet attempts to impose Russian rule over non-Russian nationalities (not because it trampled over their identity, but because it threatened to dilute the 'Russian national essence'). The problem, if you happen to have a passport from Belarus or Ukraine, is that, according to Solzhenitsyn, you are part of the Russian world.

'We all together emerged from the treasured Kyiv, "from which the Russian land began", according to the chronicle of Nestor', Solzhenitsyn writes. He argues that, in Lithuania and Poland, 'White Russians [Belarusians] and Little Russians [Ukrainians] acknowledged that they were Russians and fought against Polonization and Catholicism . . . The return of these lands to Russia was at the time viewed by everyone as "reunification".' (Coalson 2014)

The *Russkiy Mir* (the Russian world), claims Putin, is defined not by any Western category such as self-determination (ethnic or otherwise) but by blood – the blood that the Russians have spilled over the centuries to keep the Russian 'world' united, and especially the blood that was shed in the Great Patriotic War. In other words, there is a Russian world larger than the Russian Federation (cited in Kozelsky 2014: 232). And with a large Russian diaspora living outside Russia itself, protection seems to demand a strategy of forward defence. When Dimitri Medvedev was president he outlined one of Russia's new policy goals: that of creating a sphere of 'civilizational privilege' in countries with significant Russian minorities. When asked by a reporter if sanctions were a price Russia had to pay for illegally annexing Crimea, Putin replied that it was the price the Russian people had to pay to 'preserve themselves as a civilization' (Linde 2016: 32). Putin likes to remind the West that the Russians constitute the largest ethnic group to be divided by state borders and that the protection of their cultural heritage must be one of the priorities of the Russian state – bad news if you happen to be a citizen of a neighbouring country with a significant Russian minority.

Russian *ressentiment*

What should we make of all of this, asks Robert Gottlieb, the former editor-in-chief of the publishing house Knopf? Only, perhaps, in the case of Solzhenitsyn, that he could express the views that he did because he wasn't willing to acknowledge that the nineteenth century had come to an end (Ozick 1993: 228). And we can trace this bizarre situation back to a very nineteenth-century emotion that complicated relations between East and West: fear on the part of the West, resentment on the part of the Russians.

Dugin's Eurasianism, like Solzhenitsyn's nationalism, strikes a chord with many Russians because of resentment at what it considers to be 'Euro-Orientalism'. Orientalism was a term coined by the American academic Edward Said (1935–2003) to describe the way in which the West was given to seeing the Orient as the ultimate foreign Other: exotic, backward, uncivilized and untamed. It also allowed it to see itself as the superior civilization. In caricaturing the Orient, Western writers tended to essentialize the West: it allowed them to discover a non-existent 'Occidental Rationalism' (a term coined by Max Weber (1864–1920)) and to regard their own culture as particularly dynamic and ever-changing. And that was even more relevant in the dialogue with Russia because so many Russians claimed that their country was part of the Western world when many Western intellectuals clearly believed that it wasn't. The Russians themselves have traditionally been split between the modernizers and the traditionalists; the Slavophiles and the Westerners; the Enlightenment rationalists and the mystics. (During the Cold War, the Soviet Studies Group in the British Ministry of Defence broke new ground by discovering a new distinction: between the smooth, bald Politburo members – the modernizers – and the reactionaries, the hairy ones (like Solzhenitsyn) ('Game of Thrones', *Financial Times*, 17 January 2016).)

In truth, the West must bear some of the blame for Russian resentment. Following its initial enthusiasm for Peter the Great's reforms, it came to see the country as a failed experiment. Well before the end of the eighteenth century Russia was seen as 'land of absence', as Montesquieu (1689–1755) famously called it. It appeared to be a land without a vibrant civil society, a decent middle class, or the rule of law – the very bedrock of Western liberalism. It was defined, in other words, not by what it shared with Europe, but by what it didn't. Agreeing with them, Pyotr Chaadayev famously regretted that his compatriots were condemned to live in a 'narrow present' without a history in the European understanding of the term. Russia had never experienced a Renaissance, or Reformation, and it only had the Enlightenment thanks largely to a German empress, Catherine the Great. And when Western historians tried to apply the terms that made sense of Western history, such as feudalism or the nation-state, they found such concepts simply could not be applied to the country they were studying. They found it to be largely beyond classification. The Russian people, claimed Chaadayev, only had an essential character because they found themselves 'outside of time' (Adamovsky 2006).

Russia, moreover, had met with too many setbacks and regressive phases in its journey into the modern era. Here was a country which seemed constantly to update itself with the same reference points: serfdom, anti-Semitic pogroms and repressive rule. The predominant theme of its history seemed to be one of national unhappiness. And, to be frank, the unhappiness is not imagined but very real. The Russian people know that their regimes (tsarist, Bolshevik and Putenite) have cynically exploited popular fears of the outside world to create an authoritarian state that has often needlessly sacrificed people, whether in the war against Napoleon or that against the Nazis, which is why novelists from Tolstoy to contemporary ones such as Viktor Astafyev (1924–2001) have consistently denounced the corruption, incompetence and callousness of politicians and military commanders alike.

Partly in response to Euro-Orientalism, Russian politicians have found it convenient to promote a belief in Western decadence, and that belief is echoed today in government circles. Russian values, Putin declared in an address to the Federal Assembly in 2012, are what makes Russia a civilizational state (Cadier and Light 2015: 27). The nation-states of the West, by contrast, he added, had no values, or if they did they lacked the self-belief to defend them. The Russian Church has consistently argued that the West's embrace of same-sex marriage is not only detrimental to human society but fundamentally opposed to the Christian values that constitute European civilization. The Russian state prefers what it calls the 'civilizational speci- ficity' crafted by the country's moral, religious and historical values (Yatsk 2015: 146). It is, as I have said, an old theme. As early as the 1780s Russian aristocrats were being warned that sending their sons abroad to be edu- cated would weaken their love of Russia (Shakibi 2010: 58). Writers back then even demanded the 'Westoxification' of their own middle class so that it could reconnect with the country's true spiritual values. Nothing, then, would appear to have changed. This too can be seen as part of the 'unbro- kenness' of Russian history.

The irony is that Putin himself probably doesn't buy into most of these historical myths. But by characterizing Russia as a civilizational state, anti- pathetic historically and culturally to Western values, he can attack within its borders what threatens him most at home – ideas such as liberty, freedom and democracy, of which the West still claims to be a staunch defender. And he has many partners, especially in the Church. If the Russian patriarch considers human rights to be a Jewish–Protestant invention, many mem- bers of the Russian Orthodox Church consider the 1917 revolution to have been a Jewish–Masonic plot to destroy Holy Rus (von Eggert 2017: 12). In the civilizational state, paranoia and conspiracy theories tend to feed off each other.

It might all have been very different if Gorbachev had managed to reform the Soviet system without a break-up of the Soviet Union, or if his succes- sor Boris Yeltsin had not squandered the chance to transform the Russian Federation into a democratic society. Looking back upon those wasted years, there is an unavoidable sense of opportunities lost: under Gorbachev the country did experience a democratic impulse, but under Yeltsin the promise was betrayed –that is why the first taste of democracy under Yeltsin looks like a moral defeat and Gorbachev's failure looks like a moral victory. The day after he stepped down from office he told a group of Italian journalists that Russia was indeed different: 'We have our own reality, inspired by tradition, history . . . .. Yes, like many of my compatriots I have spiritual ties to Europe, but I am too no less bound to the East . . . .. Russia must recognize that it is a bridge between two cultures . . . and simultaneously, part of human civilization' (Gratchev 1995: 190). Perhaps one day it will, but not, alas, under the present dispensation. The country continues to list in the shadow of its Soviet past during which all the usual intellectual means that allow a society to analyse itself and its anxieties – sociology, psychology, philosophy and, above all, objective historical research – were hollowed out. The result, writes Masha Gessen (2017), is more than an attack on serious scholarship; it is an attack on the humanity of Russian society that has lost the tools and even the language for understanding itself.

Why India will probably not become a civilizational state

So, are there any other countries that might aspire to become a civilizational state? The one that most comes to mind is India, if we take seriously the claims of its prime minister, Narendra Modi, and the long-stated ambitions of his political party, the BJP, a Brahminical (or upper-middle-class) movement that is deeply unsympathetic to the liberal humanism of some of the great Indian leaders of the past, including Gandhi. Instead Hindu fundamentalism has been given a boost in recent years. BJP rule, while less transformative than the party promised, has intensified Hindu majoritarian impulses. Muslims are facing increasing marginalization across the country. School textbooks have been amended to include glowing references to Hindu 'resistance' to Muslim domination under the Mogul Empire. Even the Congress Party, the founder of Indian secularism, has begun to adopt a more aggressively fundamentalist tone.

If people know one saying of Gandhi, it is probably his apocryphal reply when asked what he thought about Western civilization – 'it would be a good idea'. The Mahatma had a sense of humour, though you would not always know it from most of his public pronouncements. But the quip invites a rejoinder: Is there such a thing as an Indian civilization, and, if so, how would you go about reducing its history to a few central themes and packaging it all in a form that is easy to digest? How would even the most Machiavellian of politicians succeed in drawing his countrymen into a fictional rendition of a civilization which is marked by so many different and contradictory realities? For the country that we know as India today still defies categorization while displaying cultural fissures and fragmented identities in abundance.

'There are so many stories to tell', complains the narrator of Salman Rushdie's *Midnight's Children* (1981), 'too many, such an excess of intertwined lives events miracles places rumours.' Rushdie's novel, like India itself, is a medley of stories drawn from myth, legends and history. Of course, despite its cultural complexity, there are to be found concepts that are distinctively Indian and not, for example, Chinese or European. The word *dharma* – a Sanskrit term originating in the *Upanishads* – expresses a quintessentially Indian idea, that there is a natural law that regulates the universe and everything within it, including human behaviour. The concept was recycled through the centuries, beginning with Hinduism before migrating to Buddhism and Jainism. But Indian history, unlike that of China, has no single overarching story. It is doubtful whether even the nationalists who displaced the British on the first hour of 15 August 1947 – 'the midnight hour' – could be said to have represented all of India. All the Indian people wanted from independence was that the old values and beliefs would be defended by the Indians themselves, and that what the British had begun to undertake somewhat fitfully – the modernization of the country – should be continued in other hands.

Unfortunately, the British were a problem in more ways than one. From the beginning, they found the social diversity of India baffling. They encountered a civilization of multiple identities and faiths and, with the exception of Islam, a country in which religion was apparently absent as they understood the term (a monotheistic community). They were frankly disoriented: while they felt mysteriously drawn into a relationship with a society so very different from their own, they also felt intimidated by it. What they saw in India was *excess*. What they wanted to impose was *order*.

They did so by concluding, in the face of all evidence to the contrary, that India was a one-religion country, even though for well over a thousand years the dominant religion was not Hinduism but Buddhism (in the Middle Ages, the Chinese often referred to India as the 'Buddhist Kingdom'). India also hosted a vibrant Jewish community, as well as a Christian community two centuries before there were substantial Christian communities in Britain, and of course do not forget the Sikhs or the Jains. British writers also liked to think that the defining mark of Indian thought was its concentration upon the spiritual and that the essence of Indian life was one of mystical concerns. In reality, whenever we look at Indian poetry or fiction, or even the epics, including *The Mahabharata*, we find that those concerns are sometimes straightforwardly social and show little interest in religious life (Nussbaum and Sen 1987: 11). More important, the Vedas, which were brought to India by the Sanskrit-speaking Aryans, were not scriptures at all in the Western understanding of the term. The Vedic religion as such emerged only much later with the *Upanishads*, which appeared between the seventh and second centuries BCE. And, as Amartya Sen reminds us, they are not even Hindu so much as Indian. The translations are in Bengali and were commissioned by Muslim Pathan rulers in the fourteenth century (Sen 2006: x–xi).

In other words, there has never been an exclusive Hindu civilization in the way that most of Europe was Christian by the ninth century, and much of it well before. This should not surprise us; no civilization can lay claim to an unchanging essence. We should think of a civilization instead as a *Gestalt* – a German word for which there is no exact English equivalent. One English author, however, defines it as a 'perceptual pattern or structure possessing qualities as a whole that cannot be described merely as a sum of its parts'

(Lodge 2011: 230) –which, come to think of it, is not a bad description of India itself.

Moreover, in as far as Hinduism gradually became more of a religion than a philosophy of life, the transition was very recent. It came about because the British unintentionally allowed Hindus to reify their own cultural traditions. The nineteenth-century Hindu cultural revival was a product of British attempts to order the Indian subcontinent. One British historian talks of the 're-traditionalization of society' under British rule (Washbrook 1981: 649–72). The upshot was that, whereas at the beginning of the British Raj, a Hindu might have said he was a follower of Shiva or Vishnu, by the end he would have seen himself as a Hindu rather than a Buddhist or a Muslim. And what was ordered was mostly Brahminical literature, which the British in turn took to constitute a theology of a kind. As modernizers, they encouraged Indian schools to reform their religious conventions, practices and rituals. This eventually laid the groundwork for the emergence of the fundamentalist party the BJP, the political wing of the Rashtriya Swayamsevak Sangh (RSS), a mass movement inspired by Hindutva (or Hindu nationalism).

None of which is to deny that India constitutes a civilization quite distinct from any other that has survived into the twenty-first century. The Indian people are united by culture. They are largely Indo-European; Hinduism is of Indo-European origins, as is the Sanskrit language and even the caste system. For all these reasons, writes Octavio Paz, it might be said that India is the other pole of the West – the other version of the Indo-European world, or rather its inverted image (Paz 1985: 104). Paz was a Nobel Prize-winning poet who studied the Indian classics closely when he was Mexican ambassador in the 1960s. Perhaps for a student of Indian politics today some of his observations are far too sweeping to take seriously. Take his opinion that what made India really different was its ability to coexist with, rather than assimilate, every new import. Its vocation, he wrote, was religion and metaphysics, not historical action. It never wanted to shape history; rather, it wished to escape it. It also never really reflected upon the changes it experienced and never therefore seriously tried to change. It was drawn to accepting whatever history delivered (including Islam), with which it continues to coexist uneasily. And it displayed a historical fatalism that has enabled it so far to 'accept difference' and thus actually to keep itself intact after the trauma of the 1947 partition of the subcontinent into two countries, India and Pakistan (ibid.: 105–6).

But Paz was not alone in harbouring such thoughts. India, writes the historian Felipe Fernández-Armesto, is the Cinderella civilization. It was admired in the first millennium of our era by the Chinese and after the seventh century by Arab scholars. In the second millennium, however, it failed to fulfil its potential. It seemed to waste away. The great unifying empires disappeared from the scene. The great scientific discoveries that had captivated the Arabs were not taken further. India was exploited first by Muslims from the North and then by the British, who came by sea. China had already turned its back on it in the twelfth century (Fernández-Armesto 1995: 105).

But, then again, this possibly accounts for its tolerance of different religious faiths and cultural expressions which made it in the nineteenth century peculiarly susceptible to some of the liberal ideas that the British brought with them. Even then, liberalism didn't arrive pre-packaged with the works of John Stuart Mill (1806–1873). There was already a reforming impulse at work within Indian society that British rule seems to have brought out. One example is the eradication of *sati* – the self-immolation of widows following their husband's death that was encouraged by convention, and often ruthlessly enforced. While it is perfectly true that, without the British, state reform would have been impossible, the decision to eradicate the practice was first suggested not by British reformers but by modernist Bengali elites, who in the name of a revalued Hinduism also pressed independently for the reduction in the age of consent of marriage (Lorenzen 1999; Kaviraj 2016: 135–87). Still, it is probably nonetheless true that the main legacy of British rule was an intellectual, university-educated middle class that was predominantly liberal in its thinking. And that is one reason why India is unlikely to ever become a civilizational state committed to upholding a single version of its past. Its history is far too diverse and diversified for it ever to become a Brahminical project.

Remastering the past

Not that this has stopped the most assertive of BJP members from trying to rewrite their country's history to fit in with their own preconceived ideas. A huge controversy was ignited in the scientific community in India in January 2005 at a science congress in Mumbai, when a paper was delivered claiming that the Indians invented air flight seven thousand years ago. The author appears to have been completed unfazed by the fact that over forty years earlier a group of Indian scientists from the Department of Aerospace and Mechanical Engineering at the Institute of Science in Bengaluru (Bangalore) had looked into an earlier claim and found that the designs, if ever built, would have violated the laws of physics.

Unfortunately science is being exploited quite cynically to advance the claim that India has always been a civilizational state. It is also consistent with a growing demand on the part of institutions such as the Infinity Foundation to fit modern science into a Vedic framework. Take the concept of energy – the precise and quantifiable capacity of a system to perform a task – which is now interpreted by some ultra-nationalists as a gross-level sub-type of *Shakti*, or 'intelligent energy'. Or take physics which, because it deals with causation, is deemed by some nationalists to be an empirical species of the *karma* theory. Darwinism in turn can be seen as merely a lower-level materialistic rendering of the spiritual evolution taught in the *Yoga Sutras* (Nanda 2016). The entire approach has been denounced by one Western academic as a cynical 'power play in the guise of the defence of tradition' (Nussbaum 2009).

And yet some of these positions have even been endorsed by India's prime minister, Narendra Modi, who is not averse to trying to harness his own political future and that of his party to a reinterpretation of the Vedic texts.

Modi himself is representative of a theological school – *Shakha* – that takes them to be true historical accounts, not versions of myth. Genetic science, he claims, was present at the time of *The Mahabharata*. It is not clear whether he was going back to the origins of the text in the eighth to ninth centuries BCE or the final form in which we know it today, which is a product of the fourth century CE (*The Guardian*, 28 October 2014). Whatever the chronology, the claim itself is embarrassing. Imagine a Chinese president claiming that genetic science was thriving in Confucian China or that Chinese students in the fifth century were taught genetics at the great University of Nalanda (Bihar), to which many came for instruction. What we do know is that the students studied philosophy, complex medicine, literature, architecture and astronomy. By the time Oxford University opened for business in 1096, Nalanda had been educating students for 600 years, many from as far afield as Japan and Korea. It was also the only foreign institution to which Chinese students would go for their education outside their own country. Even so, it never offered courses in modern genetics! There was of course no genetics before the discovery of the gene as a unit of heredity; genetics had to await the twentieth century and the rediscovery of the pioneering work of an obscure German-speaking Augustinian friar, Gregor Mendel (1822–1884).

What this bizarre story may call to mind is the infamous Trofim Lysenko (1898–1976), who rejected Mendelian genetics in favour of a kind of quasi-Lamarckianism. Lysenko was a political stooge, but the perfect biologist for Stalin's ambition to re-engineer humanity. He claimed that he could change a species of spring wheat into winter wheat in just a few years, even though the first has two sets of chromosomes and the second has three. Not surprisingly, the experiment failed disastrously; the result was widespread crop failure. Lysenko was finally removed from his post in 1965, but by then his star had been on the wane for years. However, before we write him off altogether, we should also note that, in Putin's Russia, there is an attempt to restore his reputation in the field of epigenetics. The point is that Lamarck was not necessarily wrong, but that his claim was only part of a much more complex story.

There is another problem the nationalists face in trying to rewrite India's history: so much of it has been forgotten. At the same time that the Egyptians were working away at the pyramids, the Harappans – a people who began living along the Indus 5,000 years ago – were building the world's first urban settlements with roads on a grid pattern, covered drains and multi-storey buildings. Unfortunately the Vedic era has no Rameses II, writes Robert Calasso, and no Cecil B. DeMille has managed to film it. There are no ruined cities or temples which you can visit and admire. The Harappans had kings but founded no kingdoms or empires. What they did leave behind was a unique literature which allows their civilization to live on in the Indian imagination through the Vedas – the great texts which are so dense and obscure that, once you become a Vedic scholar, you are likely to be swallowed up into the vastness of the thinking (Calasso 2014: 17).

But then the same might be said of much of India's history, adds Calasso. Much of it is a quicksand – not even its seminal dates are ever certain. If you are a Westerner, tracing your origins back to the Greeks, you probably wouldn't give much thought to the fact that the West is missing all but 1 per cent of Greek literature, including most of the tragedies and much of its lyric poetry. Many Western students may be surprised by this – surely they live in the days of Project Gutenberg and have access to exhaustive databases such as Chadwyck Healey? But the West is lucky to have all Plato's works, as well as most of Aristotle's (if only in the form of lecture notes taken by his students). And if his essay the *Poetics* is to be relied upon, the best Greek tragedies have survived (the ones Aristotle quoted or named in the work).

The point I am making is that the West is infinitely more fortunate than India, which has lost so much of its literature. Take the father of Indian medicine, Charaka (sixth–second century BCE), the supposed author of the *Charaka Samhita*, a Sanskrit compendium on health composed in the first century CE. But it is still uncertain whether Charaka refers to a man or a school of thought. Or take the mathematician Aryabhata (476–550). Whether or not he compares favourably with Euclid (325?–265 BCE), he was largely forgotten until India's first satellite was named after him. More is known – or is it? – of India's Machiavelli, who wrote the *Arthashastra*. It is tentatively ascribed to Kautilya (fourth century BCE), but it is also ascribed to Chanakya and Vishnugupta, both of whom may be the same person. The complete version of the text was discovered only as recently as 1905. Imagine European history if *The Prince* had been lost for 400 years.

India and the outside world

Western civilization is not the only one that is deeply indebted to others, even if it still doesn't acknowledge the full extent of its indebtedness. Intercivilizational encounters between India and the West loom very large in its history, beginning with the invasion of Alexander the Great (356–323 BCE). Two things came out of Alexander's brief irruption into Indian history: a short-lived Indo-Greek kingdom, whose most famous king, Menander (160/155–130 BCE), so legend has it, toyed with the idea of becoming a Buddhist; and what is quite possibly the very first work of anthropology – the *Indica*, a book by a writer called Megasthenes (350–290 BCE). Only fragments have survived, but enough of them to suggest that the work was a serious attempt to understand a very different world from the author's, if the prism through which he did so was still Greek. Rather surprisingly, in its discussion of Indian society there is not a single reference to the caste system (Bosworth 1996). Here is another straw in the wind: the longest Greek inscription to survive from the Hellenistic East is an edict authored by the Indian king Ashoka (304–232 BCE), cut into the rock of modern day Kandahar and describing his Buddhist philosophy in impeccable Greek (Thonemann 2016: 90). So much of the dialogue between the two worlds is now lost, but that is no reason to apply a large pinch of proverbial salt to the claim by one Greek author that Homer's poetry was once sung on the Indus. It might well have been (Pollock 2014: 64).

The second major encounter between India and the outside world was much longer lasting, and its fallout continues to this day. Arab merchants used to call India *al-Hind*. And in the person of Al-Biruni (973–1048) they produced one of the early pioneers in the study of India's religious kaleidoscope. But when other Muslim peoples began invading the subcontinent between the twelfth and sixteenth centuries, bringing with them their own monotheistic faith, the situation changed dramatically. The relationship was certainly complex and still divides historical opinion. The hostility between Muslims and Hindus has a long history and includes the desecration of Hindu temples, the destruction of Hindu texts and particularly the disappearance of Sanskrit until its re-emergence in the eighteenth century (thanks largely to British scholarship). It is not always clear, in other words, whether we are dealing with two major religions within one civilization or two civilizations that happen to share the same territory, or possibly a synthesis of the two.

But, then again, the greatest challenge of Islam, writes André Wink, was probably cultural, and not religious. What really distinguished Hinduism in the pre-modern era was its prejudice against foreign travel. On returning home from abroad, a traveller was supposed to take a dip in the holy Ganges as part of a purification ritual. Early legal digests imposed strict restrictions on high-caste Hindus who had recently travelled by sea (Wink 2004: 73). If you were a Muslim, the situation was quite different. With extensive links to fellow Muslims across the *ummah* (the community of the faithful), you could consider yourself a citizen of the world. One of the earliest known examples of a *Futuh al-Haramayn* – a guide for Muslim pilgrims embarking on the hajj (the pilgrimage to Mecca) – was written for a Muslim Indian from Gujarat. It contains the complete sequence of the rituals and illustrations of the holy sanctuaries of Mecca and Medina.

The Muslims within Hindustan eventually adjusted, as most minorities do, but in areas further north, where they were in the majority, such adjustments did not take place. Here, writes one authority, was a real clash of civilizations, which still confronts India with an unresolved civilizational identity (Arnason 2006: 42) Indeed, the fear of being overwhelmed by a Hindu population much larger than its own was so present in Muslim minds that, when the British in the nineteenth century began classifying their Indian subjects by religion, Muslim politicians readily seized upon this to stake out their own cultural claims. Eventually this led to the creation of Pakistan, a state that has an equally problematic relationship with both the West and India.

Which brings us to the last major encounter with a power west of the Indus – the British. British colonialism was a real game-changer, for it introduced the Indians to Western ideas as well as to such material products as telegraph wires and rail lines (which were often attacked during the first War of Indian Independence (1857–8) as symbols of an alien civilization that had changed local perceptions of time – the railway produced an increase in the speed of movement and, even more unsettling, the pace of 'life'). The British also produced a sea change in social structures. They created an entirely new middle class which readily embraced ideas such as liberalism and, later, socialism. The point is neither to exaggerate nor to underestimate the impact of British rule. For the problem with all civilizational encounters is that they have their positive and negative sides: the British deliberately kept India poor. In the early eighteenth century the Indian subcontinent accounted for a quarter of the world economy; by the end of the Raj it had shrunk to 3 per cent of global GDP. In the last fifty years of the Raj India achieved zero per-capita economic growth. When independence came to the country in 1947 it still relied on bullock carts for its transport, and only 0.2 per cent of its villages had electricity (Wilson 2016).

But we shouldn't judge the British experience only through the prism of economic growth. 'The empires of our time were short-lived, but they have altered the world for ever', remarks the protagonist Ralph Singh, in V. S. Naipaul's novel *The Mimic Men* ([1967] 2012). 'Their passing away is their least significant feature.' And this may be true of India's experience of democracy. Its origins go back to the founding of the Congress Party in the late nineteenth century and the long struggle against the British Raj which took place within the framework of a liberal legal system. As Christopher Bayly (2011) remarked, British rule helped to ensure that liberalism would take root in the country's schools, in its free press and in its law courts – and that all these would convert an entire generation of Indians to a way of thinking about their own future. If you come from the West, then one gratifying fact is that India has chosen to stick with democracy; China after 1926 chose not to.

But, then again, China is in a class of its own. When the Chinese cracked down on Buddhism in the eleventh century they did indeed begin to put the outside world at some distance from themselves. In 1726-8 the state published the last of the major imperial encyclopaedic projects, *The Imperially Improved Synthesis of Books and Illustrations, Past and Present.* Extending to 852,408 pages, its aim was to ring-fence knowledge. The project represented a kind of intellectual 'great wall' against the outside world (Zeldin 2015: 374-5). Most remarkable of all, all the entries were entirely about China. Compare this with the first Arab encyclopaedias centuries earlier, which contained information about every society and culture that the Arabs encountered.

China of course has changed significantly in the last 200 years thanks to its often bruising encounters with Western ideas, including Marxism. But do we make too much of this?, asks Martin Jacques (2011). For the country, he writes, is not a conventional nation-state, but a civilizational state, and once you recognize that reality you also have to take on board two other remarkable facts. The first is its sheer longevity. This is a country that can trace its origins back several thousand years to the time when social life first emerged on the Yellow River. Even so, the Communist Party has seen fit to doctor the historical record in an attempt to claim that it's older than it actually is. In 1996 the Xia-Shang-Zhou Chronology Project (named after three of the older dynasties) was tasked with proving the Chinese civilization dates back at least five thousand years. In 2000 it arrived at this politically correct conclusion, staking out a chronology that has made its way into school textbooks. In reality, India's civilization is probably much older than China's.

Secondly, China owes its survival through the ages to its remarkable ability to assimilate its many invaders. The West has been far less successful in this respect. The barbarian tribes who snuffed out the Western Roman Empire aspired to become Roman citizens but failed to make the cut. In the course of the High Middle Ages the Roman Church managed to convert large swathes of barbarian peoples to Christianity while failing to unite them under a single theocracy. Even in the Islamic world, no single caliphate was able to keep the world of the faithful together for long. Only China and Japan survived intact – in Japan's case, thanks to its isolation, in China's, thanks to the pull of its culture. There is a famous Confucian proverb to the effect that, however many times they invaded the country, the barbarians would always fail to subdue it because over time they would become Chinese (Fernández-Armesto 2000: 256). And so they did, with one notable exception: the barbarians who came by sea, and not, as tradition dictated, on horseback from the great Central Asian steppes. The European powers in the nineteenth century never came near to colonizing China, but the fact that they were not susceptible to the pull of Chinese culture still renders them in the collective consciousness of the country the greatest cultural challenge that it has ever had to face.

So, what is the take-away? Indians are much more relaxed about the outside world just as they have been more relaxed about cultural pluralism. What Westerners like me find most amazing about the country is its cultural diversity. Take its 1,652 languages and dialects, including fifteen official ones. No language is spoken by more than 15 per cent of the population (Bryson 2015: 182). What distinguished India from Europe is that, until the British arrived, there was never a brisk business between languages. Shakespeare, for example, read Cervantes (1547–1616) and Montaigne in English translation (a few years after their works had first appeared at home). In India, by contrast, nothing was translated between Urdu, Hindi, Tamil, Marathi or any of the other languages of the subcontinent. Educated Indians had to learn one another's languages and were frequently expected to speak three or four (Bellos 2011: 8).

Possibly, the absence of a unifying language explains its people's infinite capacity for coexistence. It is true that Indian history has seen its fair share of intolerance, too: take the early expulsion of the Buddhists and the rise of Islamic fundamentalism in the reign of the last major Mogul emperor, Aurangzeb (1618–1707). And ask the Dalits (who account for one-seventh of the population), or for that matter the Kashmiris, whether they have been beneficiaries of cultural tolerance. Tellingly, Indians have always been more interested in distinguishing themselves from other Indians than from non-Indians, and the caste system trapped people into fixed social orders from which until recently it was impossible to escape. Even now caste identities still remain strong, and last names are invariably an indication of what caste a person belongs to. But, then again, where are the country's inquisitions, its witch trials, its anti-Semitic pogroms, its religious wars or crusades? If you want to essentialize European history, you might choose to identify intolerance as one of its central features. While that would not be the whole truth, it would not be entirely untrue either.

Western philosophy too is noted for its polemical bias. The great philosophers such as Plato were always arguing for the one true position; the most recent, such as Heidegger (1889–1976) and Wittgenstein, like Hegel before them, insisted that they were the last of the line; there was nothing more to say. This was the tradition of *aporia* in ancient Greece where philosophers were always arguing for the one true position. In that sense, Europe's philosophical tradition has remained in every sense of the word 'agonistic'. India's, claims Amartya Sen, is different again; it is 'argumentative' – it is grounded on the understanding that you can only sustain an argument if occasionally you allow your opponents to disagree, on the understanding that you can come back to it on a later occasion (Sen 2006: 10). Civility is a democratic virtue: the willingness to consider one's fellow citizens worth debating with even if you find their arguments unconvincing. And it is sustained by the knowledge that, while it is usually impossible to argue a religious person out of his beliefs, it is often possible to argue someone out of his political convictions. So, as long as India remains a democracy, it is difficult to envisage how it could ever be transformed by any government into a civilizational state. Civilizational states are, by definition, undemocratic; in this they differ most starkly from nation-states, which take a variety of political forms.

All of which prompts a final thought – India may even be the place where the future of human freedom is determined. Hegel tells us, does he not, that freedom marches from East to West, and that it would find its ultimate future in the New World. But why should it stop there and not continue across the Pacific, and once again find its home in Asia? Not in China, perhaps, but in India, the world's largest democracy, and soon to be its third largest economy, a country that is home to more traditions, cultures, dialects and religious beliefs than any other. And, with its tradition of *ahimsa* (non-harming), there may even be a strong likelihood, as one contemporary writer surmises, that the 'West will need the East for freedom's rising' (Fritzman 2014: 126). Hegel would have been dumbfounded, but that is his problem, not ours.

6

The Once and Future Caliphate

A picture often tells its own story. And one of the most famous from the last century, Picasso's *Guernica*, captured the horror of an air raid on the Basque town during the Spanish Civil War. The attack was planned as a gift by Goering for Hitler's forty-eighth birthday (although logistical problems delayed the bombing raid by a few days). We remember the event today largely because of this painting by Picasso (1881–1973), which, with its gallery of grotesque and distorted figures, some crying in pain, some torn apart, all intimately interlinked in each other's fate, stands as permanent testimony to the carnage.

The Guernica of the twenty-first century is the city of Aleppo. Once Syria's largest metropolis, it now lies in ruins; its medieval seminaries have been destroyed, its ancient citadel damaged beyond repair. Other fractured urban landscapes of the world's conflict zones – Grozny, Beirut, Mogadishu – tell their own stories. But here is another. A dying horse in Picasso's painting is one of its most graphic images. It stands for the Four Horsemen of the Apocalypse. The horseshoe next to the head of the dismembered soldier at the bottom left of the frame refers to the sacred crescent of Islam. Although his fear of Islam is suggested only obliquely, it can't be conjured away. The painting throws into particularly vivid relief Picasso's personal fear of the Moorish soldiers whom Franco (1892–1975) brought with him from North Africa (Irujo 2016). Even today the Spanish tend to remember the Arabs with little fondness, although they were responsible for a major, and not inglorious, moment in its history. Both Averroes (1126–1198) and Ibn Baija (1085–1138) were born in Spain, and their contribution ensured that Arab philosophy would be a footnote to Aristotle (in the same way that the whole of Western philosophy can be considered a footnote to Plato). In other words, it could even be argued, and some philosophers do so argue, that the Western philosophical tradition is in part Greek–Arab.

The Spanish fear of Islam runs deep. A few years after Picasso painted his great canvas the country's most famous philosopher, José Ortega y Gasset (1883–1955), predicted that, once the West concluded its war with Germany, the next phase of history would see a threat from points further east, from 'a Chinaman's pigtail appearing behind the Urals or a shock from the great Islamic magma'. Ortega thought himself mysteriously attuned to the seismic vibrations of history; few philosophers would claim this today. And, anyway, philosophers no longer write in such colourful terms. They can't afford to if they teach in Western universities: such a remark would be deemed politically incorrect and probably cost you your career. Western societies are metaphysically tone-deaf.

But what makes the Western world still distinctive is its belief that the future can sometimes be unscrambled and that from time to time it's possible to separate the signal from the noise. In the ebbing days of the Cold War, Western politicians frequently expressed their fears about a 'global intifada' or Islamic 'war against modernity'. There were already intimations of a 'clash' of worldviews or values or civilizations some years before Samuel Huntington translated these concerns into an academic thesis that still packs a punch, even if from the first very few Western academics were willing to concede the point. Is the 'clash of civilizations' a surrender to alliteration? Would the book be treated more seriously by academics if it bore a different title?

A prophet dishonoured?

The Clash of Civilizations (1996) has been translated into almost forty languages; it is still more frequently discussed than any other work of the last twenty years in my own field of study, International Relations. But it is also a work that has invited more criticism than any other. My students just love to trash it, and it should indeed be handled with care. There is a saying attributed to the Chinese philosopher Mengzi (372–289 BCE), who is better known in the West as Mencius – 'he who believes all of a book would be better off without books' – and this advice is probably worth heeding when reading any influential book, Huntington's included.

But how many people, I wonder, have actually read it closely? It consists, after all, of 350 densely packed pages. I suspect that most of us are acquainted with one basic claim that can be extracted without doing too much injustice to the overall argument. What Huntington was saying was that conflict would continue to shape international politics, and possibly even reshape the present international order. His critics were quick enough to see a link between this proposition and his political opinions. He was a deeply committed American patriot who had been shaped in the social and ideological world of the Cold War. His government-related work during the Vietnam War made him a target for radical students at Harvard: in the 1970s he had to be escorted by security guards to his lectures. When his thesis about civilizational clashes was first adumbrated he was reviled on the left on another count: his preoccupation with future conflict seemed to dovetail rather too neatly with his fear that the West – the political civilization that had come through after a long struggle against communism – might not survive without identifying another enemy and finding another mission. The editor of the conservative monthly *The National Interest* also expressed misgivings as to whether the political 'West' could long survive: '[It] was not a natural construct but a highly artificial one. It took the presence of a life-threatening, overtly hostile "East" to bring it into existence. It is extremely doubtful whether it can survive the disappearance of that enemy' (Harries 1993). In the early 1990s both men found themselves locked into one of the local anxieties of the day.

But Huntington was a more subtle thinker than his critics are willing to admit or his admirers to recognize. He genuinely believed that in today's world, as in the past, different civilizations could – and should – coexist in dialogue with one another. The real clash was between civilization and barbarism. Of course, even to use that word is to invite criticism. A Muslim student was once upset that I called the first Taliban minister of culture 'barbaric' for visiting Kabul's only museum on his first day in office and smashing hundreds of objects for being 'blasphemous'. I offered another example – the destruction of Baghdad in 1258 by Genghis Khan's grandson Hulagu, and with it the Islamic caliphate that today's jihadists seek to restore. He remained unmoved. Even Hulagu's brother thought he had gone beyond the pale. Today St Catherine's monastery in Sinai, which runs the oldest continually running library in the world – it has been in business for 1,500 years –is threatened by Islamic fundamentalists. If we are so frightened of being thought politically incorrect to identify what is barbaric, still less to name it, then we know what to expect.

Huntington's point was that the future of civilization itself lay in coexistence – or, as he put it, 'hanging together' to avoid 'hanging alone'. And what he meant by barbarism – a loaded term, to be sure – was fundamentalism of whatever variety. One such movement is ISIS, inspired as it is by the example of the Kharijites (or 'Assassins'), a seventh-century sect which emerged slowly after the death of Muhammad to wage total war not just on infidels but on all those they considered to be Muslim apostates. Driving the leaders of ISIS was a puritanical and apocalyptic vision of a revolutionary vanguard Islam that, in its quest to murder both apostates and unbelievers, invoked both the military record of the Prophet and his companions and a Western-derived understanding of nihilism. In that sense the movement was not medieval, as so many Western commentators claimed – its ideology reached back to the origins of Islam; it drew on nineteenth-century European ideas of positivism and nihilism and it deployed twenty-first-century technology.

Huntington was a man half enmeshed in the prejudices of his time, but he was a good enough scholar to be able to see beyond them. For he thought that there was another form of fundamentalism that was uniquely

Western: the delusion of universalism. In that respect he was far less of an American 'liberal imperialist' than many thought at the time. In his book you will find this passage: 'In the emerging world of ethnic conflict and civilizational clash, the Western belief in the universality of Western culture suffers three problems: It is false, it is immoral and it is dangerous. Imperialism is the necessary logical consequence of universalism' (Huntington 1996: 310). He insisted that the Western civilization, like the Chinese or Indian, was not universal but unique. He also argued that the West's success in the Cold War owed everything to the superiority of its technology and its application of 'organized violence' and not to the superiority of its ideas, or values, or even Christianity, its once dominant religion (ibid.: 83).

These are not exactly unthought thoughts, but they were unusual for a conservative author. Huntington was reviled on the right for being a naysayer, for questioning the inevitable triumph of liberal internationalism, for insisting that the Western moment in history was over, and that the Unipolar moment, as it was called (the time when the United States was the only superpower), would be short-lived (as indeed it was). And he was reviled on the political left for much the same reasons, for rejecting the argument that globalization had levelled the cultural playing field and that one day soon everyone would be singing from the same song sheet.

Huntington's reputation is unlikely to be salvaged in the West, and that perhaps at the end of the day is not such a big deal: many of his claims show scant respect for the complexity of history. But ironically there was a much better argument struggling to get out of his book. It involved not a spurious clash of civilizations, or even a clash *within* them. What he failed to anticipate was the emergence of a quite new political unit: the civilizational state and its challenge to the present international order.

And the civilizational state, as we've seen, actually buys into the central if least persuasive aspect of Huntington's argument, namely that there have been frequent civilizational clashes in history. If we replace the word 'clash' with that of 'encounter', the argument gains greater credibility.

Take the catastrophic descent of the Mongols on Baghdad in 1258 to which I have already alluded, when the libraries were gutted and the Tigris was said to have run black with the ink of drowned books, and the authorities were terrified at the ease with which centuries of knowledge could disappear overnight; or take the Spanish eruption into the New World at the end of the fifteenth century which wiped out two entire civilizations; and the violent inclusion of China into the Western world order in the nineteenth century which one writer describes as an *ontological rupture* (Ramo 2007: 7). The Chinese considered themselves to be the acme of civilization; so too did the Europeans, who went much further – they believed that they had arrived at the future first, and that they had been entrusted not by God but by History with a 'civilizing mission' to drag everyone else along in their wake.

But there was an even more traumatic encounter between civilizations whose aftershocks still linger on: the traumatic 'rupture' within the Arab world provoked by Napoleon's invasion of Egypt in 1798. Today's Islamist fundamentalists make much of this event (it is one of the reasons why ISIS liked to target Paris). There is always an impulse in all terrorist movements to take revenge against the West for the misfortunes of the present – the Crusades and Western colonialism as well as a post-colonial, neo-colonial order.

A clash of civilizations?

'My brothers, we are introducing the French to civilization.' No, this is not a misprint, though some of my readers will recognize it as an echo of Napoleon's famous exhortation to his soldiers as he addressed them standing before the pyramids in 1798 – 'We are introducing the Egyptians to civilization' – a word that the French had only recently coined. Imagine instead that the words are those of a Mameluke general, leading an army that had arrived in Toulon ten years earlier and which successfully marches on Paris and occupies France. Let me indulge in a piece of whimsy, or what historians call an exercise in counterfactual history, and the rest of us usually call a 'what if?'. For a historical imagination allows us both to see the world that wasn't and to understand why the world is what it is.

Imagine that the Egyptians set up an enlightened administration in Paris, a Grand Council, and invite to serve on it the great intellects of the day, men such as the mathematicians Laplace (1749-1827) and Fourier (1768-1830) and the greatest chemist of the age, Fourcroy (1755-1809). Christianity is declared a protected faith (after all, Christians are one of the people of the Book). There are no forced conversions. The occupying force preaches the virtues of coexistence between the three Abrahamic faiths. This isn't a Crusade in reverse. But the graft fails to take. It doesn't have time to do so. The powers of Western Europe launch their own jihad against the Muslims (as they did against the French revolutionaries in 1792 in support of a beleaguered monarchy). The British fleet occupies Toulon (as it was also to do one year later), cutting off the Muslims from their base in Egypt.

This 'what if?' is a mirror-image of what happened when Napoleon invaded Egypt in 1798. He too set up a Grand Council on which he invited prominent Muslim scholars to serve. And the administration he left behind him when he returned to Paris the following year was eventually ousted by a British expeditionary force. But his invasion was different from any other: it was an intellectual appropriation. Napoleon brought with him a hundred or more *savants* (or intellectuals) to map out the country, to establish the intellectual title deeds to its conquest. They measured its monuments and copied its inscriptions and brought back to France some of its antiquities (including the famous Rosetta stone, which eventually allowed the Europeans to decode hieroglyphics). The Europeans thought that the country's treasures would be safer in their hands. They were wrong: many perished when the Europeans went to war against each other 150 years later; some disappeared for good in the air raids of the Second World War.

Let me admit at once that this 'what if?' actually has very little *historical* merit. So, to the first question:

Why isn't it useful from a professional historian's point of view?

Well, we are told by historians that we can only really talk about the things that might have been – not if they could have happened, but only if they were at all likely. By narrowing down the historical alternatives to those we consider plausible, and hence by replacing the 'enigma of chance' with a calculation of probabilities, we resolve the dilemma of having to choose between a single deterministic past and an unimaginably infinite number of possible pasts (Ferguson 1997: 85). The Egyptians at the time could never have envisaged occupying any European country: they didn't have the logistical capacity to mount an expedition, and they certainly didn't have the intellectual ambition or political will. The Arabs had long since lost the original urge to expand which had taken them a thousand years earlier as far as the Pyrenees and beyond.

So, if not a proper counterfactual, is it still a useful exercise for a political scientist, if not a historian?

I think it is, because it illustrates two different worldviews. Only a modern European state would have had the ambition to rescue Egypt from its past (as it saw it). Napoleon's objective, declared the philosopher and mathematician Jean-Baptiste Fourier, who accompanied the expedition, was to transform the country into a functioning modern state. The mission took many forms. One scientist studied the optics of the mirage, another the possibilities of indigo production. The invasion of Egypt was no ordinary colonial enterprise but an early experiment in social engineering.

This proved to be doubly humiliating for the Arabs. How could a people who had been given the final truth in a revelation that superseded Judaism and Christianity have been overtaken by the non-Muslim world in science and technology, and even the art of war? And why had Christian Europe managed to airbrush out of its own historical record the great Arab achievements of the past? Back in Paris, the students who had attended the lectures of the professors Napoleon took with him on his campaign would have been surprised to learn that some of the terms they took for granted, such as 'fellows' holding a 'chair' and delivering an 'inaugural lecture', were Arab in origin. So too for that matter was another concept, that of students 'reading' a subject in order to obtain a 'degree'.

To this can be added another cultural 'affront': the French conquerors were not only modernizers but revolutionaries. The invasion began with a proclamation which tried to reassure the Egyptians that the invaders had come in the name of a universal principle: all men being born equal had equal rights. It was difficult to convey this idea in Arabic because there is no obvious translation for the word 'right' (Pagden 2009: 375). Nor for that matter was there any true understanding of what the French invaders meant by *liberté*. When the religious leader Abd al-Rahman al-Jabarti (1753–1825) debated the finer points of freedom with Napoleon, he reminded him that, for an Arab, freedom meant only that a man was not a slave (de Bellaigue 2017).

Far more challenging to Arab opinion was the insult to Islam. Napoleon was on a hiding to nothing from the first because of religion. Not so much because he was a Christian as because he clearly wasn't. Napoleon may have put together a Grand Council to advise him, but its most prominent member, al-Jabarti, was scandalized by the proclamation's suggestion that all three religions of the Book – Islam, Christianity and Judaism – were to be given equal status. It meant, in effect, that the French had no genuine regard for any of them. Instead, their clear intention was to hollow out Islam from within by replacing it with the secular principles of the revolution.

Yet another reason why the arrival of the French was so traumatic stemmed from the fact that, in the Middle Ages, Egyptian scholars had found a way to affirm Arab supremacy within the world by appropriating the ancient Greeks as their own. In his giant encyclopaedia, a 9,000 page, 33-volume compendium of knowledge, the fourteenth-century writer Shihab al-Din al-Nuwayri (1279–1333) had folded the great Greek philosophers Aristotle, Empedocles and Pythagoras into the country's own intellectual genealogy, just as European thinkers in the Renaissance would later recruit them to fashion a history of 'Western science'. After 1798 such intellectual legerdemain became impossible.

For these and other reasons, the Egyptian Islamist Sayyid Qutb (1906–1966), who is often regarded as the father of modern Salafi Islamism, claimed that Napoleon's arrival was 'the greatest rupture' in Islamic history; it was what the French call a *coup d'éclat*, the moment when Muslims were introduced to a truly revolutionary, even blasphemous idea, that human beings had the right to 'appropriate God's attributes of exclusive sovereignty' (Choueiri 1990: 133). Indeed, he declared that Muslims who came to terms with such profane sovereignty were living in a pre-Islamic state of ignorance. Qutb felt a psychological need to transcend the rupture by putting forward the notion of Islam as a totality (the word in Arabic is *Tawhid*, or the Oneness of God); in that totality there was no place for nationalism, which was considered to be a modern form of idolatry, for a Muslim the greatest of all sins. As a devout Muslim himself, Qutb had a passing respect for the other two Abrahamic faiths, but he felt that they had both betrayed their origins. Judaism had declined into a system of lifeless and rigid rituals, and the value of Jesus' message had been lost sight of as soon as his followers founded a separate religion.

But, for the French themselves, the revolution of 1789 had been a rupture of another kind – a striking example of a change *of* consciousness rather than a change *in* consciousness. All of us often experience the latter in the course of our lives; we become more aware of what is happening around us and often more open to new ideas and experiences. But a change of consciousness is very different: it involves a major transformation in our way of thinking, or, if you like, a paradigm shift, and in the case of the French Revolution the *savants* whom Napoleon brought with him to Egypt had come to believe that the future would no longer be determined by the experience of the past; that it was possible to break with authority and to abandon the Mosaic law that forbade the faithful to think about the future – as Moses was told the future was God's. History now had a design: Progress. It was self-determining and had a teleological end, namely to rescue humanity from what Kant called its own 'self-incurred immaturity'.

If we look at the 'rupture' through a Western lens, can we tell ourselves a different story?

I think we can. In his introduction to Hobbes's great work *Leviathan*, Michael Oakeshott identified the historical 'rupture' in Western thinking. True to Augustinian pessimism, Christians had tended to see man as the slave of sin. The trouble was that, when Europe began to tire of Christian dogmatism, it did not wax any more optimistic. Man was now considered to be the slave of one overwhelming emotion: fear. Only the political order appeared to offer a road to redemption (Hobbes [1651] 1960: x–xi). Only by transferring the power to legislate on ethical matters to the state could humanity ameliorate the human condition.

The Western belief in the primacy of politics emerges in a famous paragraph from *The Philosophy of Right*, where Hegel tells us that the origin of the modern state as 'a self-organizing rational and ethical organization' can be traced back to the breakdown of religious unity in the West. For ethical constraints came no longer from God, but from within – from politics. The first and most important precondition of the modern concept of the state is the formation of a distinctive language of politics. In other words, for modern politics to be made possible, it was necessary to accept that a political society was held together solely for political purposes. The political sphere is both modern and ethical at the same time. Ethics inheres in the political practice of forging and keeping together a state divided by class and other conflicting interests. The aim, claimed Marx, was to create an *illusionistische Gemeinschaft* (an illusionary society) held together by certain foundational myths. The result was that, over time, political life in the

West became a battlefield for what was practical, not spiritual. A new era of 'principled un-principledness' opened, with its glorification of paradox, pluralism, opposition and contradiction (Ankersmit 2002: 27). And that is one reason, by the way, why radical Islamists despise democracy so much.

So, what was the final outcome of Napoleon's invasion?

The French soon left, but for a time the whole episode inspired many early nineteenth-century Arab reformers and contributed to a brief period of Arab enlightenment. Visionaries such as Hassan al-Attar (1766–1835), an imam who wrote on science, logic and medicine, were eager to embrace new ideas from the West, but they were faced by two challenges. In Egypt's case, the first was the forcible modernization of society by Muhammad Ali Pasha (1769–1849), a ruler who, like so many 'modernizers', was largely indifferent to the chaos that usually ensues when a society is in a hurry to reach the future. The second challenge was Western colonialism, which was successfully rebooted when the French came back to the Islamic world, this time to Algeria in 1830. As recently as the 1950s, French schoolchildren still read in their textbooks how the Algerian people had emerged into history only when they were dragged into it by their colonial masters. The textbooks may have been rewritten, but there is still an official version of history. In 2005 the French Chamber of Deputies passed a bill insisting that only 'the positive role' of the colonial experience in Algeria should be discussed in schools. To my knowledge, France is the only European country that insists on such a positive interpretation of its colonial history. And this, writes Tzvetan Todorov, is particularly regrettable, because it still invites you to see colonialism as a 'civilizing mission' (Todorov 2009: 89).

Ironically, however, the 'revolutionary missionaries' who arrived in Egypt in 1798 would have been confounded to learn that within 200 years it would be they, not the people of the Quran, who would feel most embattled. A Pew Research Center report from 2015 forecast that, by 2050, there would be 8 billion religious people in the world (almost twenty-five times more than there were in 2010). Despite two centuries of Western imperialism and modernization, it is the people without faith who find themselves in a minority, and once again the currents of religious conviction are threatening to transform the face of the Middle East.

The Islamic caliphate

Islam is unique among the world's great religions in one respect more than any other – Muhammad was both a prophet and caliph. The caliphate may not be specifically authorized by the Quran but, in regarding a territorial state as an inherent part of the new religion, Islam was politicized from the very beginning in a way that was not true of early Christianity. We hear so much about the caliphate that it is often difficult to disentangle the reality from the aspiration. It is important to recognize that there are two versions, which might be called the 'virtual' and the 'real.' Al-Qaeda was also committed to restoring the caliphate, but for Osama bin Laden (1957–2011) it was more of an ideal than a real possibility, a fact which may well explain his more liberal vision. Jews and Christians, as people of the Book, would have been allowed to coexist with their fellow Muslims: the Jews without a homeland, Israel, and the Christians without their 'unholy' alliance with Israel. In that sense, writes Faisal Devji, bin Laden was inspired, odd though it might sound to Western ears, by a kind of 'cosmopolitan militancy'. Indeed, in one of his many indictments of the United States, you will find him critical of the Bush administration for failing to sign up to the Kyoto Accords (Devji 2005: 71).

But as the insurgency in Iraq intensified after 2004, bin Laden eventually lost control of his own narrative to subordinates such as Abu Musab al-Zarqawi (1966–2006), a Jordanian-born high-school dropout who had a concrete caliphate very much in mind. Together with thirty or more Arabs who had served with him in Afghanistan in the 1980s, al-Zarqawi set up an organization called Jama'at al-Tawhid wal-Jihad. In October 2004 he formally changed the name of his group to Al-Qaeda in the Land of Two Rivers (a reference to the Tigris and the Euphrates rivers in Iraq). He hoped to create a Sunni caliphate within Iraq as a building block to a specifically *Arab* civilizational state, whose eventual centre of gravity would have been Egypt (Gerges 2011: 111). In the end the Americans were able to take him out, destroy his movement and incarcerate the surviving members in a prisoner of war camp called Camp Bucca, so named after a New York fireman who lost his life on 9/11. There they radicalized themselves and regrouped before launching a new movement, ISIS.

Islamic State, alas, needs no introduction, but is that the name we want to apply to the organization? You can take your pick – ISIS (the Islamic State of Iraq and Syria) or ISIL (the Islamic State of Iraq and the Levant). Then there is the Arabic name Daesh as well as the French rendition Groupe État Islamique (Islamic State Group) and the Al-Jazeera Arabic term Tanzim ad-Dawla (the State Organization). The variety of names partly explains its popular appeal. In the eyes of some it is a brave 'crusading' actor taking on the might of the Western world. In the eyes of others it is the 'liberator' of Muslims from the tyranny of globalization. It is a symbol of resistance to years of Western imperialism. But behind all these claims lies what it holds most dear – it is a triumphal return of the 'once and future' caliphate that collapsed a few centuries after the Prophet first preached the message of Islam.

When it comes to names I am going to stick to ISIS precisely because of its claim to be a very different kind of state (*ad-Dawla*) from that of the Westphalian model – a civilizational state with franchises that once ran from sub-Saharan Africa to the Northern Caucasus. Its founder al-Baghdadi arrived on the scene at just the right moment. He was able to exploit the disappointment that followed the Arab Spring and its promise of a more liberal, even democratic era.

Within a year the movement was able to seize almost one-third of Iraq, found a prototype state and fund its operations by raising oil revenues and trading drugs and selling off stolen antiquities on the black market, at least those that it didn't destroy. In 2015 the GDP of the state was more than that of several Caribbean island states and even small African countries. Life in the caliphate may have been grim, but in the early days at least it offered what the region's corrupt states couldn't – public services that actually worked, a genuine crackdown on corruption and, above all, the restoration of the 'true faith'. It also appealed to many Muslims outside the Middle East, who were offered $1,500 if they joined up to fight, as well as a starter home and a free honeymoon in Raqqa – it wasn't just in the next life that jihadists were promised virgins. And it chose Raqqa as its capital because this is where the most famous of the Abbasid caliphs, Haroun al-Rashid (763/766–809), moved his court at the end of the eighth century. The choice was markedly ironic given its attack on all things modern and scientific, and especially on anything that was considered to constitute independent intellectual thought. For the city had played host in the ninth century to many great Arab scientists and intellectuals, including the renowned Syrian astronomer Al-Battani (858–929), who calculated the 365-day length of the solar year to an accuracy of within two minutes.

The ISIS caliphate ran a tight ship: men were lashed for smoking and women for not covering their bodies, their fingernails included. To be sure, as a distinctive territorial entity it barely survived more than a thousand days, a little longer than John F. Kennedy's presidency. It was finally brought to its knees by nine months of airstrikes by a US-led coalition and the ground forces of the Iraqi army, the Kurds, and the Shia/Sunni militias. But if the world was able to take back its cities, it failed to break its determination to fight on. And even should it vanish from the political landscape altogether, which seems unlikely, possibly even more militant groups are likely to be emboldened to try to create another territorial state. Unfortunately, whether virtual or real, the caliphate is not going to disappear. It may well be imagined, but it is not imaginary. It is both there and in the making; it is there in people's hearts and in the making through their deeds.

The vision of a restored Islamic caliphate offers Muslims a meontology, an account of things that are not yet, a caliphate which is in the process of being realized (Critchley 2012: 245). In other words, the idea demands that its supporters make a significant leap of faith: to see what *is* in terms of what is not yet, and to see what is not yet in terms of what is. The young jihadists who went out to Iraq to fight for the vision call to mind the mystics described by John Fowles in his last novel, *A Maggot* (1985): 'baffled . . . before the real now; far happier out of it, in a narrative past or a prophetic future, locked inside that weird tense grammar does not allow, the imaginary present.'

The caliphate as an idea is 'once and future' for that reason – it is a civilizational state in the process of eternally becoming. And it has the same appeal as other civilizational states. Like them, it embraces a model that rejects the nation-state; indeed, it goes further in denouncing it as an affront to Islam because temporal legislation usurps God's sovereignty. Like them, it peddles all three of the civilizational myths that I discussed in chapter 2. It claims to represent an unchanging Islamic civilization; it offers a version of history that suggests that most contacts with the outside world, but especially the West, have been violent and unproductive; and it espouses a cultural code, in this case Salafism, a philosophy that believes in 'progression through regression', 'a redemptive philosophy based around an idealised version of Islam that enshrines both authenticity and purity' (Maher 2016). Whether the Quran is the last word or is open to interpretation is a question, of course, that has divided Muslim theologians from the very beginning.

Let us put all three features under the spotlight, for they are all likely to infuse the next generation of radical Islamists.

Islamic civilizational state?

The first myth presupposes that there actually is an Islamic civilization. It's a common enough if misleading Western belief – Islam, we are told by Henry Kissinger, was 'at once a religion, a multiethnic superstate and a new world order' (Kissinger 2014: 156). Except that the first caliphate was never a state as we understand the term today; it was not a superpower, and it never established a world order (the conversion of much of sub-Saharan Africa and Indonesia came much later). What is true, however, is that many radical Islamists – and not just radicals – draw inspiration from what the caliphate once was and might one day be again. As one writer notes, it provides an emotionally powerful antidote to the sense of geopolitical deprivation arising from the current distribution of global power; it does indeed further a sense of Muslim unity across today's globe; and, if the idea of creating a state out of nothing seems ambitious, the fact is that the Prophet and his successors did just that in the seventh century (Cook 2014: 326).

But if we talk of an Islamic civilization, then we must ask whether it refers to the Arab world, which makes up less than 10 per cent of the Islamic world. Or do we also include Persia, a civilization which is distinctive and very different, or Turkey, which is different again? The Islamic world brought together disparate sets of linguistic communities: Syriac, Aramaic, Coptic and Persian. In reality, by the end of the twelfth century, Muslims living in Mali and India, in Indonesia and Timbuktu, were divided in language, culture, wealth and, especially, political affiliation. What, we might ask, linked the cultural centres of Samarkand, Baghdad and Herat (once the cultural heart of the Timurid Empire back in the Middle Ages)? Only perhaps the Mongol invasions of the thirteenth century, which snuffed out the cultural life of all three. As for the Ottoman Empire, which remained the greatest Islamic power for centuries, how Islamic really was it? It saw itself as the reviver, not the destroyer, of the Byzantine Empire it overthrew. Even the description of the empire as Turkish is misleading: the most committed agents of imperial rule were often not Turkish at all; thanks to the levy of boys from the Balkans for service in the military and government, the empire's governing elites were often Balkan Christian in origin (Kumar 2017).

In terms of national consciousness and linguistic nationalism, the Islamic world remains fractured. But, if it is difficult to speak of a single

Islamic civilization, Muslims across the world certainly continue to iden-tify with a *community*, which stretches from Morocco to Indonesia and includes one-fifth of the world's population. Islam offers a collective iden-tity that can be more powerful than that of the nation-state, with which the great majority also identify. But, then again, if Muslims identify with one another by their faith, the way in which they celebrate their faith takes dif-ferent forms. Sunni Arab Islamism is different from Pakistan's, with its quest for the ideal of a modern Islamic state (an ideal which is not shared by many in the Middle East). For the Shia in Iran, the cult of the martyred Hussein (625–680) is more important than anything else. Today the Shi'ite world extends from its centre in Iran to neighbouring Iraq, and thence across the Levant to Lebanon. Over time the importance of the split may have waxed and waned, but today it is especially divisive. The Islamic world is not at peace with itself. Almost 40 per cent of Muslims live in crisis zones and around 25 million are political refugees. This explains, by the way, why most victims of terrorist attacks are Muslim.

And the fact that Islam is now the fastest-growing religion in the world is likely to see an even greater diversification of religious practice. There is a famous saying: 'Islam is a river that takes the colour of the bed over which it flows.' There have always been a variety of ways in which Islam can be lived. For some it involves an emphasis on dress and daily prayers at the mosque. Others prefer to pursue the 'truth', a vain pursuit perhaps, but one that may continue to lead many young Muslims to join radical movements. The great majority, by contrast, still struggle to reconcile their religious obligations with the everyday demands of life in a Western society. In that sense, writes Olivier Roy, Islam is a universal religion precisely because, since the time of the Prophet's companions (the Salaf), it has been embedded in different cultures. And these cultures are a product of history. It is the compromise with culture that has made Islam such a successful religion; it is also that compromise that infuriates fundamentalists across the world who aspire to unite behind a truly universal message (Roy 2004: 25).

War with the West?

When Al-Qaeda tried to blow up a plane over the US in the autumn of 2010, the box in which the bomb was placed was addressed to Reynald Krak, a pseudonym for a medieval Crusading knight, Raynald de Châtillon (1125–1187), a Muslim-hating thug who, it was rumoured during his life-time, harboured ambitions to destroy the Prophet's tomb. His most recent biographer prefers to see him in a more heroic light, not so much a thug as a man at the 'cutting edge of an outward expansionist society' (Lee 2016). Others may feel that this is rather rich; it is a bit like describing the Vikings as over-enthusiastic traders with a unique negotiating style and a liking for corporate raids.

Remarkably, however, the Crusades continue to remain a point of refer-ence for many people in both the West and the Middle East. Sayyid Qutb used to complain that the Crusader spirit ran in the blood of all Westerners (Tyerman 2004: 204). Some Western historians choose to give the benefit of the doubt to the Christians, who from the seventh century regarded the Muslims as conquerors and Islam as a militant, imperialist faith. A few even see the Crusades as a reaction to centuries of Islamic expansionism, a fightback, if you will, against centuries of Muslim aggression. There is little point in taking sides in this dispute; what is striking and also rather depress-ing is the fact that attitudes laid down at the beginning of the encounter between Islam and Christianity should still continue to shape what Richard Fletcher called 'the geology of human relationships' (Fletcher 2003: 159). Or, to express it rather differently, what is also remarkable is both sides' autonoetic consciousness – their ability to travel back to the distant past and relive it in the present.

Unfortunately, it's not just that the past weighs heavy; it's that the pre-sent feels too light to bear it. If you are a European Muslim, you will be told by radical mullahs, or learn from social media sites, about the heroism of those who took part in Muhammad's battles and the cowardice of those who held back. You will be told the difference between the *mujahidin,* those who are willing to struggle in God's cause, and the *munafiqeen*, those who choose to opt out. And the prospect of restoring the caliphate is sufficiently alluring for many young Muslims in Europe to fight as jihadists. ISIS invested a lot of energy in organizing self-radicalized terrorist attacks. Small-scale localized terror operations have put Europe on the defensive. The state response to these has served only to confirm many alienated young Muslims in their belief that Europe is at its core intensely Islamophobic – a conviction that has the important function of helping terrorist movements get their recruits.

Analysts still can't agree on why they join up. Olivier Roy ascribes what is happening to a generational revolt and contends that we are not dealing with the radicalization of Islam so much as the Islamization of radicalism. Many French terrorists are second-generation Muslims who were born in France, speak French as a first language, and have little or no contact with local mosques. Often they have engaged in petty or more serious crimes, live hedonistic lifestyles, take drugs, drink to excess, and often come from dysfunctional families. So why do they turn to terrorism? If religion is the main explanation for their radicalism, why does it not affect first- or third-generation Muslims? Why does its appeal extend to the children of the successful middle class? The answer, argues Roy, is to be found in sociology. It is essentially a youth revolt (Lilla 2016b: 21–2). The psychological borders between Europe and the Muslim world, in other words, are not necessarily civilizational; they are generational and involve the displaced, the unanchored and even the terminally bored.

But then, perhaps instead of asking what are they escaping from we should also ask what they are escaping *to*. 'A person who is running away from something, the Hungarian psychoanalyst Michael Balint once remarked, is also running towards something else. If we privilege (as psychoanalysts and others do) what we are escaping from as more real – or in one way or another more valuable – than what we are escaping to, we are preferring what we fear to what we seem to desire' (Carey 2005: 38). And, clearly, what many are escaping to is a life of adventure. They join movements like ISIS for what the promise of a 'clash of civilizations' offers: a life of piety, the fight for the Crescent against the Cross, the chance for the brutal to justify their brutality – and over time the brutal tends to get more brutalized, not less. And here is an even darker thought. Violence is addictive. In the Cold War days, Western security services sought to reveal the truth of communism in an effort to dissuade people from joining the Communist Party or from subverting Western institutions from within. ISIS doesn't hide the truth of its atrocities; it posts them up on the web in an attempt to shock young Muslims into choosing sides.

But for Gilles Keppel the message carries conviction precisely because it is addressed to a generation that has never known a world before 9/11, a time when Muslims have not had to defend their own identity. Many young terrorists, he insists, are indeed inspired by Islam and are even more proud to carry out attacks in its name. One interviewed by the French journalist David Thomson was especially scathing of the claim that his actions had 'nothing to do with Islam'. They had '*everything* to do with Islam', he insisted. In the course of his interviews Thomson found that Salafist theology played a leading role in the decision of young French Muslims to join ISIS, as did the folk memory of French colonialism in North Africa. One young woman who had returned from Syria was not at all repentant. She told him that the killing of the editorial team of *Charlie Hebdo* in January 2015 had been one of the 'most beautiful days' in her life (Derbyshire 2017). Thomson himself was baffled by why so many of the young jihadists he interviewed for his book (*Les Revenants*, 2016) seemed decent enough people who had been seduced by an evil message.

'Evil is good turned cancerous', remarks one of the characters in Poul Anderson's novel *The Corridors of Time* (2012) (Walton 2012). Even so, if that may be true of some terrorists, is it true of most? In the end human motivations are difficult to fathom. We don't know why one person is moved by a work of art and another left indifferent. We don't understand why one may feel dismay, and another awe, by a picture of carnage. 'We do not know our own souls,' wrote Virginia Woolf (1882–1941), 'let alone the souls of others.

Human beings do not go hand in hand the whole stretch of the way. There is a virgin forest in each . . .' (Carey 2005: 23-4). We have to acknowledge that human nature offers evidence of irreducible psychic variation.

So, is a civilizational war shaping up? Only if French voters accept the analysis of politicians such as Marine Le Pen that Islam's present would-be holy warriors are attacking Europe, and that the only response would be a 'defensive Crusade' against an enemy that is already hiding in plain sight (Poulos 2016). The National Front is gaining credibility because the liberal consensus is breaking down. The French are being urged to stop dismissing criticism of Islam as 'Islamophobia' and recognize that Western values just happen to be superior (Žižek 2016). The attacks in Paris in 2015 would seem to have challenged many of the axiomatic beliefs that are held by French intellectuals, especially about the universal appeal of Western values. Even on the left there are claims that the values being defended are not universal but Western, and in some cases not Western but specifically French.

Islamic essentialism

Part of the appeal of ISIS as a brand is its claim to be following the example of the first three generations of Muslims and that the quest for the truth lies only through the Quran and the introduction of sharia, even though the word appears only once in the entire Quran (45.11) – and there it means simply 'the right path'. For Henry Corbin (1903–1978), the great scholar of Islamic thought, this utter rejection of culture, especially of its greatest cultural achievements, was actually symbolic of 'the very idolatry [Islamism] denounces' (Ruthven 2016: 18). For most people, religious faith is reinforced not only through theological or biblical texts but also through the arts: the Divine can be glimpsed in architectural styles such as the great Gothic cathedrals of medieval Europe and the great mosques of Granada and Cordoba. Indeed, evolutionary functionalists will tell you what artists have long intuited: that style is vital to any comprehension of reality, and that the architecture of something like a church or a temple has immense communal appeal.

Poetry and religion, argues Harold Bloom, have always accompanied each other 'in a cosmological emptiness marked by the limits of truth and of meaning' (Bloom 1991: 4). Poets, claimed Shelley (1792–1822), are the 'founders of civil society' because they help to nurture the imagination; poetry, he added, was the greatest instrument of moral good (Carey 2005: 97). And for many Christians the kernel of religiosity in Western civilization can be found not only in the Bible but in the poetry of Homer, Dante (1265–1321) and Milton (1608–1674), and even for some in the nihilistic vision of Samuel Beckett (1906–1989). What is truly impressive about *The Divine Comedy*, writes Rowan Williams, a former archbishop, is that the poem seeks to enact its subject matter: we are invited as readers to allow the being of God to become transparent and actively transformative in the words we read (Williams 2017: 3).

In the case of Islam, we are stumbling into the middle of a very old and often heated debate about whether or not the Quran is the only legitimate source of religious inspiration. Either the word of God as conveyed to the Prophet is beyond the scope of human argument, or we humans are so fallible that we are condemned to reason out what it means. Perhaps the Quran can only be read in the context of the times and our understanding of them. In other words, while God's word may indeed be timeless, the application of it in the world may well be time-bound. Put another way, Muslims too have had to live with the 'death of God' – or, rather, his absence from history.

I think the only realistic conclusion to reach is that the caliphate will continue to remain more aspirational than real. It may be remembered in years to come more for the scope of its ambition than for the intelligence of its design. Even if ISIS proved to be unable to stop the world from taking back its cities, the world is unlikely to break the will of radical Islamists to continue the fight. ISIS is already adapting to the loss of its territorial base. Its children who have grown up under ISIS rule – the 'young cubs', as they are called – have been trained for the next war against its many enemies: the *Rawafidh* (Shia), the *Murtaddeen* (apostate Sunnis), the *Safavids* (Iranians) and, of course, the *Crusaders* – the West. Radical Islam is here to stay.

One day, perhaps, it will go the way of the Anabaptists, one of the most extreme of the Protestant millenarian groups spawned by the Reformation. The Anabaptists preached a strict interpretation of the Sermon on the Mount and looked forward to the imminent end of the world. They even managed to establish a short-lived religious state in Münster (1534–5) which abolished private property and allowed its leaders many wives. It is easy to forget how terrifying radical Protestantism once seemed to most Europeans. When the Anabaptist leaders were finally dislodged, their corpses were exhibited in iron cages, which can still be seen today hanging from the city's cathedral tower.

One day, too, the passion for jihad will die, and angry young Muslims will come back into the fold. One day the nightmare will end. But, alas, not soon.

Many young Muslims in the West will continue to fault their own governments for propping up the regimes of Arab states that are either irredeemable or incapable of reform. More to the point, how can you renew a political order such as the one in the Middle East, which is clearly in urgent need of renewal, until you can imagine something radically different in its place? The failure of ISIS ironically may give the idea of the caliphate a renewed lease of life; if the pan-Arabism of the late 1950s went nowhere, a pan-Islamic movement may surprise us yet.

So, what should the rest of the world do to defend civilization against fundamentalism of this particularly egregious form? Perhaps it might heed the advice that Arnold Toynbee proffered seventy years ago: to keep fighting the zealots while continuing to support the Herodians, or what Islamists denounce as the *Tawaghit* – the rulers who believe that Islam lies more in the hearts of the believers than in the dogma of sharia. Back in 1948 Toynbee wrote a largely forgotten essay, 'Islam and the West', which can be found in one of his last works, *Civilization on Trial* (1948). And it has the author's imprimatur – it is at times moralistic, historically sweeping and insufferably didactic. But it is also characteristically thought-provoking. Toynbee argued that the Islamic world had been in crisis since the early nineteenth century. As a historian of civilization, he compared the crisis with the one that had been faced by another, much older religion: Judaism, in the first century BCE. The Jews, too, were a monotheistic people with an equally inflated view of their own importance. After the Roman occupation of Palestine they fell back on two strategies: collaborating with Rome and fighting it.

Toynbee called the two strategies Herodianism and Zealotism (Toynbee 1948). To be pedantic, it was not only the Jews around Herod who remained 'on side'; so did those of the diaspora who spoke Greek, read their own scriptures in Greek and had no problem with the Roman Empire. The zealots, on the other hand, were never reconciled to Roman rule: they kept faith with the past and dreamed of restoring the former glory of the Jewish state; they waited impatiently for the appearance of the Messiah. Even then, the era of Jewish history Toynbee was describing had many other divisions, into Sadducees, Pharisees and Essenes, plus a host of fringe holy men of whom Jesus was one. Today's Middle East has its Shia and Sunni divisions, its constitutional and revolutionary Islamists, its democrats and secular authoritarians, its Alawites in Syria, and the Kurds who see themselves as a separate nationality from the Arabs. But Toynbee, it might be claimed, grasped the rules of engagement that the world has chosen to adopt in its fightback against the once and future caliphate long before radical Islam penetrated our collective consciousness.

7

A Post-Liberal World

In a speech at the NATO summit in Warsaw in July 2017, Trump asked his fellow Western leaders: Do we have the confidence in our values to defend them at any cost? Trump brought with him into office a set of assumptions that was summed up best, perhaps, by the now disgraced Steve Bannon, his former chief strategist. One of his aims in joining the Trump bandwagon, he told *The Economist*, was that the West should continue to dominate the high ground of history. And he had a much larger mission in mind than just seeing off Islamic fundamentalism: 'I want the world to look back in a hundred years and say that their mercantilist Confucian system lost, and that the Judeo-Christian-liberal West won' (*The Economist*, 26 August 2017, p. 34). Bannon himself was driven by a propulsive indignation about what the future might hold. His remarks expressed a despairing sense that the West is losing its place in the world and that it is time to push back. It also reflected a zero-sum view of international politics in which the winner takes all.

Whatever Trump's record in office will be, the next American president is likely to find him- or herself constrained by some of the forces which got Trump elected. As America's position in the world continues to erode, s/he is likely to be much more mindful of American domestic concerns. Trumpism may merely be a mild foreshadowing of what is to come. Western leaders are beginning to recognize that, although the West was once powerful enough to set the rules, its power to enforce them is diminishing fast; that the Russians are now powerful enough to break them; and that China, one day quite soon, will be powerful enough to remake them.

The civilizational state is an eclectic concept: it's largely a device to legitimize the power of a particular regime and to help it shape the political landscape in its own interests. But if it has one overarching theme it is this: the total rejection of universalism, the great dream of Western writers. Towards the end of his life, one of the great writers on civilization, Pitirim Sorokin, suggested that one day all the world's civilizations might converge around an 'integral culture', though even he found himself at a loss to explain what shape it might eventually take (Sorokin 1964). Fernand Braudel, too, chose to conclude his book *A History of Civilizations* with a prediction by his compatriot Raymond Aron that humanity was in the process of forging a single civilization, 'truly universal in its appeal' (Braudel 1994: 8). Such comforting predictions now seem rather dated. The civilizational state, or at least the most important one, China, is likely to come up with some truly transformative ideas to end the dominance of the Westphalian state system. Whatever happens, I think it is safe to predict that we will see an essential upgrade and not, as many Americans hope, merely the addition of a few new updates.

The end of Western exceptionalism

Rummaging through the library stacks of his university while researching his senior thesis, the young Saul Bellow was surprised to learn from one of the books that two of the French ships in the slave trade had been named the *Jean-Jacques Rousseau* and the *Contrat Social* (Bellow 2015: 408). *Anorak moment*: there was also another ship, *Le Voltaire*, which was apparently named with the express authorization of the philosopher himself (Miller 2008). Hypocrisy, of course, is not the speciality of any one civilization, though the West lends itself to criticism more than most because of the immodesty of its claims. The Enlightenment may be one of the supreme accomplishments of Western civilization, in Western eyes, at least, but it is also the principal source of what Martin Jacques (2011) calls

'Euro-provincialism'. It is still the yardstick by which the West tends to judge those it deems to be less enlightened, democratic or cosmopolitan than itself.

It would be foolish, nevertheless, to deny that there is still a Western 'differential'. In the world literature stakes, Western authors such as Shakespeare are quoted far more often than their non-Western peers. This can be laid at the door of cultural imperialism, of course, but that is only part of the story. In the last 200 years the West has also managed to craft a set of values and norms that, though grounded in its own historical experience, still enjoy immense cross-cultural appeal. The point is that, although the human rights revolution may have begun in late nineteenth-century Europe, it didn't remain tied to its roots. The abolition of the slave trade, the emancipation of women and social welfare provision, as well as universal education, may have originated in the West, but they have now become part of a world culture (Boli and Thomas 1999: 35).

Then again, one mustn't exaggerate the West's originality. Many societies in the non-Western world discovered human 'wrongs' long before they were introduced to the world of 'Rights'. Let me offer a particularly graphic example. Back in the fifteenth century a samurai warrior needed to be sure that he could dispatch his enemy nicely, i.e., with a neat downward thrust on the shoulder. It was taxing work; a samurai warrior could spend years perfecting his swordplay, which is one of the reasons why guns were banned a century later. Who could take swordplay seriously if a peasant hiding behind a wall could take you out with a single shot? The problem was that the samurai were allowed by law to test their skills against any wayfarer they encountered on the road – provided, of course, that he wasn't another samurai. The practice even had a name, *tsujigiri*, or the 'cross-roads cut'. Over time, however, even the samurai found the practice unethical; instead of targeting innocent wayfarers, they tested out their sword skills on condemned criminals (Midgley 1981: 69). What the story illustrates is that the behaviour that a society finds acceptable at a particular time in its history may well be found unacceptable in another. Cultural practices invoke normative judgements, and norms are subject to constant change. Civilizations, as we've seen, have no historical core – even the samurai experience, which is probably what most people know about Japan outside karaoke, sushi and perhaps the haiku, is only part of a much more varied and interesting history.

There is very little likelihood, I think, of the Japanese reverting to the practice any time soon, or the Chinese reintroducing foot-binding, or the Russians engaging in the anti-Semitic pogroms of the late nineteenth century, or, for that matter, the Europeans returning to the witchcraft trials of the sixteenth century. By the beginning of the twenty-first century we have come to recognize that the behaviour of ISIS in throwing gays off roofs, or selling girls as young as nine into sexual slavery, or burning prisoners alive, consists of 'wrongs' that have long been held to have no place in civilized thinking. They are an outrage against what the Geneva Conventions call 'the public conscience of mankind'.

But how far does that conscience extend, and what is its imaginary scope? The Rights of Man back in 1789 meant just that: women only had rights that their husbands were willing to concede. Since then rights have been extended to racial and ethnic minorities, refugees and people without citizenship, political exiles, the physically or mentally challenged, and people of different sexualities or none. The West seems anxious to extend the scope still further: a few years ago the legal committee of the European Parliament debated the rights of robots. The New Zealand Parliament is the first in the world to recognize the rights of the higher primates. But clearly not all these rights are recognized by other cultures, or the governments that claim to speak in their name, and the rights of dolphins are well down the list in those countries in which a large percentage of human beings still find themselves living at a subsistence level.

The rich countries of the world, the majority of them still Western, are in the vanguard of the human rights crusade. But this is very different from claiming that liberal civilization is the only successful form of future-proofing. The West may well have to accept, wrote the late Richard Rorty, that the ideas of John Stuart Mill may have little appeal to the 3 billion people coming into the world between now and 2050. Its values may not in fact be universal. Rorty has come in for a lot of criticism in his own country, particularly from the right, for telling his fellow countrymen that their own human rights narrative was the wholly fortuitous outcome of a particular set of historical circumstances. It was not a 'discovery' of some eternal truth that had managed to escape everyone else, and upon which the West had stumbled thanks to a superior ability to reason out the meaning of history. And, as he also insisted, if you really believe in the brand, you have to have faith that it will eventually come through. Besides which, even if the liberal experiment fails to take elsewhere in the world, that is no reason to give up on liberalism, any more than the impending demise of the Western Roman Empire persuaded St Augustine to give up on Christianity.

Historians are still given to finding inevitability in the history they relate. But there are also discontinuities: the roads not taken, the intellectual journeys that ended abruptly. Civilizations display 'emergent properties' – i.e., they are shaped by different experiences and contingent events. If you're interested in the contingency of European history, there is an excellent volume of essays entitled, rather tellingly, *Unmaking the West* (Tetlock et al. 2006). Would the West as we know it, asks one author, have been stillborn if Themistocles (524–459 BCE) had lost the battle of Salamis? Would it have been 'modern' as we understand the term today if William III's invasion of England had failed? Counterfactual history may be a Western invention, but it encourages Westerners to question some of the presuppositions to which they hold tenaciously, especially about their own historical trajectory. My favourite 'what if?' is to be found in another volume: Victor Davis Hanson's take on what would have happened had Socrates been killed at the battle of Delium. It was, after all, his third battle, and he fought it at what was then an advanced age. What indeed? Certainly, no Plato (he turned to philosophy, spurning politics, only as a result of Socrates' later trial). And, without neo-Platonism, where would Christianity be? Would it even have been possible to conceive of a Christian God (Hanson 2002).

'We claim only an experimental success: we have come up with a way of bringing people into some degree of comity,' wrote Rorty, 'and of increasing human happiness, which looks more promising than any other way which has been proposed so far' (Rorty 1999: 273). There are those who would take issue with the idea that the West is happier than anyone else, even if Denmark regularly appears near the top of the Human Happiness Index. And anyway, since the global financial crisis, the experiment may look a little less compelling. Has the West really discovered the formula for the best form of government or the most enlightened way of life? These days many Westerners seem deeply unhappy with their lot.

Rorty is such a bugbear to many of his fellow Americans that I feel bound to quote an impeccable conservative writer, the little-known Englishman T. E. Hulme (1883–1917), who was felled by a German shell in 1917. Hulme died convinced that the First World War had vindicated his pessimistic view of life. Far from being appalled by the 'horror' (as most First World War poets saw the blood-letting), he thought it perfectly consistent with his understanding that history is not for the faint-hearted. He died defending a liberal vision that, as a conservative, he could no longer take entirely on trust. 'From time to time', he wrote, 'great and useless sacrifices become necessary, merely that whatever precarious "good" the world has achieved may just be preserved' (Jenkins 2014). He entered the war with few illusions anyway: he didn't share the official view that the Allies were fighting for a better world; he went to the front for a very practical end – to prevent Europe from falling under German domination.

Hulme even entertained serious doubts about whether democracy could be exported. The 'evolution towards democracy', he wrote, 'is not inevitable; it is

the most precarious, difficult and exigent task political man has ever conceived. And ... far from it being the predestined path of every nation and race, only one or two nations have attempted to pursue it, while the rest deliberately and even, we might say, intelligently, pursue another path altogether, as if that were progress, and are thus sincerely hostile to our own. (Hulme 1994: 333)

Hulme was disinclined to put humanity before the individual; instead he thought that humanity was reflected through the particularity of an individual life. He rejected such abstractions as Freedom, which were frequently invoked by the Allies during the war. Of course, Woodrow Wilson might well have been right in thinking that the world had to be made 'safe for democracy'; but, if so, the West has certainly paid a high enough price for that belief. A century later we are more inclined to ask whether the world can be made safe for democracy promotion. Anyway, Hulme was simply of a different persuasion. Reading his work again, what I find beguiling is not only his refreshing lack of cant but the supreme honesty of his sacrifice.

In the future, even the Americans may have to give up on their liberal interventionist ambitions, but I doubt whether they will give up on liberalism. Nor should they, whatever Trump's message. The West in general would be well advised to continue to tell itself that its values are true, or at least true for it, even if others increasingly lose interest in them. The principal reason for telling those stories is the terrible weight of *its own* history. We don't know how universal Western values actually are, though the historians of the future will eventually tell us. We don't stand at the end of history, in the privileged position of being able to look back. It is impossible to prove that human beings have rights; we can only continue to tell ourselves that they do. But, from even a passing knowledge of its own history, the West knows the appalling consequences of believing that they don't.

The civilizational state and non-Western values

But just at the time Western exceptionalism is losing traction, the civilizational state is encouraging its own citizens to think of their own civilization as exceptional, at times even 'immemorial' or 'eternal' (like ancient Rome), something that can be analysed, catalogued and studied as a single entity because it is deemed to have an essence, or a spirit, and, in the case of Russia, even a 'soul'. All this is nonsense of course. Nothing has an essence, wrote Nietzsche, unless it is without a history. Ronald Hayman introduced his biography of the philosopher with these wonderfully insightful words. For a biographer, every philosopher's work is biographical (i.e., historical). A person's beliefs, for example, often change over time as life moves on; his personal philosophy is usually shaped by the circumstances of his career; his writing is influenced by events, not all of them significant, perhaps, in the eyes of others, but which may be certainly significant in his own (Hayman 1995: 1). Every civilization likewise has a biography (those that fail to evolve tend to ossify and go out of business).

But, of course, many Russian and Chinese writers now insist that their own civilization has an essence which is essentially unchanging. Take a familiar concept, the Russian 'soul'. As it happens, it too has a distinct history, one more recent than many Russians might think. Liah Greenfield claims that it first made an appearance in the nineteenth-century Russian novel as a reaction to a perceived failure to live up to Western expectations. In European eyes, Russia was hardly a land infused with progressive possibilities. In response, Russian writers such as Dostoevsky took comfort in mysticism; the Russian soul served as a basis for individual self-esteem (Greenfeld 1990: 582) And to compensate for their hurt feelings they saw the Western world in turn as 'decadent' and 'rotten'. *Gniloy* ('rotten') and *gnilyushchik* ('rotten man') are terms that are often heard in political discourse today (Neumann 2016: 1393).

The attack on liberal civilization should be seen for what it is, of course – less an attack on the ideology of globalism or Western exceptionalism than a cynical ploy by the state to reinforce its own cultural credentials in the eyes of its citizens. What is being secured against the West is not civilization as such but the interests of a particular regime. That is why it rewrites history. In 2013 the Russian government set out to create a series of textbooks that would 'eliminate the possibility of internal contradictions . . .

and encourage exclusive interpretations of historical events'. Three years later the Russian National Security Council claimed that one of its principal mandates was to prevent alleged 'distortions' of Russian history by foreign powers. The minister for culture, Vladimir Medinsky, was unexpectedly frank in maintaining that facts would only get in the way of producing 'the historical mythology' that is at the heart of the Russian civilizational state (Johnston 2016: 1–2). In a classic defence of post-truth history, he insisted that 'the facts themselves don't mean too much. I will be more brutal: in the historical mythology they do not mean anything. Facts only exist in the context of the concept. Everything begins not with facts but with interpretations' (Prus 2015: 1). 'If you like your motherland, your people, your history, what you'll be writing will always be positive', he added for good measure (Johnston 2016).

And there's the rub. The problem with every mythology is that it doesn't allow you to remain faithful to the individuality of experience. Myths are usually immune to factual rebuttal for that reason – they tend to operate on a deeper level of consciousness in their claim to communicate a more immediate, metaphysical truth. And that truth is conveyed by only one source of authority: the state. Not surprisingly, the chairman of the Russian Historical Association is not an academic historian but the director of the SVR – the Russian Foreign Intelligence Service. History, joked the authors of that popular English classic *1066 and All That*, is the sum of all you can remember (which is usually not very much). Today it's what the state remembers for you or what it chooses to flag up on your behalf.

The Russian authorities also insist that the state is under threat, together with its ability to protect the nation. Putin likes to issue dire warnings about the country's imminent 'de-sovereignization' – the threat that it will disappear as an independent cultural entity if Western ideas are allowed to circulate unchallenged. The patriarch of Moscow talks of defending its values against the 'contamination' of Western ideas such as human rights, which he deems to be the product not of the European Enlightenment but, more narrowly, of Western Protestantism and, more ominously, Jewish thinking (cited in Lunde 2016: 251). Many Chinese writers believe that they are building what one of them calls a 'homo-ecological symbiosis' which, in fostering 'cultural togetherness', will make the Chinese people immune from the infection of such Western ideas as democracy (Wu 1998: 342).

Of course, to reiterate, what is being defended – and asserted at the same time – is the primacy of the state. The state insists that only it can be entrusted to secure its basic values and that it is the embodiment of the civilization itself. The Chinese Communist Party likes to claim that the Reform Programme which opened the country to rampant capitalism after 1979 springs 'from the soil of China' (Fenby 2014). And just as there must be no dilution of sovereignty, so there must be no dilution of security in the name of cosmopolitanism or multilateralism. Hard power remains the hard reality. In China, internet firewalls have replaced the stone walls of the past. The ideological journal *Red Flag* warned its readers in 2013 that the West was trying to use the internet to bring China down. The same year Chinese academics were warned to avoid discussing subjects which the regime considered off-limits, such as universal values, citizen rights and freedom of information; all of these were held to be not only alien to China's tradition but a deliberate tool of the West to weaken it from within (ibid.: 34). Even in the case of music, the defence of Chinese values now includes a crackdown on the Western religious music tradition – no more performances of Handel's *Messiah* or Verdi's *Requiem*, which are seen to pose a danger in the form of cultural contamination.

In Russia the situation is no better, with the minister of culture accusing Netflix – the global film-streaming company – of being part of an American plot to subvert Russian society. In an effort to upgrade its defences against outside influences, his ministry has now introduced licences banning the media from showing any films that are deemed to 'defile the national culture' (*The Times*, 24 June 2016). And, given that it considers the country to be under siege, the state demands the unconditional loyalty of its own citizens. They may be allowed to hold to other affinities, elective or otherwise, but they are not encouraged to entertain affinities that are judged to cut across cultural identities. Civil society networks and NGOs certainly exist, but they are still strictly controlled. And meanwhile the state continues to lure people into complicity with many of its nastier nationalist prejudices, which is why the adoption of Russian orphans by American families has been banned and why a large number of Russian civil servants are not allowed to travel abroad (according to one estimate, about 4 million people are on the list), not to mention the fact that foreign stakes in the Russian media have been restricted to a maximum of 20 per cent (Lipman 2015).

All of which calls into question whether the world's civilizational states have much interest in entering into a dialogue with anyone else – why should they, when they largely prohibit an open dialogue between themselves and their own citizens? In China, instead of celebrating a polyphony of voices from the past, the regime embraces just one, Confucianism, in order to further an agreed narrative – the China story. When Czech reformers in 1968 tried to liberalize the system, they talked of 'socialism with a human face'. When the Chinese government talks of defending the system in the face of a Western liberal challenge, it talks of 'socialism with Chinese characteristics'. The regime, in fact, has no interest in tonal variety in politics or in speaking a 'human language' (*shuo ren hua*), a popular expression in today's China that rejects the party-speak as inhuman. Putin's Russia, meanwhile, finds itself imprisoned in its own private grief, and its message calls attention to emotions that most countries would prefer to keep hidden: shame, resentment, even envy of other people's good fortune. If there is a difference between the two countries it's surely this: that, whereas Putin would still like all Russians to think like him, Xi Jinping would rather have his subjects not think at all but instead buy into the party's understanding of what makes China 'Chinese'.

As I argued in chapter 2, the myths that governments spin shape our thoughts and feelings. They are real enough even if they are not objectively true. And you don't need to buy into fantasies about Chinese 'cultural nativism' or Russian Eurasianism to see why the appeal to civilization tends to diminish the appeal of Western ideas. It is still difficult to assess how far the language and concepts have reshaped popular thinking, but the longer such concepts are invoked, and the more they lodge in the popular consciousness, the more likely that the next generation of politicians will come to find themselves imprisoned by them.

Reshaping the international order

For post-colonial and world-systems theorists, the contemporary global order is the product of a global structure that was shaped by Western imperialism in the nineteenth century. In other words, the modern world is the product of empire and the interactions among the major European players who competed against each other for power and influence. The international order is still managed in a fashion by a declining hegemonic power, the United States, and institutions of global governance such as the World Bank and the IMF. But for how much longer?

'For the first time in many years', we are told by Sergei Lavrov, the Russian foreign minister, 'a real competitive environment has emerged on the market of ideas' between opposing value-systems and development models. The West, he insists, has 'lost its monopoly over the globalization process' (Sherr 2008: 9). The Russians have come to believe that they are engaged in a bleak and existential struggle, writes Edward Lucas, and one that they can win as the West weakens. And one of the reasons for the West's lack of resolve, he adds contentiously, is that it still chooses to see itself as a liberal world civilization interested in the things that *really* matter, such as democracy promotion in the Middle East or the fate of indigenous people around the world, none of which figure highly, if at all, on anyone else's agenda (Lucas 2016).

As for China, Singapore's founder, Lee Kuan Yew (1923–2015), was right to warn the West that it should expect that one day soon it would want to reshape the present world order according to its own interests and values. After all, China is a nation that has already put cosmonauts in space and shot down one of its own satellites with a missile. As a 4,000-year-old culture, with 1.3 billion people, the Chinese can potentially tap into the greatest fund of cultural capital in history. Why should they want to join the West? Why should they not want to make history on terms of their own making (Allison and Blackwell 2013)? Why not indeed?

China's ambitions, however, are difficult to pin down. It is still remarkably reticent about its wider ambitions. Its vision of the future remains frustratingly out of focus, like a Chinese painting, much of whose genius consists of leaving things out. That said, there are some straws in the wind, some suggestions for how the liberal global order might be restructured to reflect the imprint of 'Chinese characteristics' (Zeng and Breslin 2016). And it's not particularly good news for the West, which is seen in Beijing as a distinctive 'democratic civilization' that cynically still uses its own cover story (human rights and international law) to shape the world according to its own interests.

'China is destined to lead, but not ready', is the title of an article posted in September 2016 by Liang Xiaojun, a professor at the China Foreign Affairs University. Unfortunately, that is the first problem. Even if the liberals were to push a more enlightened agenda, the Chinese people, he argues, simply don't have enough interest in the fate of the outside world to want their country to provide the 'public goods' that are on offer from Western countries (Liang 2016). Moreover, even if they *were* interested in the fate of others – if there were frequent public protests by human rights activists against their own government's cynical support for brutal regimes in Africa, this would still presuppose that human rights would be seen as a public good. As Michael Sandel argues, the concept of justice is inescapably judgemental because it rests on unprovable visions of the goals of humanity. We cannot define, let alone defend, the principles of justice without first making assumptions about the meaning of the good life (Sandel 2010: 261). So the eventual outcome might be disappointing. Indeed, in his book *Every Nation for Itself: Winners and Losers in a G-Zero World* (2012), Ian Bremmer imagines a world run by a caucus whose members no longer share the same political or economic values, let alone the same social priorities. Instead of witnessing the birth of a new international order, the world may find itself confronting a profound global governance gap, or what another American author prefers to call 'No one's world', a world in which there will be no cultural centre of gravity (Kupchan 2012: 3).

A second problem is that, if China is a one-party state, it is not monolithic when it comes to the exchange of ideas. Witness the present debate between the extreme nationalists and the New Leftists when they look back to the Song Empire as one of the most deluded or enlightened dynasties in Chinese history. Even today the Song dynasty is generally remembered with affection because of its meritocratic philosophy. The examination system for the civil service was reformed to test a candidate's social awareness as well as textual mastery of the classics. The dynasty also sealed the reunification of the densely populated valleys of the Yangtze and Yellow rivers, and thus gave permanent shape to the China we know today (Fernández-Armesto 1995: 39–40). Nevertheless, the empire eventually collapsed following the Mongol invasions of the thirteenth century, and for the nationalists this is an object lesson of what happens when you put too much emphasis on culture and soft power (Hughes 2011: 610). For them, hard power, not moral leadership, is what counts, and, if they share little in common among themselves other than a suspicion of all things Western, most appear genuinely to believe that the West is pushing a value agenda at the very point that it is about to be eclipsed historically.

Even so, a vision of a new world order is beginning to emerge, based largely on civilizational values. Addressing the United Nations in September 2005, China's President Hu Jintao insisted that the next international order should be one of diverse civilizations, on the understanding that both those that had survived and many that haven't had contributed more than anyone else to human progress (Hurrell 2007: 30). The buzzword now is not only a 'harmonious society' but also a 'harmonious world'. We can catch a glimpse of something more concrete in the writings of Zhao Tingyang and the importance that he attaches to *tianxia*, a concept which is difficult to translate into English but which can be rendered, at a push, as 'the world'. China, he claims, is the first authentic world power with a truly global vision precisely because its approach to world politics has been civilizational, not imperialist. In Chinese eyes, the present world order is inherently zero-sum because it was created by a bunch of European states which were almost permanently at war with each other (Zhao 2006: 30). My own country, Britain, has invaded, attacked or occupied 173 out of the 193 members of the UN (a record that one can safely assume will never be surpassed!). So, if you are reading this book and you happen to hail from Hungary, Bolivia or Belarus, you may consider your ancestors got lucky.

And, whereas when they arrived in Asia the Europeans pursued nakedly power-related goals, the Chinese for centuries demanded only the recognition that theirs was not only a unique civilization but the only one that really made the cut. Remember that the tribute system which functioned for almost 700 years was not essentially coercive (though China was ready to punish countries that tried to escape from it). The point was that it cost the Chinese far more than they received. Every new tributary state drove the Chinese economy even further into the red. What made the Chinese different from the Europeans was that they impressed others by their power to *give* (Boorstin 1983: 192).

China claims to be a uniquely ethical power because it has no notion of the 'other' outside the system. It has never wished to colonize anyone; it has never had a civilizing mission. Critical to the story is the eunuch admiral Zheng He (1371–1433), who is seen as a supreme navigator and explorer. In reality he was a typical imperialist whose junks carried, as well as a crew, entire armies whose only purpose was to subjugate others. Ming China was a classic gunpowder empire which, like every other, bullied neighbouring countries by using new technologies that its neighbours had not yet mastered (French 2017). What killed off the Sinosphere in the mid-nineteenth century was the prosaic fact that the Europeans had better guns and were able to impose a very different normative order on East Asia. Westphalian conceptions of international order are theoretically egalitarian (even if some countries are deemed to be more equal than others); and additionally they are intensely legalistic in character, particularly in the emphasis they place on contractual relationships. And, unfortunately for the Chinese, the Western powers had little time for the hierarchical assumptions upon which the East Asian international order was based. In place of what Andrew Phillips calls the 'paternal moralism characteristic of East Asian diplomacy', Westerners preferred to mediate international relationships through a 'de-personalized, formal, rationalized caucus of international law' (Phillips 2011: 180).

It is that 'order' which the Chinese are now challenging in the South China Sea. The Hague Tribunal which considered and rejected its insistence on its 'historical rights' in the South China Sea explicitly objected to the fact that it claimed rights 'outside the Convention'. Is this going to be true of other international understandings that China has signed? Indeed, some American commentators are beginning to suspect that what the regime is really after is ontological primacy (Zhang 2016: 801). The word ontology, remember, comes from the Greek: it means all things we take for granted, including our place in the world. The idea in this case is to move China back to the centre, to return to the future, to the days when it saw itself and was seen by others as the acme of civilization itself by countries such as Vietnam. When the French arrived in Indochina in the nineteenth century, success in the civil service exams still required a knowledge of Confucianism and a facility in writing with Chinese characters. In this regard, Chinese hegemony was always more cultural than political or economic; when envoys bowed before the emperor they were acknowledging his cultural superiority, not his political authority (Kang 2010: 99). Perhaps twenty-first-century China will be willing to settle for something similar. Like Russia, it seems to want 'special civilizational rights', either in the absence of an agreed rewrite of the rules or as a way of challenging them.

Is anyone else giving voice to a conception of what a new world order might look like? India seems to be torn between three competing visions: sticking with the liberal international order, as a leading liberal democracy itself; embracing the BRICS (Brazil, Russia, India, China and South Africa), an eclectic club of coming powers which have almost nothing in common other than the fact that they are 'rising'; or falling back on a very Indian concept – a *Dharma Rajya*, a world that is finally at peace with itself. Whatever path it eventually chooses it is likely to strike a different posture from China; true to its own traditions, it is likely to show not only a tolerance for intercivilizational dialogue but also a genuine respect for it.

As democracy seemed to be in retreat after 9/11, so some Westerners, prominently Senator John McCain in the United States, floated the idea of a League of Democracies. It is illuminating that it had much more appeal to American Democrats than to Republicans. Indeed, it had been suggested first by such liberal internationalists as Madeleine Albright, the former US secretary of state, before being taken up by academics such as Ivo Daalder, a senior adviser to Barack Obama, and Anne-Marie Slaughter, who also worked in the Obama administration (Kagan 2008). And it's not difficult to see why the idea had traction, or at least appeared to do so in the corridors of power in Washington. What could be more alluring than inviting India to join the club, not only as the largest democracy in the world but also as the oldest in Asia, and, what's more, an English-speaking democracy to boot?

For the moment, at least most Indian politicians continue to remain sceptical; if this really is the Asian Century, why should they want to take part in a belated Western fightback against the coming changing of the guard? Instead some Indian pundits have begun arguing for a fairer international order. The call is not for 'unity in diversity' so much as 'mutual cooperation' – a true harmony of interests between civilizations, one that is more ecologically friendly in reflecting the balance of nature. If all this sounds vague, that's because it is; for that reason it is unlikely to appeal to the realists, Democrat or Republican, in the 'Washington Beltway'. But you'll find the basic arguments outlined in the book *Integral Humanism* (1965) by Deendayal Upadhyaya (1916–1968), which soon became the political platform of the Bharatiya Jana Sangh (BJS), the forerunner of today's BJP. So far the idea would appear to have fallen by the wayside; you won't find it promoted by many of the country's leading politicians. For the moment, given their own increasing concerns about China's rise, they seem to be sticking with the present world order.

What appears to be emerging is a world of two different blocs or two different orders – a US-centric and a Sino-centric system – with Russia ready to do deals with whoever shows it greater respect. But, then again, as Henry Kissinger warned in his book *World Order*, competing regional visions (and especially civilizational ones) can easily collide, and such a struggle might be far more dangerous than the struggle between states (Kissinger 2014: 371).

Russia as eternal spoiler?

In 2015 a senior European official told a *New York Times* columnist, Roger Cohen, that Russia was a 'loser's challenge' to the West because it had given up on globalization and modernization at the same time. China was a 'winner's challenge' because it was embarking on both with a vengeance (Cohen 2015). Whereas China's policy is perceived to be driven by strength, Russia's is perceived to be driven by weakness. One is experiencing an economic uplift unique in history; the other appears to be in terminal decline. The result would appear to be that Russia has resolved to be selectively obstructive and disruptive, both to frustrate the West and to give it leverage with countries such as China. Breaking the international rules without being punished for doing so seems to be Putin's peculiar definition of being a Great Power.

Is Russia really interested in reframing the world order? Strong militarily, but weak in most other respects, is the role of spoiler its only realistic option? The West tends to hold Russia responsible for much of what is going wrong in the world, from the destabilization of Ukraine to the war in Syria. For its part, Russia is equally suspicious of the West and its ambitions, both stated and unstated. After all, it holds it responsible for much of the disorder across the world, for the 'colour revolutions' in Ukraine and Georgia; the Russians have even coined a new term, 'Maidanarchy' (a reference to the large-scale demonstrations in 2014 in Maidan Square in Kiev which led to the ousting of Ukraine's pro-Russian president). Russian politicians often refer to an 'arc of crisis' in the same way that back in 1979 many experts in the US talked of 'an arc of instability' stretching from North Africa to Afghanistan. But, whereas the US attributed the latter to the rise of Islamic fundamentalism, those close to Putin attribute the former to democratic fundamentalism – the West's apparent determination to export its own values come what may (Goble 2014). For Putin and his friends, the world is simply not amenable to the application of the universal standards and values that Western countries are still in the business of promoting. Instead, they see their immediate geopolitical space as one that is divided into three cultural zones: *Russkiy Mir*, a Russian world which has been historically determined not by the principle of national self-determination but by 'blood' – the blood shed over the centuries by the Russian people; the historical West, a world west of the Neisse River, together with the countries of Scandinavia; and 'a grey zone' in between (Putin 2001). It is the 'political West' (not the historical West, whose existence Russia accepts) that has intervened in the 'grey zone' and even in part of *Russkiy Mir*, pushing its own value agenda and producing in the process a new 'civilizational schism' in Europe (Shevtsova 2010: 101).

So, do the Russians entertain any constructive vision of an alternative world order? Does Putin want to return to the world of the Yalta Conference, when the allies carved out separate 'spheres of influence'? Does he want to reset European security back to 1944? Or, instead of re-establishing an Iron Curtain separating two ideological blocs, does Russia want a 'zone of privileged civilizational interest' (Sutyagin 2016: 88)? Remember that its privileged interests extend well beyond the Russian Federation. The Russian view is perfectly clear on this point. It adheres to international law for one reason only: to defend Russian interests and not the values of a fictional 'international community', or an even more fictitious 'global civil society' (Staib 2016: 211). An early example of this was the attempt in

2002–3 to get its interpretation of law into a UN resolution on peacekeeping. The reasoning was pretty transparent: whenever the UN proposed to send a peacekeeping force into a country, it would have to seek the approval of neighbouring states. In other words, Russia would have been able to have vetoed any intervention in its neighbouring region, the so-called Near Abroad.

Putin would like to change the international order if he could, but he is not powerful enough to do so. Accordingly he has been forced back on a compromise: to return to the future, to the nineteenth-century concert of powers. And, in the absence of either economic or diplomatic clout, he has been forced to rethink war. Hybrid warfare, claims Fyodor Lukyanov, is merely an attempt by classical realists such as Putin to find a way to deal with the complexities of a world where the notion of 'power' has become much more fluid and its use likely to produce non-linear effects. Every act of Russian 'aggression' as the West understands it, from the military intervention in Georgia in 2008 to the hybrid operations in Ukraine six years later, should be seen not so much as acts of aggression as the expression of a wish to return to the viability of national sovereignty. After the Cold War the West tried to redefine sovereignty in ways that allowed it to intervene in the internal affairs of other countries, usually in the name of human rights and the right to protect citizens from their own governments. Today Russia finds itself in a much better position to defend the old rules. Whatever interpretation we prefer, writes Lukyanov, 'the era of restoration is over; it is time to start building a new world' (Lukyanov 2017: 20).

But how civilized are we?

Which brings me back to my point of departure and the question I raised in the preface. Do you give much thought to civilization? It is possible that, wherever you hail from, you may well think that your civilization is superior to every other because – in a word – it's more 'civilized'. The adjective is more generally used than the noun. It's almost never used to qualify the noun – it would be odd, wouldn't it, to talk of a 'civilized' civilization: wouldn't that be an exercise in tautology? Except that it really wouldn't. How civilized are the world's great civilizations?

We all seem to have screened out some of the elements that we once thought central to a civilized life, and that most depressingly includes the concept of 'humanity', a term we invented to denote not only a particular species but also the qualities that it was deemed to embody. Cast your eye around the world and you'll soon see how inhumane it still is. In an article in *Le Monde* in April 2011, the former French prime minister Michel Rocard (1930–2016) warned that what we are witnessing is the impending 'dehumanization of the species'. The striking inequality, he concluded, between those who have and those who have not would have made 'the inventors of the modern project blush for shame'. In the early nineteenth century only 20 per cent of global inequality owed anything to the difference in a country's geographical position. There was no place on earth where the standard of living in the richest part of the world was more than twice as high as in the poorest. Today the richest country, Qatar, boasts an income per head 428 times higher than the poorest, Zimbabwe (Bauman 2013). And if you consider 'the bottom 1 billion', as Paul Collier calls them, the world's poorest people, who find themselves living in the fourteenth century while coexisting with the twenty-first, we might also ask whether there has been any progress at all. Some writers, seeing no chance of improvement, have come to conclude that the only possible meaning of 'Progress' has become the avoidance of regression.

And then of course there is climate change, a threat to all of us, as climate refugees and rising seas and increasing heatwaves undermine 'civilized rights'. Is it possible, asks Amitav Ghosh (2016), that the things we take to be the acme of civilization – the arts and literature of this age – will be remembered one day only for their complicity in what he calls 'the great derangement'? Is our cultural self-regard (or what he calls our obsession with the 'individual moral adventure') so predominant that we will continue to shut our eyes to what we are colluding in: the trashing of the planet? Is it because we think of civilization as uniquely human (remember the termites?) that we have arrogated for ourselves the right to dispose of the planet and its other species as we see fit. We may have accepted that the sun no longer revolves round the earth or that we are above the animal kingdom, but we still think we are cosmologically unique, that, in the words of Carl Sagan (1934–1996), we are 'the universe's way of knowing itself'.

To sum up: we are still far from being as civilized as we like to think. In fact, even a rudimentary study of history suggests that a huge gap has always existed between civilization and its pretensions to civility. The great material achievements of the former are only part of the reality. The cruelties contrast markedly with the achievements – so how best to bring the paradox into focus? Only if we are willing to go back to our historical experience and confront it honestly. What, then, will we discover? We will find that the depressing features of history – its constant wars and dynastic struggles and the relentless exploitation of human beings – have remained much the same across time and across culture. All that has changed over time has been our attitudes to them – the emphasis we have placed on them, the attention we have paid them, the priority we have given them, and the importance and meaning we have attached to them (Midgley 2002: 16) – none of which is reason to embrace the post-modern belief that civilization is a myth.

James Clifford, a famous historian of ideas, once wrote of culture that it was a deeply compromised concept that we still couldn't do without (Clifford 1988: 10). The same is also true, I would suggest, of civilization, a concept that is no less compromised and equally contested. But the idea even more than the reality is still, I would suggest, indispensable if we aspire to become more civilized. Indeed, the idea may be the most important object of study.

References and Bibliography

Abe, Shinzo (2007) 'Japan and NATO: toward further collaboration', Statement to the North Atlantic Council, 12 January, www.nato.int/docu/speech/2007/s070112b.html.

Adamovsky, Ezequiel (2006) *Euro-Orientalism: Liberal Ideology and the Image of Russia in France (c.1740–1880)*. Bern: Peter Lang.

Adams, Douglas (1980) *The Restaurant at the End of the Universe*. Bath: Chivers Audio Books.

Al-Khalili, Jim (2010) *The Pathfinders*. Harmondsworth: Penguin,

Allison, Graham, and Blackwell, Robert (2013) 'Interview: Lee Kuan Yew on the future of U.S.–China relations', *The Atlantic*, 5 March, www.theatlantic.com/china/archive/2013/03/interview-lee-kuan-yew-on-the-future-of-us-china-relations/273657/.

Allison, Graham, and Simes, Dimitri K. (2015) 'Russia and America: stumbling to war', *The National Interest*, 20 April, http://nationalinterest.org/feature/russia-america-stumbling-war-12662.

Almond, Mark (1994) *Europe's Backyard War: The War in the Balkans*. London: Mandarin.

Ankersmit, Frank (2002) 'Representational democracy: an aesthetic approach to conflict and compromise', *Common Knowledge*, 8(1): 24–46.

Appiah, Kwame Anthony (2010) *The Honour Code: How Moral Revolutions Happen*. New York: W. W. Norton.

Appiah, Kwame Anthony (2016) 'There is no such thing as Western civilization', *The Guardian*, 9 November, www.theguardian.com/world/2016/nov/09/western-civilisation-appiah-reith-lecture.

Arnason, Johann P. (2006) 'Understanding intercivilizational encounters', *Thesis Eleven*, 86(1): 39–53.

Asad, Talal (1993) *Genealogies of Religion: Discipline and Reasons of Power in Christianity and Islam.* Baltimore: Johns Hopkins University Press.

Aslan, Reza (2010) *How to Win a Cosmic War: Confronting Radical Religion.* London: Arrow Books.

Balabar, Étienne (2004) *We, the People of Europe? Reflections on Transnational Citizenship.* Princeton, NJ: Princeton University Press.

Balcer, Adam, Buras, Piotr, Gromadzki, Grzegorz, and Smolar, Eugeniusz (2016) *Change in Poland, but What Change? Assumptions of Law and Justice Party Foreign Policy.* Warsaw: Stefan Batory Foundation.

Ball, Philip (2016) *The Water Kingdom: A Secret History of China.* London: Bodley Head.

Balladur, Edouard (2008) 'For a union of the West', *Freedom & Union*, 3(1): 5–11.

Banks, Iain (1996) *Excession.* London: Orbit.

Bannerman, Patrick (1988) *Islam in Perspective: A Guide to Islamic Society, Politics and Law.* London: Routledge.

Bark, Dennis L. (2007) *Americans and Europeans Dancing in the Dark.* Stanford, CA: Hoover Institution Press.

Barras, Colin (2015) 'Chimpanzees and monkeys have entered the Stone Age', *BBC Earth*, 18 August, www.bbc.com/earth/story/2015 0818-chimps-living-in-the-stone-age.

Barth, John (1960) *The Sot-Weed Factor.* New York: Doubleday.

Bauman, Zygmunt (1997) *Postmodernity and its Discontents.* Cambridge: Polity.

Bauman, Zygmunt (2002) *Society under Siege.* Cambridge: Polity.

Bauman, Zygmunt (2004a) *Europe: An Unfinished Adventure.* Cambridge: Polity.

Bauman, Zygmunt (2004b) *Identity: Conversations with Benedetto Vecci.* Cambridge: Polity.

Bauman, Zygmunt (2007) *Consuming Life.* Cambridge: Polity.

Bauman, Zygmunt (2013) 'Does the richness of the few benefit us all?', *Social Europe*, 28 January, www.socialeurope.eu/2013/01/does-the-rich ness-of-the-few-benefit-us-all/ .

Bayly, C. A. (2011) *Recovering Liberties: Indian Thought in the Age of Liberalism and Empire*. Cambridge: Cambridge University Press.

BBC News (2014) 'Britain is a post-Christian country says former archbishop', 27 April, www.bbc.com/news/uk-politics-27177265.

Beck, Ulrich (2000) *What is Globalization?* Cambridge: Polity.

Beinhart, Peter (2006) *The Good Fight: Why Liberals, and Only Liberals, Can Win the War on Terror*. New York: HarperCollins.

Bell, Daniel (2000) *The End of Ideology*. Cambridge, MA: Harvard University Press.

Bell, Daniel (2007) *China's New Confucianism: Politics and Everyday Life in a Changing Society*. Princeton, NJ: Princeton University Press.

Bellos, David (2011) *Is That a Fish in Your Ear? Translation and the Meaning of Everything*. Harmondsworth: Penguin.

Bellow, Saul (2015) *There Is Simply Too Much to Think About: Collected Nonfiction*. New York: Penguin.

Berman, Marshall (1982) *All That Is Solid Melts into Air: The Experience of Modernity*. London: Verso.

Bettelheim, Bruno (1982) *Freud and Man's Soul: An Important Re-Interpretation of Freudian Theory*. New York: Vintage.

Betzig, Laura (2015) 'Culture', in John Brockman (ed.), *This Idea Must Die: Scientific Theories that are Blocking Progress*. New York: Harper Perennial, pp. 429–31.

Billington, Michael (2015) *101 Greatest Plays: From Antiquity to the Present*. London: Faber & Faber

Bissell, Tom (2016) *Apostle: Travels among the Tombs of the Twelve*. London: Faber & Faber.

Blomberg, Catharina (1994) *The Heart of the Warrior: Origins and Religious Background of the Samurai System in Feudal Japan*. Richmond, Surrey: Curzon Press.

Bloom, Harold (1991) *Ruin the Sacred Truths: Poetry and Belief from the Bible to the Present*. Cambridge, MA: Harvard University Press.

Bloom, Harold (2000) *How to Read and Why*. New York: Touchstone Books.

Blue, Gregory (2001) 'Xu Guangqi in the West: early Jesuit sources and the construction of an identity', in Catherine Jami, Peter Engelfriet and Gregory Blue (eds), *Statecraft and Intellectual Renewal in Late Ming China: The Cross-Cultural Synthesis of Xu Guangqi (1562–1633)*. Leiden: Brill, pp. 42–3.

Bogdanor, Vernon (2016) 'Europe's peace dividend', *The World Today*, June/July: 40–1.

Boli, John, and Thomas, George M. (eds) (1999) *Constructing World Culture: International Nongovernmental Organizations since 1875*. Stanford, CA: Stanford University Press.

Bonnett, Alastair (2004) *The Idea of the West: Culture, Politics and History*. New York: Palgrave Macmillan.

Boorstin, Daniel J. (1983) *The Discoverers*. New York: Random House.

Borges, Jorge Luis (1973) *Other Inquisitions 1937–1952*, trans. Ruth L. C. Simms. London: Souvenir Press.

Bosworth, A. B. (1996) 'The historical setting of Megasthenes' Indica', *Classical Philology*, 91(2): 113–27.

Braudel, Fernand (1994) *A History of Civilizations*. London: Allen Lane.

Bremmer, Ian (2012) *Every Nation for Itself: Winners and Losers in a G-Zero World*. London: Penguin.

Bridenthal, Renate, and Koonz, Claudia (1977) *Becoming Visible: Women in European History*. Boston: Houghton Mifflin.

Brown, Peter (2016) 'The glow of Byzantium', *New York Review of Books*, 14 July, p. 117.

Bryson, Bill (2015) *Mother Tongue: English and How it Got That Way*. New York: HarperCollins.

Brzezinski, Zbigniew (1983) *Power and Principle: Memoirs of the National Security Adviser 1977–1981*. London: Weidenfeld & Nicolson.

Bull, Hedley (2012) *The Anarchical Society: A Study of Order in World Politics*. London: Macmillan.

Buras, Piotr (2015) 'Driving Poland apart', *New York Times*, 22 December.

Burk, Kathleen (2002) *Troublemaker: The Life and History of A. J. P. Taylor*. New Haven, CT: Yale University Press.

Burkert, Walter (1992) *The Orientalizing Revolution: Near Eastern Influence on Greek Culture in the Early Archaic Age*. Cambridge, MA: Harvard University Press.

Burleigh, Michael (2010) *Moral Combat: A History of World War II*. London: HarperPress.

Buruma, Ian (2014) *Theater of Cruelty: Art, Film, and the Shadow of War*. New York: New York Review of Books.

Buruma, Ian, and Margalit, Avishai (2004) *Occidentalism: A Short History of Anti-Westernism*. New York: Atlantic Books.

Cadier, David, and Light, Margot (eds) (2015) *Russia's Foreign Policy: Ideas, Domestic Politics and External Relations*. London: Palgrave Macmillan.

Calasso, Robert (2014) *Ardour*. Harmondsworth: Penguin.

Callahan, William A. (2004) 'Remembering the future – utopia, empire, and harmony in 21st-century international theory', *European Journal of International Relations*, 10(4): 569–601.

Callahan, William A. (2008) 'Chinese visions of world order: post-hegemonic or a new hegemony?', *International Studies Review*, 10(4): 749–61.

Callahan, William A. (2012) 'Sino-speak: Chinese exceptionalism and the politics of history', *Journal of Asian Studies*, 71(1): 33–55.

Callahan, William A. (2016) 'China's "Asia Dream": the Belt Road Initiative and new regional order', *Asian Journal of Comparative Politics*, 1(3): 226–43.

Caplin, Justin (1975) *Lincoln Steffens: A Biography*. London: Jonathan Cape.

Carey, John (2005) *What Good are the Arts?* London: Faber & Faber.

Carter, Jimmy (1982) *Keeping Faith: Memoirs of a President*. New York: Bantam Books.

Casey, John (2014) *Beyond the First Draft: The Art of Fiction*. New York: W. W. Norton.

Castro, Jorge, and Lafuente, Enrique (2007) 'Westernalization in the mirror: on the cultural reception of Western psychology', *Integrative Psychological and Behavioural Science*, 41(1): 106–13.

Chakrabarty, D. (2007) *Provincializing Europe: Post-Colonial Thought and Historical Difference*. Princeton, NJ: Princeton University Press.

Choueiri, Youssef M. (1990) *Islamic Fundamentalism*. London: Pinter.

Clifford, James (1988) *The Predicament of Culture: Twentieth-Century Ethnography, Literature, and Art*. Cambridge, MA: Harvard University Press.

Coalson, Robert (2014) 'Is Putin "rebuilding Russia" according to Solzhenitsyn's design?', 1 September, www.rferl.org/a/russia-putin-solzhenitsyns-1990-essay/26561244.html.

Cochran, Gregory, and Harpending, Henry (2009) *The 10,000 Year Explosion: How Civilization Accelerated Human Evolution*. New York: Basic Books.

Cohen, Roger (2015) 'Counterrevolutionary Russia', *New York Times*, 25 June, p. 7.

Conrad, Peter (1998) *Modern Times, Modern Places*. London: Thames & Hudson.

Conrad, Peter (2016) *Mythomania: Tales of our Times, from Apple to ISIS*. London, Thames & Hudson.

Cook, Michael (2003) *A Brief History of the Human Race*. London: Granta.

Cook, Michael (2014) *Ancient Religions, Modern Politics: The Islamic Case in Comparative Perspective*. Princeton, NJ: Princeton University Press.

Coonan, Clifford (2008) 'Jiang Rong's "Wolf Totem": the year of the wolf', 7 January, www.independent.co.uk/arts-entertainment/books/features/jiang-rongs-wolf-totem-the-year-of-the-wolf-768583.html.

CORAB (Commission on Religion and Belief in British Public Life) (2015) *Living with Difference: Community, Diversity and the Common Good*. Cambridge: Woolf Institute.

Cox, Robert W. (2000) 'Thinking about civilizations', *Review of International Studies*, 26(5): 217–34.

Craig, Gordon A. (1996) 'The Mann nobody knew', *New York Review of Books*, 29 February, p. 38, www.nybooks.com/article/1996/02/29/the-mann-nobody-knew/.

Crawford, James (2015) *Fallen Glory: The Lives and Deaths of 20 Lost Buildings, from the Tower of Babel to the Twin Towers*. London: Old Street.

Critchley, Simon (2012) *The Faith of the Faithless: Experiments in Political Theology*. London: Verso.

Curtis, Henry (2016) 'Constructing cooperation: Chinese ontological security seeking in the South China Sea dispute', *Journal of Borderlands Studies*, 31(4): 537–49.

Damasio, Antonio (2004) *Looking for Spinoza*. London: Vintage.

D'Angour, Armand (2011) *The Greeks and the New: Novelty in the Greek Imagination and Experience*. Cambridge: Cambridge University Press.

Darczewska, Jolanta, and Żochowski, Piotr (2015) *Russophobia and the Kremlin's Strategy: A Weapon of Mass Destruction*, Point of View no. 56, Warsaw: Centre for Eastern Studies.

Davison-Hunter, James (1991) *Culture Wars: The Struggle to Define America*. New York: Basic Books.

de Bellaigue, Christopher (2017) *The Islamic Enlightenment: The Modern Struggle between Faith and Reason*. London: Bodley Head.

Debashi, Hamid (2015) *Can Non-Europeans Think?* London: Zed Books.

DeLillo, Don (2016) *Zero K*. New York: Charles Scribner's Sons.

Dennett, Daniel (2017) *From Bacteria to Bach and Back: The Evolution of Minds*. London: Allen Lane.

Derbyshire, Jonathan (2017) 'The voices of France's jihadist foot-soldiers', *Financial Times*, 5 February.

Derrida, Jacques (1992) *The Other Heading: Reflections on Today's Europe*. Bloomington: University of Indiana Press.

Desmond, William, and Grange, Joseph (eds) (2000) *Being and Dialectic: Metaphysics as a Cultural Presence*. Albany: State University of New York Press.

Devji, Faisal (2005) *Landscapes of the Jihad: Militancy, Morality, Modernity*. London: Hurst.

Dhal, Ann-Sofie (2016) *A Continent in Chaos: The Security Implications of the European Migration Crisis*. College Station, TX: Scowcroft Institute of International Affairs.

Dick, Philip K. ([1978] 1995) 'How to build a universe that doesn't fall apart two days later', in *The Shifting Realities of Philip K. Dick: Selected Literary and Philosophical Writings*. New York, Vintage, pp. 259–80.

Dobson, Miriam (2017) 'What did Khruschev say?', *London Review of Books*, 2 November.

Doctorow, E. L. (2007) *Creationists: Selected Essays 1993–2006*. New York: Random House.

Doerries, Bryan (2016) *The Theatre of War: What Ancient Greek Tragedies Can Teach Us Today*. New York: Vintage.

Dugin, Alexander (2014) 'Civilization as a political concept', interview, www.4pt.su/en/content/civilization-political-concept.

Dumont, Louis (1991) *German Ideology: From France to Germany and Back*. Chicago: University of Chicago Press.

Dusenbury, D. L. (2016) 'Beware of Greeks,' *Times Literary Supplement*, 2 December.

Eagleton, Terry (2016) *Hope without Optimism*. New Haven, CT: Yale University Press.

Eakin, Hugh (2016) 'Ancient Syrian sites: a different story of destruction', *New York Review of Books*, 29 September.

Eco, Umberto (2007) *Turning Back the Clock: Hot Wars and Media Populism*. New York: Harvill Secker.

The Economist Intelligence Unit (2017) *Democracy Index: Free Speech under Attack*, www.eiu.com/public/topical_report.aspx?campaignid=Democracy Index2017.

Eltsov, Peter (2015) 'What Putin's favorite guru tells us about his next target', *Politico*, 10 February, www.politico.com/magazine/story/2015/02/vladimir-putin-guru-solzhenitsyn-115088.

Emmott, Bill (2017) *The Fate of the West: The Battle to Save the World's Most Successful Political Idea*. London: The Economist.

Engelke, Matthew (2017) *Think Like an Anthropologist*. Harmondsworth: Penguin.

Esposito, John L. (1992) *The Islamic Threat: Myth or Reality?* Oxford: Oxford University Press.

Etulain, Richard W. (ed.) (1991) *Writing Western History: Essays on Western Major Historians*. Albuquerque: University of New Mexico Press.

Etzioni, Amitai (2016) 'Making a US–Sino war "thinkable?"', *The Diplomat*, 22 September, http://thediplomat.com/2016/09/making-a-us-sino-war-thinkable.

Feeney, Dennis (2016) *Beyond Greek: The Beginnings of Latin Literature*. Cambridge, MA: Harvard University Press.

Fenby, Jonathan (2014) *Will China Dominate the 21st Century?* Cambridge: Polity.

Ferdinand, Peter (2016) 'Westward ho – the China dream and "one belt, one road": Chinese foreign policy under Xi Jinping', *International Affairs*, 92(4): 941–57.

Ferguson, Niall (ed.) (1997) *Virtual History: Alternatives and Counterfactuals*. London: Picador.

Ferguson, Niall (2011) *Civilization: The West and the Rest*. Harmondsworth: Penguin.

Ferguson, Niall (2016) 'Donald Trump's new world order', *The American Interest*, 21 November, https://the-american-interest.com/2016/11/21/donald-trumps-new- world-order/.

Fernández-Armesto, Felipe (1995) *Millennium: A History of our Last Thousand Years*. London, Bantam Press.

Fernández-Armesto, Felipe (2000) *Civilizations: Culture, Ambition, and the Transformation of Nature*. London: Macmillan.

Fernández-Armesto, Felipe (2011) *The World: A History*. Boston: Prentice Hall.

Finnemore, Martha, and Sikkink, Kathryn (1998) 'International norm dynamics and political change', *International Organization*, 52(4): 887–917.

Fletcher, Richard (2003) *The Cross and the Crescent: Christianity and Islam from the Prophet Muhammed to the Reformation*. London: Allen Lane.

Ford, Christopher A. (2012) 'A state of moral Confucian', *New Paradigms Forum*, 13 July, www.newparadigmsforum.com/NPFtestsite/?p=1360.

Frankopan, Peter (2015) *The Silk Roads: A New History of the World*. London: Bloomsbury.

French, Howard (2017) *Everything under the Heavens: How the Past Helps Shape China's Push for Power*. New York: Alfred Knopf.

Freud, Sigmund ([1936] 1985) *Civilization and its Discontents*, trans. James Strachey. Harmondsworth: Penguin.

Friedman, Thomas L. (2016) *Thank You for Being Late: An Optimist's Guide to Thriving in the Age of Accelerations*. London: Allen Lane.

Fritzman, J. M. (2014) *Hegel*. Cambridge: Polity.

Fukuyama, Francis (1989) 'The end of history', *The National Interest*, summer.

Fukuyama, Francis (2002) 'The West may be cracking up', *International Herald Tribune*, 8 September.

Gao, Xingjiang (2007) 'The case for literature', in *Nobel Lectures: From the Literature Laureates. 1986–2006*, New York: New Press.

Gardner, Lloyd (1982) *A Covenant with Power: America and World Order from Wilson to Reagan*. Oxford: Oxford University Press.

Garton Ash, Timothy (1994) *In Europe's Name: Germany and the Divided Continent*. New York: Vintage.

Gekoski, Rick (2013) *Lost, Stolen or Shredded: Stories of Missing Works of Art and Literature*. London: Profile Books.

Gelber, Harry (2016) *Battle for Beijing, 1858–1860: Franco-British conflict in China*. London, Palgrave Macmillan.

Gel'man, Vladimir (2015) *Authoritarian Russia: Analyzing Post-Soviet Regime Changes*. Pittsburgh: University of Pittsburgh Press.

Gerges, Fawaz A. (2011) *The Rise and Fall of Al-Qaeda*. Oxford: Oxford University Press.

Gerges, Fawaz A. (2016) *ISIS: A History*. Princeton, NJ: Princeton University Press.

Gessen, Masha (2017) *The Future is History: How Totalitarianism Reclaimed Russia*. London: Granta.

Ghosh, Amitav (2016) *The Great Derangement: Climate Change and the Unthinkable*. Chicago: University of Chicago Press.

Gibson, William (2004) *Pattern Recognition*. Harmondsworth: Penguin.

Giegerich, Bastian, and Terhalle, Maximilian (2016) 'The Munich consensus and the purpose of German power', *Survival*, 58(2): 155–66.

Goble, Paul (2014) 'Putin has re-awakened Russian Messianism, Pastukhov says', *The Interpreter*, 26 March, www.interpretermag.com/putin-has-re-awakened-russian-messianism-pastukhov-says/.

GoGwilt, Christopher Lloyd (1995) *The Invention of the West: Joseph Conrad and the Double-Mapping of Europe and Empire*. Stanford, CA: Stanford University Press.

Goldsworthy, Adrian (2009) *The Fall of the West: The Slow Death of the Roman Superpower*. London: Weidenfeld & Nicolson.

Goldsworthy, Vesna (2015) *Gorsky: A Novel*. London: Overlook Press.

Goody, Jack (1995) *The Domestication of the Savage Mind*. Cambridge: Cambridge University Press.

Goody, Jack (1996) *The East in the West*. Cambridge: Cambridge University Press.

Gotschall, Jonathan (2012) *The Storytelling Animal: How Stories Make us Human*. New York: Houghton Mifflin.

Graham, Gordon (1997) *The Shape of the Past: A Philosophical Approach to History*. Oxford: Oxford University Press.

Grant, Charles (2008) *Can Europe and China Shape a New World Order?* London: Centre for European Reform.

Gratchev, Andrei (1995) *Final Days: The Inside Story of the Collapse of the Soviet Union*. Boulder, CO: Westview Press.

Gray, John (2007) *Black Mass: Apocalyptic Religion and the Death of Utopia*. Harmondsworth: Penguin.

Gray, John (2010) 'Philosophy for the all-too-common man', *The National Interest*, no. 107.

Gray, John (2011) 'The triumphalist', *New Republic*, 9 November.

Greenfeld, Liah (1990) 'The formation of the Russian national identity: the role of status insecurity and ressentiment', *Comparative Studies in Society and History*, 32(3): 549–91.

Guizot, François ([1846] 1997) *The History of Civilization in Europe*, trans. William Hazlitt. Harmondsworth: Penguin.

Habermas, Jürgen (2006) *The Divided West*. Cambridge: Polity.

Haig, David (2016) 'Genomic imprinting', in John Brockman (ed.), *Life: The Leading Edge of Evolutionary Biology, Genetics, Anthropology, and Environmental Science*. New York: Harper Perennial.

Hall, David (2000) 'On looking up "dialectics" in a Chinese dictionary', in William Desmond, and Joseph Grange (eds), *Being and Dialectic: Metaphysics as a Cultural Presence*. Albany: State University of New York Press, pp. 197–212.

Hall, David L., and Ames, Roger T. (1999) *The Democracy of the Dead: Dewey, Confucius and the Hope for Democracy in China*. Chicago: Open Court.

Hall, Edith (2014) *Introducing the Ancient Greeks: From Bronze Age Seafarers to Navigators of the Western Mind*. New York: W. W. Norton.

Hall, Robert King (ed.) (1949) *Kokutai no Hongi: The Cardinal Principles of the National Entity of Japan* (1949), trans. John Owen Gauntlett. Cambridge, MA: Harvard University Press.

Hall, Stuart (1987) 'Minimal selves', in Lisa Appignenesi (ed.), *Identity – the Real Me: Postmodernism and the Question of Identity*. London: Institute of Contemporary Arts.

Hamid, Mohsin (2008), *The Reluctant Fundamentalist*. Harmondsworth: Penguin.

Hamid, Mohsin (2015) *Discontent and its Civilizations: Dispatches from Lahore, New York, and London*. Harmondsworth: Penguin.

Handelman, Stephen (1997) *Comrade Criminal: Russia's New Mafia*. New Haven, CT: Yale University Press.

Hanson, Victor Davis (2002) 'Socrates dies at Delium, 424 BC', in Robert Cowley (ed.), *More What If? Eminent Historians Imagine What Might Have Been*. London: Macmillan, pp. 1–23.

Hanson, Victor Davis (2010) *The Father of Us All: War and History, Ancient and Modern*. London: Bloomsbury.

Harari, Yuval N. (2014) *Sapiens: A Brief History of Mankind*. London: Harvill Secker.

Harari, Yuval N. (2016) *Homo Deus: A Brief History of Tomorrow*. New York: Penguin Random House.

Harding, Joel (2015) 'Putin's Russia: madness "from Lisbon to Vladivostok"', *Information Resistance*, 8 May, http://sprotyv.info/en/news/putins-russia-madness-lisbon-vladivostok.

Harries, Owen (1993) 'The collapse of "the West"', *Foreign Affairs*, September/October.

Harris, Jonathan (2015) *The Lost World of Byzantium*. New Haven, CT: Yale University Press.

Harris, Myles (2015) 'The Islamic Republic of Poland', *Salisbury Review*, 34(2): 4–6.

Havel, Václav (1994) 'A call for sacrifice', *Foreign Affairs*, 73(2): 2–7.

Havel, Václav (1997) *The Art of the Impossible: Politics as Morality in Practice*. New York: Alfred A. Knopf.

Hayman, Ronald (1995) *Nietzsche: A Critical Life*. London: Phoenix.

Heraclitus (2001) *Fragments*, trans. Brooks Haxton. Harmondsworth: Penguin.

Higgins, Charlotte (2010) 'The Iliad and what it can still tell us about war', *The Guardian*, 30 January.

Himmelfarb, Gertrude (1996) 'The illusions of cosmopolitanism', in Martha Nussbaum, *For Love of Country?*, ed. Joshua Cohen. Boston: Beacon Press, pp. 72–7.

Hobbes, Thomas ([1651] 1960), *Leviathan*, ed. Michael Oakeshott. Oxford: Blackwell.

Hosking, Geoffrey (2001) *Russia and the Russians: A History.* Cambridge, MA: Harvard University Press.

Hrabal, Bohumil (2015) *Mr Kafka and Other Tales.* New York: New Directions.

Huang Yasheng (2014) 'Why democracy still wins: a critique of Eric X. Li's "A Tale of Two Political Systems"', *Global Policy*, 25 April 2014, www.globalpolicyjournal.com/blog/25/04/2014/why-democracy-still-wins-critique-eric-x-li%E2%80%99s-%E2%80%9C-tale-two-political-systems%E2%80%9D.

Hughes, Christopher (2011) 'Reclassifying Chinese nationalism: the *geopolitik* turn', *Journal of Contemporary China*, 20(71): 601–20.

Hulme, T. E. (1994) *The Collected Writings of T. E. Hulme*, ed. Karen Csengeri. Oxford: Clarendon Press.

Huntington, Samuel (1996) *The Clash of Civilizations and the Remaking of World Order.* New York: Simon & Schuster.

Hurrell, Andrew (2007) *On Global Order: Power, Values and the Constitution of International Society.* Oxford: Oxford University Press.

Huxley, Aldous (1994) *Music at Night and Other Essays.* London: HarperCollins.

Ibn Khaldûn (1980) *The Muqaddimah: An Introduction to History*, Vol. 1. Princeton, NJ: Princeton University Press.

Ignatieff, Michael (1994) *Blood & Belonging: Journeys into the New Nationalism.* New York: Farrar, Straus & Giroux.

Ignatieff, Michael (2017) 'Which way are we going?', *New York Review of Books*, 6 April.

'Inside the Bear', special report, Russia (2016), *The Economist*, 22 October.

Ioffe, Julia (2016) 'Russians tighten their belts for a great cause', *Financial Times*, 19 February, p. 11.

Iqbal, Muhammed (1962) *The Reconstruction of Religious Thought in Islam.* Lahore: Muhammad Ashraf.

Irujo, Xabier (2016) *Gernika 1937: The Market Day Massacre.* Reno: University of Nevada Press.

Jacques, Martin (2011), 'Civilization state versus nation-state', *Süddeutsche Zeitung*, 15 January, www.martinjacques.com/articles/ civilization-state-versus-nation-state-2/.

James, Peter, and Thorpe, Nick (1994) *Ancient Inventions.* London: Michael O'Mara.

Jaspers, Will (2016) *Lusitania: The Cultural History of a Catastrophe.* New Haven, CT: Yale University Press.

Jenkins, Alan (2014) 'T. E. Hulme's ways of seeing', *Times Literary Supplement Blog*, 20 November.

Jenkyns, Richard (2016) *Classical Literature: The Epic Journey from Homer to Virgil and Beyond.* New York: Basic Books.

Jiang, Rong (2008) *Wolf Totem*, trans. Howard Goldblatt. Harmondsworth: Penguin

Johnson, Ian (2017) *The Souls of China: The Return of Religion after Mao.* London: Allen Lane.

Johnston, Cameron (2016) 'Russia: history as myth', *European Union Institute for Security Studies*, November, www.iss.europa.eu/sites/ default/files/EUISSFiles/Alert_40_Russia.pdf.

Jullien, François (1995) *The Propensity of Things: Toward a History of Efficacy in China.* New York: Zone Books.

Kadare, Ismail (2001) *The Palace of Dreams.* London: Vintage.

Kagan, Robert (2008) 'The case for a league of democracies', *Financial Times*, 13 May, www.ft.com/content/f62a02ce-20eb-11dd-a0e6-000077b07658.

Kagan, Robert (2014) 'Superpowers don't get to retire', *New Republic*, 26 May, https://newrepublic.com/article/117859/superpowers-dont-get-retire?utm_medium=App.net&utm_source=PourOver.

Kahneman, Daniel (2012) *Thinking, Fast and Slow*. Harmondsworth: Penguin.

Kang, David (2010) 'Civilization and state formation in the shadow of China', in Peter J. Katzenstein (ed.), *Civilizations in World Politics: Plural and Pluralist Perspectives*. London: Routledge.

Kapuściński, Ryszard (1993) *Imperium*. New York: Alfred A. Knopf.

Karsh, Ifraim (2016) 'Holding the balance of power', *Times Literary Supplement*, 24 June.

Katzenstein, Peter J. (2010) '"Walls" between "those people"? Contrasting perspectives on world politics', *Perspectives on Politics*, 8(1): 11–25.

Katzenstein, Peter J. and Weygandt, Nicole (2017) 'Mapping Eurasia in an open world: how the insularity of Russia's geopolitical and civilizational approaches limits its foreign policies', *Perspectives on Politics*, 15(2): 428–42.

Kauffman, Stuart (2008) *Reinventing the Sacred: A New View of Science, Reason and Religion*. New York: Basic Books.

Kaviraj, Sudipta (2016) 'Disenchantment deferred', in Akeel Bilgrami (ed.), *Beyond the Secular West*. New York: Columbia University Press.

Kearney, Richard (ed.) (2016) *Reimagining the Sacred*. New York: Columbia University Press.

Kelly, Joan (1977) 'Did women have a Renaissance?', in Renata Bridenthal and Claudia Koonz (eds), *Becoming Visible: Women in European History*. Boston: Houghton Mifflin.

Kelly, Stuart (2005) *The Book of Lost Books*. Edinburgh: Polygon.

Kim, Key-hiuk (1980) *The Last Phase of the East Asian World Order: Korea, Japan and the Chinese Empire, 1860-1882*, Berkeley: University of California Press.

Kissinger, Henry (2014) *World Order*. New York: Allen Lane.

Kohn, Hans (1950) *The Twentieth Century: A Midway Account of the Western World*. London: Victor Gollancz.

Kohn, Hans (1953) *Pan-Slavism: Its History and Ideology*. Notre Dame, IN: University of Notre Dame Press.

Kołakowski, Leszek (1989) *The Presence of Myth*. Chicago: University of Chicago Press.

Kozelsky, Mara (2014) 'Religion and the crisis in the Ukraine', *International Journal for the Study of the Christian Church*, 14(3): 219–41.

Krauthammer, Charles (1989–90) 'Universal dominion: toward a unipolar world', *The National Interest*, no. 18: 46–9.

Kristeva, Julia (2000) *Crisis of the European Subject*. New York: Other Press.

Kumar, Krishan (2014) 'Civilized values: the return of Arnold Toynbee', *Times Literary Supplement*, 22 October.

Kumar, Krishan (2017) *Visions of Empire: How Five Imperial Regimes Shaped the World*. Princeton, NJ: Princeton University Press.

Kundera, Milan ([1979] 1992) *The Book of Laughter and Forgetting*. London: Faber & Faber.

Kundera, Milan (1984) 'The Tragedy of Central Europe', *New York Review of Books*, 26 April.

Kundera, Milan (2007) *The Curtain: An Essay in Seven Parts*. London: Faber & Faber.

Kupchan, Charles A. (2012) *No One's World: The West, the Rising Rest and the Coming Global Turn*. New York: Oxford University Press.

Laruelle, Marlene (2006) *Aleksandr Dugin: A Russian Version of the European Radical Right?* Washington, DE: Woodrow Wilson International Center for Scholars, Occasional Paper 294.

Lee, Jeffrey (2016) *God's Wolf: The Life of the Most Notorious of All Crusaders, Reynald de Chatillon*. London: Atlantic Books.

Lee, Michael (2012) *Knowing Our Future: The Startling Case for Futurology*. Oxford: Infinite Ideas.

Lévi-Strauss, Claude (1966) *The Savage Mind*. London: Weidenfeld & Nicolson.

Lévi-Strauss, Claude (1969) *The Raw and the Cooked*. London: Jonathan Cape.

Li, Eric (2017) 'China, America and "nationalism"', *American Affairs*, 26 October, http://americanaffairsjournal.org/2017/10/china-america-nationalism.

Liang, Xiaojun (2016) 'China is destined to lead, but not ready', *East Asia Forum*, 13 September, www.eastasiaforum.org/2016/09/13/china-is-destined-to-lead-but-not-ready/.

Lilla, Mark (2016a) *The Shipwrecked Mind: On Political Reaction*. New York: New York Review of Books.

Lilla, Mark (2016b) 'France: is there a way out?', *New York Review of Books*, 10 March.

Lin, Yutang ([1937] 1949) *The Importance of Living*. London: Heinemann.

Linde, Fabian (2016) 'State civilisation: the statist core of Vladimir Putin's civilisational discourse and its implications for Russian foreign policy', *Politics in Central Europe*, 12(1): 21–35.

Lipman, Maria (2015) 'How Russia has come to loathe the West', *European Council on Foreign Relations*, 13 March, www.ecfr.eu/article/commentary_how_russia_has_come_to_loathe_the_west311346.

Litwak, Robert S. (2002) 'The imperial republic after 9/11', *Wilson Quarterly*, 26(3): 76–82.

Lloyd, G. E. R. (2012) *Being, Humanity, and Understanding: Studies in Ancient and Modern Societies*. Oxford: Oxford University Press.

Locke, John (1997) *Political Essays*, ed. Mark Goldie. Cambridge: Cambridge University Press.

Lodge, David (2011) *The Art of Fiction*. London: Vintage.

Lorenzen, David N. (1999) 'Who invented Hinduism?', *Comparative Studies in Society and History*, 41(4): 630–59.

Losurdo, Domenico (2001) *Heidegger and the Ideology of War: Community, Death, and the West*. Amherst, NY: Humanity Books.

Losurdo, Domenico (2015) *War and Revolution: Rethinking the Twentieth Century*. London: Verso.

Lucas, Edward (2016) 'Western weakness is the ace in Putin's hand', *The Times*, 30 August.

Lukacs, John (2005) *Democracy and Populism: Fear and Hatred*. New Haven, CT: Yale University Press.

Lukacs, John (2010) *The Legacy of the Second World War*. New Haven, CT: Yale University Press.

Lukyanov, Fyodor (2017) 'Russia 100 years on: Putin's Viennese waltz', *The World Today*, August/September, www.chathamhouse.org/publications/twt/putin-s-viennese-waltz.

Lunde, Nils (2016) 'Asymmetric ethics: Russian and Western perceptions of war', in Janne Haaland Matláry and Tormod Heier (eds), *Ukraine and Beyond: Russia's Strategic Security Challenge to Europe*. London: Palgrave Macmillan.

Luttwak, Edward N. (2010) *The Grand Strategy of the Byzantine Empire*. Cambridge, MA: Harvard University Press.

MacIntyre, Alasdair (1998) *A Short History of Ethics*. London: Routledge.

Macintyre, Ben (2016) 'Don't be fooled by the lovable new-look Stalin', *The Times*, 16 September.

Mackinnon, Mark (2014) 'Sergey Karaganov: the man behind Putin's pugnacity', *Globe and Mail*, 30 March, www.theglobeandmail.com/news/world/sergey-karaganov-the-man-behind-putins-pugnacity/article17734125/.

MacMillan, Margaret (2013) *The War that Ended Peace: How Europe Abandoned Peace for the First World War*. London: Profile Books.

McNeill, William Hardy (1989) *Arnold J. Toynbee: A Life*. Oxford: Oxford University Press.

Mahbubani, Kishore (1998) *Can Asians Think? Understanding the Divide between East and West*. Hanover, NH: Steerforth Press.

Maher, Shiraz (2016) *Salifi-Jihadism: The History of an Idea*. Oxford: Oxford University Press.

Mansour, Kholoud (2016) 'Let Syria have its voice', *The World Today*, February/March.

Marias, Javier (2006) *Written Lives*. Harmondsworth: Penguin.

Marsh, Christopher (2013) 'Eastern orthodoxy and the fusion of national and spiritual security', in Chris Seiple, Dennis R. Hoover and Pauletta Otis (eds), *The Routledge Handbook of Religion and Security*. Abingdon: Routledge, pp. 22–32.

Maull, Hanns W. (1990) 'Germany and Japan: the new civilian powers', *Foreign Affairs*, 69(5): 91–106.

Mayne, Richard (1983) *Postwar: The Dawn of Today's Europe*. London: Thames & Hudson.

Meineck, Peter, and Konstan, David (eds) (2014) *Combat Trauma and the Ancient Greeks*. New York: Palgrave Macmillan.

Midgley, Mary (1981) *Heart and Mind: The Varieties of Moral Experience*. Brighton: Harvester Press.

Midgley, Mary (2002) *Evolution as a Religion: Strange Hopes and Stranger Fears*. London: Routledge.

Midgley, Mary (2004) *The Myths We Live By*. London: Routledge.

Miller, Christopher (2008) *The French Atlantic Triangle: Literature and the Culture of the Slave Trade*. Durham, NC: Duke University Press.

Mishra, Pankaj (2016) 'Welcome to the age of anger', *The Guardian*, 8 December, www.theguardian.com/politics/2016/dec/08/welcome-age-anger-brexit-trump.

Mishra, Pankaj (2017) *The Age of Anger: A History of the Present*. London: Allen Lane.

Moïsi, Dominique (2003) 'Reinventing the West', *Foreign Affairs*, 82(6): 67–73.

Moretti, Franco (2013) *Distant Readings*. London: Verso.

Móricz, Zsigmond (1995) *Be Faithful unto Death*. London: Central European University

Morozov, Viatcheslav (2010) 'Western hegemony, global democracy and the Russian challenge', in Christopher S. Browning and Marko Lehti (eds), *The Struggle for the West: A Divided and Contested Legacy*. London: Routledge, pp. 185–200.

Morris, Ian, and Scheidel, Walter (2016) 'What is ancient history?', *Daedalus*, 145(2): 113–21.

'Muslim scholar discovered America 500 years before Columbus' (2014) *World Bulletin*, 4 January, www.worldbulletin.net/islamic-history/126 242/muslim-scholar-discovered-america-500-years-before-columbus.

Naipaul, V. S. ([1967] 2012) *The Mimic Men*. London: Picador.

Nanda, Meera (2016) 'Hindutva's science envy', *Frontline*, 16 September, www.frontline.in/science-and-technology/hindutvas-science-envy/article9049883.ece.

Neumann, Iver B. (2016) 'Russia's Europe, 1991–2016: inferiority to superiority', *International Affairs*, 92(6): 1381–99.

Newberg, Andrew (2008) 'Brain science and belief', in Alex Bentley (ed.), *The Edge of Reason? Science and Religion in Modern Society*. London: Bloomsbury, pp. 109–18.

Nietzsche, Friedrich ([1886] 1966) *Beyond Good and Evil*, trans. Walter Kaufman. New York: Random House.

Nussbaum, Martha (2009) *The Clash Within: Democracy, Religious Violence, and India's Future*. Cambridge, MA: Harvard University Press.

Nussbaum, Martha, and Sen, Amartya (1987) *Internal Criticism and Indian Rationalist Traditions*, World Institute for Development Economics Research (UNO), Working Paper 30.

Oakeshott, Michael (2007) 'The voice of poetry in the conversation of mankind', https://mikelove.wordpress.com/2007/01/14/oakeshotts-conversation-of-mankind [excerpt].

O'Rourke, P. J. (2004) *Peace Kills: America's Fun New Imperialism*. London: Picador.

Ortega y Gasset, José (1961) *History as a System, and Other Essays Toward a Philosophy of History*. New York: W. W. Norton.

Orton, Kyle W. (2015) 'ISIS' debt to Saddam Hussein', *International New York Times*, 24 December.

Orwin, Clifford (1994) *The Humanity of Thucydides*. Princeton, NJ: Princeton University Press.

Ory, Pascal (2016) *Ce que dit Charlie: treize leçons d'histoire*. Paris: Gallimard.

Osterhammel, Jürgen (2014) *The Transformation of the World: A Global History of the Nineteenth Century*. Princeton, NJ: Princeton University Press.

Overy, Richard (2016) *A History of War in 100 Battles*. London: William Collins.

Ozick, Cynthia (1993) *What Henry James Knew and Other Essays on Writers*. London: Jonathan Cape.

Packer, George (ed.) (2003) *The Fight is for Democracy: Winning the War of Ideas in America and the World*. New York: Harper Perennial.

Pagden, Anthony (2009) *Worlds at War: The 2,500-Year Struggle between East and West*. New York: Random House.

Pagel, Mark (2012) *Wired for Culture: The Natural History of Human Cooperation*. London: Allen Lane.

Patterson, Orlando (1991) *Freedom in the Making of Western Culture*. London: I. B. Tauris.

Paz, Octavio (1985) *One Earth, Four or Five Worlds: Reflections on Contemporary History*, London: Carcanet.

Paz, Octavio (1990) *Convergences: Essays in Art and Literature*. London: Bloomsbury.

Pfaff, William (2005) 'EU's problem with "no"', *International Herald Tribune*, 23 June.

Phillips, Andrew (2011) *War, Religion and Empire: The Transformation of International Orders*. Cambridge: Cambridge University Press.

Plumb, J. H. (1969) 'Churchill as historian', in A. J. P. Taylor et al., *Churchill: Four Faces and the Man*. London: Allen Lane.

Plumb, J. H. (1972) *The Death of the Past*. Harmondsworth: Penguin.

Pollock, Sheldon (2014) 'Indian classicity', in Kurt Almqvist and Alexander Linklater, *Civilisation: A Perspective from the Engelsberg Seminar*. Stockholm: Axel and Margaret Ax:son Johnson Foundation.

Pomfret, John (2016) *The Beautiful Country and the Middle Kingdom: America and China from 1776 to the Present*. New York: Henry Holt.

Popper, Karl (1946) *The Open Society and its Enemies*, Vol. 1: *The Spell of Plato*. London: Routledge

Poulos, James (2016) 'How to start a clash of civilizations', *Foreign Policy*, 26 July, http://foreignpolicy.com/2016/07/26/how-to-start-clash-of-civilisations-catholic-france-islamic-state-crusades.

Prus, Justyna (2015) *Russia's Use of History as a Political Weapon*, Policy Paper no. 12. Warsaw: Polish Institute of International Affairs.

Puchala, Donald J. (1997) 'International encounters of another kind', *Global Society*, 11(1): 5–29.

Putin, Vladimir (2001) Speech at the Congress of Compatriots, 11 October, http://kremlin.ru/events/president/transcripts/21359 [in Russian].

Pye, Lucian (2000) 'Asian values: from dynamos to dominoes?', in Lawrence E. Harrison and Samuel Huntington (eds), *Culture Matters: How Values Shape Human Progress*. New York: Basic Books.

Qing, Jiang (2013) *A Confucian Constitutional Order: How China's Ancient Past Can Shape its Political Future*. Princeton, NJ: Princeton University Press.

Qing, Jiang, and Bell, Daniel A. (2012) 'A Confucian constitution for China', *New York Times*, 10 July, www.nytimes.com/2012/07/11/opinion/a-confucian-constitution-in-china.html?r=0.

Rachman, Gideon (2015) 'Do Paris terror attacks highlight a clash of civilisations?', *Financial Times*, 16 November.

Rachman, Gideon (2017) 'Merkel, Trump and the end of the West', *Financial Times*, 30 May.

Ramo, Joshua Cooper (2007) *Brand China*. London: Foreign Policy Centre.

Raphael, Frederick (2017) *Antiquity Matters*. New Haven, CT: Yale University Press.

Renan, Ernest (1882) 'What is a nation?', trans. Ethan Rundell, http://ucparis.fr/files/9313/6549/9943/What_is_a_Nation.pdf.

Roberts, Adam (2000) *Science Fiction*. London: Routledge.

Romano, Flavio (2006) *Clinton and Blair: The Political Economy of the Third Way*. New York, Routledge.

Rorty, Richard (1989) *Contingency, Irony, and Solidarity*. Cambridge: Cambridge University Press.

Rorty, Richard (1999) *Philosophy and Social Hope*. Harmondsworth: Penguin.

Rovere, Crispin (2016) 'A review of RAND Corporation's "War with China': Thinking through the Unthinkable"', *The Interpreter*, 24 August, www.lowyinstitute.org/the-interpreter/review-rand-corpora tions-war-china-thinking-through-unthinkable.

Roy, Arundhati (2017) *The Ministry of Utmost Happiness*. Harmondsworth: Penguin.

Roy, Olivier (2004) *Globalized Islam: The Search for a New Ummah*. New York: Columbia University Press.

Rushdie, Salman ([1981] 2010) *Midnight's Children*. New York: Random House.

Russian Federation (2009) *Russia's National Security Strategy to 2020* http:// rustrans.wikidot.com/russia-s-national-security-strategy-to-2020.

Rutherford, Adam (2016) *A Brief History of Everyone Who Has Ever Lived: The Stories in Our Genes*. London: Weidenfeld & Nicolson.

Ruthven, Malise (2016) 'Inside obedient Islamic minds', *New York Review of Books*, 7 April.

Sandel, Michael (2010) *Justice: What's the Right Thing to Do?* Harmondsworth: Penguin.

Sauerbrey, Anna (2016) 'What is German?', *New York Times*, 26 May.

Schiavone, Aldo (2000) *The End of the Past: Ancient Rome and the Modern West*. Cambridge, MA: Harvard University Press.

Sen, Amartya (2006) *The Argumentative Indian: Writings on Indian Culture, History and Identity*. Harmondsworth: Penguin.

Shakibi, Zhand (2010) *Khatami and Gorbachev: Politics of Change in the Islamic Republic of Iran and the USSR*. London: I. B. Tauris.

Shankman, Steven, and Durrant, Stephen (2000) *The Siren and the Sage: Knowledge and Wisdom in Ancient Greece and China*. London: Cassell.

Sherr, James (2008) 'A dangerous game', *The World Today*, 64(10).

Shevtsova, Lilia (2010) *Lonely Power: Why Russia has Failed to Become the West and the West is Weary of Russia*. Washington, DC: Carnegie Endowment for International Peace.

Sloterdijk, Peter (2013) *Philosophical Temperaments: From Plato to Foucault*, trans. Thomas Dunlap. New York: Columbia University Press.

Smail, David Lord (2008) *On Deep History and the Brain*. Berkeley: University of California Press.

Smith, Tony (1994) *America's Mission: The United States and the Worldwide Struggle for Democracy in the Twentieth Century*. Princeton, NJ: Princeton University Press.

Solomon, Scott (2017) *Future Humans: Inside the Science of our Continuing Evolution*. New Haven, CT: Yale University Press.

Sontag, Susan (1977) 'Unguided tour', *New Yorker*, 31 October.

Sorokin, Pitirim (1964) *The Basic Trends of Our Times*. New Haven, CT: College & University Press.

Spencer, Richard (2008) 'Confucius, he has many descendants', *The Telegraph*, 19 February.

Spengler, Oswald ([1918] 1980) *The Decline of the West*. London: Allen & Unwin.

Stahl, William A. (2001) *God and the Chip: Religion and the Culture of Technology*. Waterloo, Ontario: Wilfrid Laurier University Press.

Staib, J. T. (2016) 'Russian and Western views of international law: the case of Crimea', in Janne Haaland Matláry and Tormod Heier (eds), *Ukraine and Beyond: Russia's Strategic Security Challenge to Europe*. London: Palgrave Macmillan.

Steiner, George (1960) *Tolstoy or Dostoevsky: An Essay in Contrast*. London: Faber & Faber.

Steiner, George (2008) *My Unwritten Books*. London: Weidenfeld & Nicolson.

Stone, Norman (2007) *World War One: A Short History*. London: Allen Lane.

Strange, Susan (1990) 'The name of the game', in Nicholas X. Rizopoulos (ed.), *Sea-Changes: American Foreign Policy in a World Transformed*. New York: Council on Foreign Relations Press.

Strange, Susan, and Stopford, John (1991) *Rival State, Rival Firms: Competition for Market Shares*. Cambridge: Cambridge University Press.

Sutyagin, Igor (2016) 'Driving forces in Russia's strategic thinking', in Janne Haaland Matláry and Tormod Heier (eds), *Ukraine and Beyond: Russia's Strategic Security Challenge to Europe*. London: Palgrave Macmillan.

Tal, Uriel (1981) 'On structures of political theology and myth in Germany prior to the Holocaust', in Yehuda Bauer and Nathan Rotenstreich (eds), *The Holocaust as Historical Experience*. New York: Holmes & Meier.

Tan, Clarissa (2012) 'China's civilising mission', *The Spectator*, 30 June, www.spectator.co.uk/2012/06/chinas-civilising-mission.

Tanaka, Stefan (1993) *Japan's Orient: Rendering Pasts into History*. Berkeley: University of California Press.

Taylor, Charles (2016) *The Language Animal: The Full Shape of the Human Linguistic Capacity*. Cambridge, MA: Harvard University Press.

Taylor, Timothy (2010) *The Artificial Ape: How Technology Has Changed the Course of Human Evolution*. London: Palgrave Macmillan.

Temperley, Howard (1972) *British Antislavery, 1833–70*. London: Longman.

Tetlock, Philip E., and Gardner, Dan (2015) *Superforecasting: The Art and Science of Prediction*. New York: Penguin Random House.

Tetlock, Philip E., Lebow, Richard Ned, and Parker, Geoffrey (eds) (2006) *Unmaking the West: 'What-if' Scenarios That Rewrite World History*. Ann Arbor: University of Michigan Press.

Thonemann, Peter (2016) *The Hellenistic Age*. Oxford: Oxford University Press.

Thorne, Christopher (1988) *Border Crossings: Studies in International History*. London: Hamish Hamilton.

Todorov, Tzvetan (2009) *In Defence of the Enlightenment*. London: Atlantic Books.

Toner, Jerry (2015) *The Ancient World*. London: Profile Books.

Toynbee, Arnold (1948) *Civilization on Trial*. Oxford: Oxford University Press.

Traverso, Enzo (2003) *The Origins of Nazi Violence*. New York: New Press.

Trifonov, Yuri ([1983] 1999) *Another Life*, trans. Michael Glenny. Evanston, IL: Northwestern University Press.

Trilling, Daniel (2016) 'Perspectives on the refugee crisis', *Times Literary Supplement*, 22 June.

'Trump spells out foreign aims on grand tour' (2017) *The World Today*, June/July, p. 7, www.chathamhouse.org/publications/twt/trump-spells-out-foreign-aims-grand-tour.

Tsygankov, Andrei (2016) 'Crafting the state-civilization: Vladimir Putin's turn to distinct values', *Problems of Post-Communism*, 63(3): 146–58.

Turner, Frederick Jackson ([1894] 1963) *The Significance of the Frontier in American History*. New York: Frederick Ungar; excerpts at www.mtholyoke.edu/acad/intrel/afp/turner.htm.

Tusk, Donald (2016) 'Brexit could destroy Western political civilisation', *BBC News*, 13 June, www.bbc.com/news/uk-politics-eu-referendum-36515680.

Tyerman, Christopher (2004) *Fighting for Christendom: Holy War and the Crusades*. Oxford: Oxford University Press.

Updike, John (2011) *Higher Gossip: Essays and Criticisms*. Harmondsworth: Penguin.

Varouxakis, Georgios (2008) 'On the origins of the idea of the West', in Kurt Almqvist (ed.), *What is the West? Perspectives from the Englesberg Seminar, 2007*. Stockholm: Axel and Margaret Ax:son Johnson Foundation.

Vermes, Timur (2015) *Look Who's Back*. London: MacLehose Press.

Veyne, Paul (2010) *When Our World Became Christian, 312–394*, trans. Janet Lloyd. Cambridge: Polity.

Veyne, Paul (2017) *Palmyra: An Irreplaceable Treasure*, trans. Teresa Lavender Fagan. Chicago: University of Chicago Press.

Vico, Giambattista ([1725] 2001) *New Science*. Harmondsworth: Penguin.

Victoria, Brian Diazen (1997) *Zen at War*. New York: Weatherhill.

Vidal, Gore (1981) *Creation*. New York: Random House.

Voegelin, Eric (1944) 'Nietzsche, the crisis and the war', *Journal of Politics*, 6(2): 177–212.

Voll, John Obert (1996) 'The mistaken identification of "the West" with "modernity"', *American Journal of Islamic Social Sciences*, 13(1): 1–12.

von Eggert, Konstantin (2017) 'It's not a good time to revel in revolution', *The World Today*, August/September.

Walden, George (2011) '*Why the West Rules – for Now* by Ian Morris: Review', *The Observer*, 30 January.

Walt, Stephen M. (2017) 'America's new president is not a rational actor', *Foreign Policy*, 25 January, http://foreignpolicy.com/2017/01/25/americas-new-president-is-not-a-rational-actor.

Walton, Jo (2012) 'What is living for? Poul Anderson's *The Corridors of Time*, 11 May, http://www.tor.com/2012/05/11/what-is-living-for-poul-andersons-the-corridors-of-time/.

Wang Zheng (2012) *Never Forget National Humiliation: Historical Memory in Chinese Politics and Foreign Relations*. New York: Columbia University Press.

Washbrook, David A. (1981) 'Law, state and agrarian society in colonial India', *Modern Asian Studies*, 15(3): 649–721.

Watson, David (1992) *Hannah Arendt*. London: Fontana.

Watson, Peter (2012) *The Great Divide: History and Human Nature in the Old World and the New*. London: Weidenfeld & Nicolson.

Webb, Justin (2013) 'America's future is Latin, Asian and liberal', *The Times*, 4 June.

Wilcox, Robert K. (1995) *Japan's Secret War: Japan's Race against Time to Build its Own Atomic Bomb*. New York: Marlowe.

Williams, David (2014) *The Philosophy of Japanese Wartime Resistance: A Reading, with Commentary, of the Complete Texts of the Kyoto School Discussions of 'The Standpoint of World History and Japan'*. London: Routledge.

Williams, R. John (2010) 'The *technê* whim: Lin Yutang and the invention of the Chinese typewriter', *American Literature*, 82(2): 389–419, https://rjohnwilliams.files.wordpress.com/2010/05/williams-american-litera ture-82-21.pdf.

Williams, Rowan (2017) 'Meet the author', *Times Literary Supplement*, 15 September.

Wilson, Edward O. (1997) *In Search of Nature*. London: Allen Lane. check the quote p. 24, 25

Wilson, Jon E. (2016) *India Conquered: Britain's Raj and the Chaos of Empire*. New York: Simon & Schuster.

White, Donald W. (1992) 'The "American century" in world history', *Journal of World History*, 3(1): 105–27.

Windsor, Philip (2002) *Studies in International Relations: Essays by Philip Windsor*, ed. Mats Berdal. Brighton: Sussex Academic Press.

Wink, André (1990–2004) *Al-Hind: The Making of the Indo-Islamic World*, 3 vols. Leiden: Brill.

Woolf, Leonard (1935) *Quack, Quack!* London: Hogarth Press.

Woolf, Leonard (1969) *The Journey Not the Arrival Matters: An Autobiography of the Years 1939–1969*. London: Hogarth Press.

Wright, Ronald (2004) *A Short History of Progress*. Edinburgh: Canongate.

Wu, Kuang-ming (1998) 'Time in China', in *On the 'Logic' of Togetherness: A Cultural Hermeneutic*. Leiden: Brill.

Xinhuanet (2016) 'China's Xi calls for better development of internet', 19 April, www.xinhuanet.com/english/2016-04/19/c_135293965.htm.

Xu, Zhiyuan (2016) *Paper Tiger: Inside the Real China*. London: Head of Zeus.

Yanov, Alexander (2013) 'Putin and the "Russian Idea"', *Institute of Modern Russia*, 1 July, http://imrussia.org/en/society/504-putin-and-the-russian-idea.

Yaqing Qin (2011) 'The possibility and inevitability of a Chinese school of international relations theory', in William Callahan (ed.), *China Orders the World: Normative Soft Power and Foreign Policy*. Baltimore: Johns Hopkins University Press.

Yatsk, A. (2015) 'Refracting Europe: bio-political conservatism and art protest in Putin's Russia', in David Cadier, and Margot Light (eds) (2015) *Russia's Foreign Policy: Ideas, Domestic Politics and External Relations*. London: Palgrave Macmillan.

Zeldin, Theodore (2015) *The Hidden Pleasures of Life: A New Way of Remembering the Past and Imagining the Future*. London: Maclehose Press.

Zeng, Jinghan, and Breslin, Shaun (2016) 'China's "new type of Great Power relations": a G2 with Chinese characteristics?', *International Affairs*, 92(4): 773–94.

Zhang, Weiwei (2012) *The China Wave: Rise of a Civilizational State*. Hackensack, NJ: World Century.

Zhang, Yongjin (2016) 'China and liberal hierarchies in global international society: power and negotiation for normative change', *International Affairs*, 92(4): 795–816.

Zhao, Tingyang (2006) 'Rethinking empire from a Chinese concept "all-under-heaven"', *Social Identities*, 12(1): 29–41.

Žižek, Slavoj (2015) 'Sinicisation', *London Review of Books*, 16 July, www.lrb.co.uk/v37/n14/slavoj-zizek/sinicisation.

Žižek, Slavoj (2016) *Against the Double Blackmail: Refugees, Terror and Other Troubles with the Neighbours*. London: Allen Lane.

Index